FOCUS

FOCUS ON VOCABULARY

Thematischer Wortschatz in Texten

NEW EDITION

von
Steve Williams

Cornelsen

Focus on Vocabulary wurde geplant und entwickelt von Cornelsen Berufliche Bildung, Berlin.

Verfasser:	Steve Williams, Melbourne
Beraterin:	Susanne Burkhardt, Berlin

Projektleitung:	Jim Austin
Verlagsredaktion:	Kari-ann Seamark
Außenredaktion:	Christine House
Redaktionelle Mitarbeit:	Fritz Preuss
Layout und technische Umsetzung:	Stephan Hilleckenbach, Berlin
Bildredaktion:	Gertha Maly
Umschlaggestaltung:	werkstatt für gebrauchsgrafik, Berlin
Illustrationen:	Oxford Designers & Illustrators

www.cornelsen.de

1. Auflage, 3. Druck 2012

Alle Drucke dieser Auflage sind inhaltlich unverändert und können im Unterricht nebeneinander verwendet werden.

Druck: H. Heenemann, Berlin

ISBN 978-3-06-024152-1

Inhalt gedruckt auf säurefreiem Papier aus nachhaltiger Forstwirtschaft.

Vorwort

Focus on Vocabulary richtet sich an Englisch Lernende, die das Abitur oder die Fachhochschulreife anstreben. Doch auch für fortgeschrittene Lernende aus anderen Bereichen, die ihre Englischkenntnisse vertiefen wollen, ist es ein ebenso sinnvoller wie nützlicher Begleiter.

Focus on Vocabulary ist kein „Wörterbuch" im tradierten Sinne, sondern geht von einem kontextbezogenen Lernansatz aus. Demnach ist es weitaus effektiver, Wörter in einem zusammenhängenden, eingängigen und interessanten Text zu lernen oder zu wiederholen, statt sich lange Wortlisten einzuprägen. Darüber hinaus vermittelt kontextbezogenes Wörterlernen nicht nur den grammatisch richtigen Gebrauch, sondern auch den Sinnzusammenhang, in dem ein Wort üblicherweise erscheint. Ein einzelnes Wort in einer Liste steht immer für sich, dagegen ist der Kontext für die Erinnerung eines Wortes eine Eselsbrücke, die in Prüfungen, beim Verfassen von Aufsätzen und beim Lesen von englischen Texten hilfreich ist. Das Lesen in einer fremden Sprache hilft den Lernenden wiederum, ihre Gedanken gleich in dieser Sprache zu formulieren, statt den Umweg über das Deutsche und die Übersetzung zu nehmen.

Eine weitere sinnvolle Lernmethode ist, sich verwandte Wörter, also Wörter aus Wortfamilien, einzuprägen. Deshalb werden in *Focus on Vocabulary* Antonyme, Synonyme und Wortfamilien in einer separaten Spalte aufgeführt. Kennt man ein Wort aus der Familie, lässt sich ein weiteres oder eine Wortkombination leichter herleiten.

Focus on Vocabulary ist in sieben thematische Einheiten untergliedert, von denen jede einen Bereich der englischsprachigen Welt betrachtet. Jede dieser thematischen Einheiten ist in mehrere Abschnitte gegliedert, in denen die facettenreichen Aspekte eines Themas aus unterschiedlichen Perspektiven beleuchtet werden. Die Themen, um die es auf den 83 Textseiten geht, stammen aus den für die Oberstufe typischen Themengebieten. Somit bieten die Texte auch ausgezeichnete Anregungen für Diskussionen und Aufsätze.

Focus on Vocabulary eröffnet vielfältige Möglichkeiten, Wörter zu lernen und zu wiederholen. Hier nur einige Anregungen für die Handhabung des Buches:

- als Wiederholungshilfe für eine Klausur
- als Anregung für Aufsätze, Textaufgaben und Diskussionen
- als Anregung für die Wortbildung
- um den Gebrauch eines bestimmten Wortes nachzuschlagen

Das Buch hat einen Index, der die erklärten Wörter und Begriffe und deren Fundstellen enthält. So können alle Wörter rasch kontextbezogen im Buch gefunden werden. Das Auffinden wird zudem durch die farbige Markierung im Text erleichtert.

Wir hoffen, dass Ihnen *Focus on Vocabulary* ein ebenso interessanter wie auch nützlicher Begleiter ist und wünschen Ihnen viel Freude und Erfolg.

Inhalt

Abkürzungen und Symbole

abbr. ...... abbreviation (*Abkürzung*)
adj .... adjective
adv. .... adverb
attr adj ... attributive adjective
coll. .... colloquial (*umgangssprachlich*)
n .... noun (*Substantiv/Nomen*)
sb. .... somebody (*jemand*)
sth .... something (*etwas*)
vi .... intransitive verb
vt .... transitive verb
vti. .... transitive and intransitive verb
v prep .... prepositional verb
≈ .... synonym
<> ...... antonym (*Gegensatz*)
⚠ .... warning (*Achtung, Falle!*)

BE .... British English
AE .... American English

A

Society

1 Health and well-being

2 Education

3 Family and community

4 Law and order

http://about.info/health/tears.php

Adolescence and body image

Images of impossibly thin models overwhelm today's teenage girls. Open any teen magazine, switch on primetime TV or walk through a department store. These images are both unhealthy and unattainable: most of these models are thinner than 98% of American girls and women.

Adolescents are particularly vulnerable to these images because their bodies and minds are undergoing huge changes as they move from childhood to adulthood. They are generally seeking to define their identity and looking for role models; during this transition they often have to struggle with problems of low self-esteem.

Of course, pressure to conform to an impossible ideal doesn't just come from the media. It also comes from their peers and even from well-meaning but misguided parents. It's understandable therefore that appearance is the biggest concern for many girls. A study indicates that 90% of teenage girls frequently think about their body shape and that 86% are either on a diet, or think they should be.

It's no surprise that 5–10 million girls in the USA suffer from eating disorders such as anorexia and bulimia. Of course, boys aren't immune to body image issues either. Men and boys account for an estimated 5–15% of patients with anorexia or bulimia and an estimated 35% of those with binge eating disorder. Excessive gym usage and steroid abuse can result from young men's obsession with achieving a 'perfect' body.

There are no quick fixes for these problems, but one approach is to improve teenagers' media literacy, so that they recognize more easily that the media promote idealized images that encourage excessive thinness for females and muscularity for boys.

1 Health and well-being

▸ **adolescence** [ˌædə'lesns]	*Jugendalter, Pubertät*	cf	youth – *Jugend*
▸ **body image**	*(äußeres) Erscheinungsbild*	cf	self image – *Selbstverständnis*
▸ **model**	*Model*	vti	to model
▸ **to overwhelm**	*überwältigen*	≈	to overpower
▸ **primetime TV**	*Hauptfernsehzeit*	cf	off-peak, late-night TV
▸ **unattainable**	*unerreichbar*	phr	~ dream, ideal, goal
▸ **adolescent** [ˌædə'lesnt]	*Jugendliche/r*	≈	teenager, youth
▸ **vulnerable to**	*anfällig für*	n	vulnerability
▸ **mind**	*Vorstellung, Geist*	≈	brain, intellect
▸ **to undergo**	*erleben*	≈	to experience
▸ **childhood**	*Kindheit*	cf	infancy – *frühe Kindheit*
▸ **adulthood**	*Erwachsenenalter*	cf	old age – *Alter*
▸ **to define**	*definieren*	n	definition
▸ **identity**	*Identität*	≈	individuality, personality
▸ **role model**	*Vorbild*	≈	example
▸ **transition**	*Übergang*	phr	a period of ~
▸ **to struggle with**	*kämpfen mit*	n	struggle
▸ **self-esteem**	*Selbstwertgefühl*	≈	self-respect
▸ **pressure**	*Druck*	vt	to pressure/pressurize
▸ **to conform to**	*entsprechen*	≈	to comply with
▸ **the media**	*die Medien*	≈	the mass media
▸ **peer**	*Gleichaltrige/r*	phr	~ group pressure
▸ **well-meaning**	*wohlmeinend*	≈	well-intentioned
▸ **misguided**	*irregeleitet*	≈	ill-advised
▸ **appearance**	*Aussehen*	≈	looks
▸ **concern**	*Anliegen, Sorge*	≈	worry
▸ **to indicate**	*anzeigen*	adj	indicative
▸ **diet**	*Diät*	vi	to diet
▸ **to suffer from**	*leiden an*	n	suffering
▸ **eating disorder**	*Essstörung*	cf	eating habits – *Essgewohnheiten*
▸ **anorexia**	*Magersucht*	adj	anorexic
▸ **bulimia**	*Bulimie*	adj	bulimic
▸ **immune to**	*immun gegen*	n	immunity
▸ **binge eating**	*Fressanfälle*	cf	binge drinking – *Komasaufen*
▸ **excessive** [ɪk'sesɪv]	*übermäßig*	<>	insufficient
▸ **gym**	*Fitnessstudio*	⚠	≠ *Gymnasium*
▸ **abuse** [ə'bjuːs]	*Missbrauch*	≈	misuse
▸ **obsession**	*Besessenheit*	vi	to be obsessed with
▸ **quick fix**	*rasche Lösung*	≈	stop-gap solution
▸ **approach**	*Herangehen(sweise)*	≈	method
▸ **media literacy**	*Medienkompetenz*	adj	media literate
▸ **to promote**	*anpreisen*	n	promotion
▸ **idealized**	*idealisiert*	n	ideal
▸ **to encourage**	*fördern*	n	encouragement
▸ **thinness**	*Dünnheit*	<>	fatness
▸ **muscularity**	*starke Muskeln*	adj	muscular ['mʌskjələ]

Say no to drugs

Josh and Anna are youth workers in south London. They are discussing a new government anti-drugs initiative over their morning coffee.

Josh Have you heard about the new drug campaign targeting teenagers?

Anna Yes, I have, and I've seen one of the ads. I thought it was pretty hard-hitting and it showed the consequences of substance abuse very graphically.

Josh Yes, but do you think it will have an impact?

Anna No, I'm afraid I don't. The trouble is, teenagers tend to believe that they are totally invulnerable. They aren't impressed by ads that use shock tactics. At best, they warn off some of the more cautious kids who might otherwise be tempted to give drugs a try.

Josh Well, with over 40% of 15-year-old boys admitting that they've used illicit drugs, there's a real crisis and something has to be done.

Anna True, true. All the same, that statistic presents a distorted picture of the situation. It doesn't mean that 40% of boys are hardened drug users, it just means that they have experimented at some time, probably with cannabis or ecstasy.

Josh Yes, and it really worries me that these so-called soft drugs are regarded as somehow more socially acceptable than ice or heroin. I'm opposed to moves to decriminalize cannabis, for example.

Anna Well, I disagree with you there. I don't see the point in prosecuting cannabis users. Big-time dealers are another matter.

Josh But it's a well-documented fact that cannabis is a gateway drug – it's often the first step to serious addiction to hard drugs. Plus there is the danger of brain damage from smoking cannabis …

Anna Oh, come on! There are plenty of studies that contradict those claims.

▸ **government**	*Regierung*	adj	governmental
▸ **anti-drugs**	*Antidrogen-*	<>	pro-drugs
▸ **initiative**	*Initiative*	phr	to take the ~
▸ **campaign**	*Kampagne*	v prep	to campaign for/against
▸ **to target**	*abzielen auf*	n	target – *Ziel*
▸ **ad**	*Anzeige*	≈	advert, advertisement
▸ **hard-hitting**	*zur Sache gehend*	≈	powerful
▸ **consequence** ['kɒnsɪkwəns]	*Folge, Konsequenz*	≈	result, outcome
▸ **substance abuse** [ˌsʌbstəns ə'bju:s]	*Drogenmissbrauch*	≈	drug abuse
▸ **graphically**	*anschaulich*	≈	vividly
▸ **impact**	*(Aus-)Wirkung*	≈	effect
▸ **to tend to**	*dazu neigen*	n	tendency
▸ **invulnerable**	*unverwundbar*	n	invulnerability
▸ **to impress**	*beeindrucken*	n	impression
▸ **shock tactic**	*Abschreckungstaktik*	≈	scare tactic
▸ **to warn off**	*warnen, abschrecken*	≈	to scare off
▸ **cautious**	*vorsichtig*	n	caution
▸ **tempted**	*versucht*	n	temptation
▸ **to give sth a try**	*etw ausprobieren*	≈	to give sth a go
▸ **to admit**	*zugeben*	<>	to deny
▸ **illicit**	*illegal, verboten*	≈	illegal
▸ **crisis**	*Krise*	pl	crises
▸ **to present**	*darstellen*	≈	to give
▸ **distorted**	*verzerrt*	≈	falsified
▸ **hardened**	*hart*	phr	~ drug user, criminal
▸ **drug user**	*Drogenkonsument/in*	cf	drug addict – *Drogenabhängige/r*
▸ **to experiment with**	*experimentieren mit*	n	experiment
▸ **soft drug**	*weiche Droge*	≈	recreational drug
▸ **to regard sth as sth**	*etw betrachten als*	≈	to consider sth sth
▸ **socially acceptable**	*gesellschaftsfähig*	vt	to accept
▸ **to be opposed to**	*dagegen sein*	≈	against
▸ **to decriminalize** [di:'krɪmɪnəlaɪz]	*entkriminalisieren*	n	decriminalization
▸ **to prosecute**	*strafrechtlich verfolgen*	n	prosecution
▸ **dealer**	*(Drogen-)Händler/in*	vt	to deal (in)
▸ **well-documented**	*gut dokumentiert*	≈	proven
▸ **gateway drug**	*Einstiegsdroge*	cf	gateway – *Tor, Zugang*
▸ **step**	*Schritt*	≈	move
▸ **addiction to**	*Abhängigkeit von*	v pass	to be addicted to
▸ **danger**	*Gefahr*	adj	dangerous
▸ **brain damage**	*Hirnschäden*	vt	to damage
▸ **to contradict**	*widersprechen*	n	contradiction
▸ **claim**	*Behauptung*	≈	assertion

www.netdoctor.co.uk

Smoking – health risks

Dr Carl J Brandt

You can eat five portions of fruit and vegetables a day and exercise regularly, but these healthy habits mean little if you continue to smoke. The message that 'smoking is bad for you' is an old one, so not everyone gives it their full attention.

Most people know that smoking can cause lung cancer, but it can also cause many other cancers and illnesses. Smoking kills around 114,000 people in the UK each year. Of these deaths, about 42,800 are from smoking-related cancers, 30,600 from heart disease and 29,100 die slowly from chronic lung diseases.

Cigarettes contain at least 400 toxins. The products that are most damaging are: tar, a carcinogen, nicotine, which is addictive and increases cholesterol levels in your body, and carbon monoxide, which reduces oxygen in the body.

Research has shown that smoking reduces life expectancy by seven to eight years. On average, each cigarette shortens a smoker's life by around 11 minutes.

There are many health-related reasons to give up cigarettes – not just for smokers, but to protect those around you from the effects of passive smoking. Babies born to mothers who smoke during pregnancy are twice as likely to be born prematurely and with a low birth weight. Being exposed to cigarette smoke puts children at risk of asthma and other health problems and may also be harmful to adults.

Quitting smoking is the single biggest thing you can do to improve your health, but it's a difficult task. Smokers who are trying to kick the habit may be disappointed to find there's no single method that guarantees success.

On average it takes four to five attempts to give up. Fortunately there are a number of things that can aid willpower, including medicines and alternative therapies such as acupuncture and hypnosis.

[www.netdoctor.co.uk/health_advice/facts/smokehealth.htm]

▸ **health**	*Gesundheit*	adj	healthy
▸ **risk**	*Risiko*	adj	risky
▸ **to exercise**	*sich körperlich bewegen*	n	exercise
▸ **habit**	*Gewohnheit*	adj	habitual
▸ **bad for**	*schlecht für*	<>	beneficial to
▸ **to cause**	*verursachen*	n	cause
▸ **lung cancer**	*Lungenkrebs*		
▸ **illness**	*Krankheit*	≈	disease
▸ **death**	*Tote/r*	adj	dead
▸ **related**	*im Zusammenhang stehend mit*	≈	connected
▸ **heart disease**	*Herzkrankheit*	cf	heart attack
▸ **chronic** ['krɒnɪk]	*chronisch*	≈	long-term
▸ **toxin**	*Gift(stoff)*	≈	poison
▸ **damaging**	*schädlich*	n	damage
▸ **tar**	*Teer*	adj	tarry
▸ **carcinogen** [kɑː'sɪnədʒən]	*Krebs erregender Stoff*	adj	carcinogenic [ˌkɑːsɪnə'dʒenɪk]
▸ **addictive**	*süchtig machend*	n	addiction, addict
▸ **cholesterol level**	*Cholesterinspiegel*	phr	a high/low ~
▸ **carbon monoxide**	*Kohlenmonoxid*		
▸ **oxygen**	*Sauerstoff*		
▸ **research**	*(die) Forschung*	phr	to do ~
▸ **life expectancy**	*Lebenserwartung*	vt	to expect
▸ **on average**	*im Durchschnitt*	adj	average
▸ **to shorten**	*verkürzen*	<>	to lengthen
▸ **to give up**	*aufgeben*	≈	to kick, to quit
▸ **to protect from**	*schützen vor*	n	protection
▸ **effect**	*Auswirkung*	vt	to affect
▸ **passive smoking**	*Passivrauchen*	cf	passive smoker
▸ **pregnancy**	*Schwangerschaft*	vi	to be pregnant
▸ **likely**	*wahrscheinlich*	n	likelihood
▸ **prematurely** ['premətʃəli]	*frühzeitig*	≈	too early/soon
▸ **birth**	*Geburt*	<>	death
▸ **weight**	*Gewicht*	vti	to weigh
▸ **to be exposed to**	*ausgesetzt sein*	≈	to be subjected to
▸ **to put at risk**	*gefährden*	≈	to endanger
▸ **asthma** [æsmə]	*Asthma*	adj	asthmatic
▸ **harmful**	*schädlich*	v	to harm
▸ **to quit**	*aufgeben*	≈	to stop
▸ **to kick the habit**	*es sich abgewöhnen*	≈	to give up
▸ **to guarantee**	*garantieren*	n	guarantee
▸ **success**	*Erfolg*	vi	to succeed
▸ **attempt**	*Versuch*	≈	try
▸ **to aid**	*unterstützen*	≈	to support, to assist
▸ **willpower**	*Willenskraft*	≈	determination

Binge drinking costs billions

Britain's binge drinking culture is costing the country £20 billion a year, according to a government report. The study shows 17 million working days are lost to hangovers and alcohol-related illness each year.

Billions more are spent dealing with alcohol-related crime and social problems. In addition, alcohol is responsible for 22,000 premature deaths each year. The report found that there are 1.2 million incidents of alcohol-related violence a year. Accidents due to intoxication and alcohol-related illnesses land around 150,000 people in hospital each year.

It shows that one in three men and one in five women indulge in binge drinking. In addition, youngsters are starting to binge-drink at an earlier age. The binge-drinking period that was once confined to the late teens now often runs from 16 to 24, it said.

Ministers are planning to publish a strategy to tackle binge drinking and other alcohol-related problems next year.

Home Office Minister Hazel Blears said there would be a drive to give more information to young people about the risks of drinking too much. Ms Blears told Radio 4's Today programme: 'Information means young people can make choices, so I think education and prevention are going to be a big part of our policy.'

Professor Ian Gilmore, of the Royal College of Physicians, urged ministers to act on the report's findings: 'It's crucial that the government follows up this report urgently with strong recommendations to tackle the problem, including labelling of alcohol content and health warnings on drinks.'

Rob Hayward, chief executive of the British Beer and Pub Association, said: 'Alcohol misuse needs to be tackled and treated. We also need to get to the root causes. What motivates a significant number of people to go out on a Friday or Saturday night, get drunk and indulge in drunken, antisocial behaviour?'

[Slightly adapted: news.bbc.co.uk]

1 Health and well-being

binge drinking	*Komasaufen*	phr	to go on a (drinking) binge
working day	*Arbeitstag*	cf	weekday – *Wochentag*
hangover	*Kater*	phr	to have a ~
illness	*Krankheit*	≈	sickness, disease
to deal with	*fertig werden mit*	≈	to cope with
crime	*Kriminalität*	adj	criminal
responsible for	*verantwortlich für*	n	responsibility
premature ['premətʃə]	*vorzeitig, frühzeitig*	≈	(too) early
death	*Tod(esfall)*	≈	fatality
incident	*Zwischenfall*	≈	occurrence
violence	*Gewalt*	adj	violent
accident	*Unfall*	adj	accidental
intoxication	*Trunkenheit*	adj	intoxicated
to indulge in	*Gefallen finden an*	adj	indulgent
confined to	*beschränkt auf*	≈	limited to
teens	*Jugend(jahre)*	≈	teenage years
to tackle	*in Angriff nehmen*	≈	to deal with
drive	*Aktion*	≈	(concerted) effort
to make choices	*Entscheidungen treffen*	cf	to choose (between)
prevention	*Vorbeugung*	vt	to prevent
policy	*Politik*	phr	government ~
to urge sb to do sth	*jdn drängen, etw zu tun*	≈	to advise sb strongly to do sth
to act on sth	*handeln nach*	adj	active
findings	*Ergebnisse*	≈	results
crucial ['kru:ʃl]	*äußerst wichtig*	≈	vital
to follow sth up	*etw weiterverfolgen*	n	follow-up
urgently	*dringend*	n	urgency
recommendation	*Empfehlung*	vt	to recommend
to label	*kennzeichnen*	n	label
content	*Gehalt*	vt	to contain
health warning	*Hinweis auf Gesundheitsgefahren*	vt	to warn (sb about sth)
misuse [ˌmɪs'ju:s]	*Missbrauch*	≈	abuse
to treat	*behandeln*	n	treatment
root cause	*Fehlerursache*	≈	underlying cause
to motivate	*motivieren*	n	motivation
to get drunk	*sich betrinken*	<>	to stay sober
drunken	*betrunken*	n	drunkenness
anti-social	*asozial*	≈	offensive
behaviour	*Verhalten*	vi	to behave

Sports forum: drugs in sport

Thread: Brad Cameron a drugs cheat??

I couldn't believe it when I read that Brad Cameron was a drugs cheat. Brad Cameron, the greatest Australian athlete ever! Surely it can't be true?

posted by: Green and Gold

Reply *posted by: TroubleMaker*

Come on! All professional sportspeople take performance-enhancing drugs. Brad's problem is not that he cheated, but that he was found out ;-) Sportspeople are always finding new ways of getting around the regulations.

Reply *posted by: quick wheels*

That's a very cynical view of the state of professional sport. I know from my own experience as a cyclist that drugs testing in sport is extremely rigorous. Of course, there is a minority of athletes who want to gain an advantage over others and are prepared to use artificial means to do so. It's not only unfair, it's also extremely risky because there's a good chance you'll get caught eventually.

Reply *posted by: GirlGymnast*

Sometimes I think the enforcement of the rules is too strict. The list of banned substances is huge, including not just steroids and human growth hormones but also common nutritional supplements and even cold and flu remedies you can buy in any pharmacy over the counter. Testing positive for drugs doesn't mean that you actually intended to cheat. Andreea Raducan's gold medal for gymnastics at the Sydney Olympics in 2000 was revoked because she had taken two painkillers for a cold. Her low body weight meant that these drugs had a stronger effect and showed up in a test as being over the legal limit for painkillers.

Reply *posted by: soccer crazy 09*

Then of course there's always the possibility that blood samples could be contaminated before testing in the laboratory ...

Reply *posted by: get real*

It's part of the coach's job to make sure that the athlete doesn't accidentally take a banned substance. Besides, all professionals know the rules, so there's no excuse for breaking them. As for contaminated samples – don't make me laugh!

1 Health and well-being

▸ **cheat**	*Betrüger/in*	cf	cheating – *Mogeln*
▸ **athlete**	*Athlet,/in, Sportler/in*	adj	athletic
▸ **professional**	*Profi-, Berufs-*	<>	amateur
▸ **sportsperson**	*Sportler/in*	pl	sportspeople
▸ **performance-enhancing**	*leistungssteigernd*	vti	to perform
▸ **to cheat**	*betrügen, mogeln*	phr	to ~ at sth
▸ **to find out**	*erwischen*	≈	to catch (out)
▸ **to get around**	*umgehen*	≈	to circumvent
▸ **regulation**	*Vorschrift, Bestimmung*	vt	to regulate
▸ **cynical** ['sɪnɪkl]	*zynisch*	n	cynicism ['sɪnɪsɪzəm]
▸ **cyclist**	*Radsportler/in*	vi	to cycle
▸ **testing**	*Kontrollen*	phr	to test sb for drugs
▸ **rigorous** ['rɪgərəs]	*streng*	≈	strict
▸ **advantage**	*Vorteil*	<>	disadvantage
▸ **artificial**	*künstlich*	<>	natural
▸ **risky**	*riskant*	n	risk
▸ **to get caught**	*erwischt werden*	cf	to catch sb
▸ **eventually**	*schließlich*	⚠	≠ *eventuell*
▸ **enforcement**	*Durchsetzung*	vt	to enforce
▸ **rule**	*Regel*	phr	rules and regulations
▸ **strict**	*streng*	<>	lax
▸ **banned**	*verboten*	≈	forbidden
▸ **growth**	*Wachstum*	vi	to grow
▸ **nutritional** [nju'trɪʃənl]	*Nahrungs-*	n	nutrition
▸ **supplement** ['sʌplɪmənt]	*Ergänzungsmittel*		
▸ **remedy**	*(Heil-)Mittel*	≈	cure
▸ **pharmacy**	*Apotheke*	≈	chemist
▸ **to test positive**	*positiv getestet werden*	<>	to test negative
▸ **actually**	*tatsächlich*	⚠	≠ *aktuell*
▸ **to intend to do sth**	*beabsichtigen, etw zu tun*	n	intention
▸ **gold medal**	*Goldmedaille*	cf	gold medallist
▸ **to revoke** [rɪ'vəʊk]	*aberkennen*	≈	to take back
▸ **painkiller**	*Schmerzmittel*	≈	analgesic [ˌænəl'dʒiːsɪk]
▸ **body weight**	*Körpergewicht*	vti	to weigh
▸ **to show up**	*erscheinen*	≈	to be detected
▸ **limit**	*Grenze*	≈	boundary
▸ **blood**	*Blut*	phr	to have a ~ test
▸ **sample**	*Probe*	vt	to sample
▸ **to contaminate**	*verunreinigen*	n	contamination
▸ **laboratory**	*Labor*	abbr	lab
▸ **coach**	*Trainer/in*	≈	trainer
▸ **accidentally**	*aus Versehen*	<>	deliberately
▸ **excuse** [ɪk'skjuːs]	*Entschuldigung*	vt	to excuse [ɪk'skjuːz]

www.blogspot.de/annalytisch

Annas Blog

16.9.2009 ◀ ▶ Suche Kommentare

At school in England

Hi everyone,

I'm writing this page of my blog in English, as I'm spending the week with my English exchange partner, Emily. She goes to a big secondary school here in Brighton and today I went with her.

First a few words about the English education system – there are a few differences to the German one.

Compulsory education begins at the age of five with primary school, which children usually attend until the age of 11, followed by secondary school from 11 to 16. Over 90% of secondary school students attend comprehensive schools, like Emily's, which accepts all levels of ability, including children with learning difficulties or special needs. There are also a few grammar schools, which select pupils according to academic ability, and around 9% of students attend independent schools.

Oh, yes, I almost forgot: they have three terms a year in Britain.

Anyway, Emily looked funny in her school uniform! She explained that casual dress isn't allowed until students are 16. Even then there's a strict dress code. In general there seem to be a lot of rules at Emily's school :(

We had to be at school by 9.00 but lessons didn't start until 9.15 because we had assembly, then we went to Emily's classroom for registration. Assembly is when the whole school meets in the school hall for announcements by the head teacher.

After that there was the first lesson, Maths – Emily's worst subject. She's worried because she has to sit her GCSE exams soon. GCSE stands for General Certificate of Secondary Education and is a public examination that most students do at the age of 16. Emily's grades depend partly on her exam results and partly on her coursework, including homework and project work, which she has to do throughout the year. As in Germany there's a combination of compulsory and optional subjects, and, of course, Maths is compulsory.

In the lunch break we went to the school canteen and Emily told me about her plans for next year. She wants to go to a sixth-form college to study for her A levels (A = 'Advanced') so that she can go on to higher education when she's 18 – but she has to pass her Maths GCSE first …

◀ ▶

exchange partner	*Austauschpartner/in*	phr	to go on an exchange
secondary school ['sekəndri]	*weiterführende Schule*	AE	high school
education	*Bildung, Erziehung*	vt	to educate
compulsory	*Pflicht-*	<>	voluntary, optional
primary school	*Grundschule*	AE	elementary school
to attend	*besuchen*	⚠	≠ to visit
comprehensive school [ˌkɒmprɪ'hensɪv]	*Gesamtschule*	cf	comprehensive – *umfassend*
level	*Niveau*	adj	high/low-level
ability	*Fähigkeit, Begabung*	adj	able
learning difficulty	*Lernschwäche*	phr	to have a ~
special needs	*Förderunterricht benötigend*	phr	a ~ pupil
grammar school	*Gymnasium*	⚠	≠ gym(nasium)
to select	*auswählen*	n	selection
according to	*entsprechend*	≈	depending on
academic	*schulisch*	<>	practical
independent	*frei*	<>	state
term	*Trimester*	AE	semester/trimester
casual dress ['kæʒuəl]	*Freizeitkleidung*	<>	formal dress
dress code	*Kleiderordnung*	phr	a strict ~ ~ applies
rule	*Regel, Vorschrift*	≈	regulation
assembly	*(morgendliche) Versammlung*	vti	to assemble
registration	*Anwesenheitskontrolle*	vt	to register
announcement	*Ankündigung*	vt	to announce
head teacher	*Schulleiter/in*	AE	principal
subject	*Schulfach*	cf	topic – *Thema*
to sit an exam	*eine Prüfung machen*	cf	exam candidate
general	*allgemein*	<>	specific
certificate [sə'tɪfɪkət]	*Zeugnis*	cf	diploma – *Diplom*
public examination	*staatliche Prüfung*	<>	class test
grade	*(Schul-)Note*	≈	mark
to depend on	*abhängen von*	≈	to be dependent on
exam results	*Prüfungsergebnisse*	≈	exam scores
coursework	*eingereichte Arbeiten*	phr	~ assignment
homework	*Hausaufgaben*	phr	to do your ~
optional ['ɒpʃənl]	*Wahl-*	n	option
lunch break	*Mittagspause*	cf	to take a break
canteen	*Kantine, Cafeteria*	≈	cafeteria
sixth-form college	*Oberstufenzentrum*	cf	sixth-former – *Primaner/in*
advanced	*fortgeschritten*	<>	basic
higher education	*Hochschulausbildung*	≈	university education
to pass an exam	*eine Prüfung bestehen*	<>	to fail an exam

www.bullying.co.uk

Bullying

Bullying isn't confined to schools, and the emails we receive reflect the fact that college and university students are affected as well as members of youth clubs, sports clubs and other young peoples' organizations. Cyberbullying offers bullies a new dimension through threatening or abusive emails and text messages, offensive comments on websites, etc.

More work needs to be done in class and in youth organizations, from a very early age, and regularly repeated, so that everyone understands what bullying behaviour is, and that what one person thinks of as just a harmless joke may be very upsetting and traumatic for someone else.

If there has been a complaint from a parent to the class teacher, or if organization leaders are concerned that one member is being singled out for victimization, time could be given to group discussion on bullying. The discussion should take place in small groups, with the target in a different group to the bullies.

The person who leads the session could ask for words to describe bullying and write them on a chart. Then the group could be asked for words which describe the feelings of the victim or the bully, and then finally for ways they think bullying could be prevented in their own school or club.

The discussion could also involve asking about what witnesses to bullying should do about it. If the issue is approached in this way, the bullies probably won't suspect that the target has 'sneaked' about the bullying.

Involving bystanders is a very important aspect of tackling bullying because there are always people who know what is going on. Young people regularly tell us that they are afraid of being bullied because they've seen it happening to others.

Schools should make it clear that they encourage their pupils to report incidents – so that even if the victim is too intimidated to say anything, the bully will know he/she cannot get away with abusive behaviour.

Contact us on help@bullying.co.uk if you need more help.

[Slightly adapted: www.bullying.co.uk]

bullying	*Mobbing*	vt	to bully
confined to	*beschränkt auf*	≈	limited to
to reflect	*wiederspiegeln*	n	reflection
to affect	*betreffen*	n	effect
youth	*Jugend*	adj	youthful
cyberbullying	*Mobbing im Internet*	cf	cyberspace
bully	*Mobber/in*	<>	victim of bullying
to threaten ['θretn]	*drohen*	adj	threatening
abusive [ə'bju:sɪv]	*beleidigend*	vt	to abuse [ə'bju:z]
text message	*SMS(-Nachricht)*	vti	to text
offensive	*beleidigend*	vt	to offend
harmless	*harmlos*	<>	harmful
joke	*Witz*	≈	trick
to upset	*verletzen*	≈	to distress
traumatic [trɔ:'mætɪk]	*traumatisch*	vt	to traumatize
complaint	*Beschwerde*	vi	to complain
leader	*Leiter/in*	vti	to lead
concerned	*besorgt*	≈	worried
to single out	*auswählen*	≈	to isolate
victimization [ˌvɪktɪmaɪ'zeɪʃn]	*Schikanierung*	vt	to victimize
target	*Opfer*	vt	to target
session	*Sitzung, Stunde*	phr	group ~, one-to-one ~
victim	*Opfer*	<>	perpetrator
to prevent	*verhindern*	n	prevention
to involve	*einbeziehen*	n	involvement
witness	*Zeuge/Zeugin*	vt	to witness
issue	*Problem, Thema*	≈	problem
to approach	*angehen*	n	approach
to suspect	*vermuten*	n	suspicion
to sneak (coll)	*petzen*	≈	to tell tales
bystander	*Zuschauer/in*	≈	witness
to tackle	*(erfolgreich) bewältigen*	≈	to deal with
to go on	*vor sich gehen*	≈	to happen
to be afraid of	*sich fürchten vor*	≈	to be frightened of
to make clear	*klar machen*	≈	to clarify
to encourage	*ermutigen*	<>	to discourage
to report	*melden*	n	report
incident	*Vorfall, Ereignis*	≈	event
to intimidate [ɪn'tɪmɪdeɪt]	*einschüchtern*	n	intimidation
to get away with	*sich erlauben können*	<>	to be punished for

Apprenticeships in the UK

FREQUENTLY ASKED QUESTIONS

What sort of person is accepted on an apprenticeship?

All sorts of people, from all walks of life, are working towards or have successfully completed an apprenticeship. In order to achieve success an element of commitment is required and expected on your part.

Apprenticeships can be demanding, but rewarding. Being an apprentice has enabled many people to fulfil their career goals and it can help you do the same too.

What happens in the application process?

There are two ways to apply for an apprenticeship. You can approach an employer who takes on apprentices and see if they are willing to give you a job. You can also apply through the Learning and Skills Council, who will put you in touch with a training provider who will then try to match you with an employer.

The selection process is just like any other job application process. You could be put through interviews and even asked to take tests to see if you're a suitable person. This process can be carried out by both the training provider and employer, so you need to be prepared to sell yourself and convince others that an apprenticeship is for you. After all, there's no such thing as an automatic place; employers can refuse to take you on if they don't think you're right for the job.

How do apprenticeships work?

Apprenticeships are a mixture of on- and off-the-job training. On the job you will work with a mentor, learning skills on site. Off the job you will spend time with a training provider, working towards a National Vocational Qualification (NVQ) at Level 2 or 3.

You will gain key transferable skills – like working in teams, problem-solving, communication and using new technology as well as studying (in most cases) for a technical certificate, which will give you further knowledge and understanding of your job.

The amount of time you'll spend studying varies; it can be anything from 100 to 1,000 hours over the course of your apprenticeship, depending on your chosen profession.

[http://www.apprenticeships.org.uk/wanttobecomeanapprentice/faqs/]

apprenticeship [ə'prentɪʃɪp]	*Ausbildung*	≈	traineeship
to accept	*akzeptieren*	<>	to reject
walk of life	*soziale Stellung*	≈	social position
successfully	*erfolgreich*	vi	to succeed (in)
to complete	*abschließen*	n	completion
to achieve	*erreichen*	n	achievement
success	*Erfolg*	<>	failure
commitment	*Engagement*	adj	committed
to require	*verlangen*	n	requirement
demanding	*anstrengend*	≈	challenging
rewarding	*lohnend*	vt	to reward sb with sth
apprentice	*Auszubildende/r*	≈	trainee
to enable to	*(es) ermöglichen*	<>	to prevent from
career goal	*Berufsziel*	≈	career aspiration
application	*Bewerbung*	phr	letter of ~
to apply for	*sich bewerben um*	n	applicant
to approach	*sich wenden an*	≈	to contact
employer	*Arbeitgeber/in*	<>	employee
to take on	*einstellen*	≈	to employ
skill	*Fertigkeit*	phr	job ~s, interpersonal ~s
to put in touch with	*in Verbindung bringen mit*	≈	to put in contact with
training provider	*Lehrstellenvermittler*	vt	to provide
to match (with)	*zuordnen*	≈	to pair up
selection	*Auswahl*	vt	to select
suitable	*geeignet*	n	suitability
to convince	*überzeugen*	≈	to persuade
on-the-job training	*Ausbildung am Arbeitsplatz*	cf	coaching
off-the-job training	*Berufsschule*	cf	evening class, day release
mentor	*Ausbilder/in*	vt	to mentor
on site	*vor Ort*	<>	off site
vocational [vəʊ'keɪʃənl]	*beruflich*	≈	job-related
key skill	*Schlüsselfähigkeit*	≈	vital skill
transferable skill	*übertragbare Fähigkeit*	vt	to transfer
problem-solving	*Problemlösung*	vt	to solve
technology	*Technologie*	adj	technological
technical	*technisch, Fach-*		
knowledge ['nɒlɪdʒ]	*Wissen, Kenntnisse*	adj	knowledgeable
understanding	*Verständnis*	vti	to understand
over the course of	*im Verlauf von*	≈	during
profession	*Beruf*	adj	professional

www.vistawide.com

Why study abroad?

1. It's the best way to learn a language. You'll be immersed in a culture that speaks the language you are learning. You're surrounded by the language on a daily basis and are seeing and hearing it in the proper cultural context.

2. It provides the opportunity to travel. Weekends and academic breaks allow you to explore your surroundings. Some programmes even have field trips planned in or around the curriculum.

3. It allows you to get to know another culture first-hand. Cultural differences affect more than just language, food, appearance and personal habits. A person's culture reflects deep perceptions, beliefs and values that influence his or her way of life.

4. It will help you develop skills and give you experiences a classroom setting will never provide. You will encounter situations that are wholly unfamiliar to you and will learn to adapt and respond in effective ways.

5. It affords you the opportunity to make friends around the world. You will meet not only natives to the culture in which you are studying, but also other international students.

6. It helps you to learn about yourself. You'll return home with new ideas and perspectives about yourself and your own culture. It may challenge you to reconsider your beliefs and values.

7. It expands your world view. Students who study abroad return home with an informed and much less biased perspective toward other cultures.

8. It gives you the opportunity to break out of your academic routine. You will get to know an entirely new academic system, and you will have the chance to take courses not offered at your home university.

9. It enhances employment opportunities. The world continues to become more globalized. Through an employer's eyes, a student who has studied abroad is self-motivated, independent, willing to embrace challenges and able to cope with diverse problems and situations.

[Slightly adapted: www.vistawide.com]

abroad	*im Ausland*	<>	at home
to be immersed in	*eintauchen in*	n	immersion
surrounded by	*umgeben von*	adj	surrounding
on a daily basis	*jeden Tag*	≈	every day
cultural	*kulturell*	n	culture
opportunity	*Möglichkeit*	≈	chance
academic break	*Semesterferien*	≈	university/college holidays
to explore	*erkunden*	n	exploration
surroundings	*Umgebung*	vt	to surround
field trip	*Exkursion*	cf	excursion – *Ausflug*
curriculum	*Lehrplan*	cf	extra-curricular
to get to know	*kennenlernen*	≈	to acquaint yourself with
first-hand	*aus erster Hand*	<>	indirectly
appearance	*Aussehen*	vi	to appear
habit	*Gewohnheit*	adj	habitual [həˈbɪtʃuəl]
to reflect	*widerspiegeln*	n	reflection
perception	*Vorstellung*	vt	to perceive
belief	*Glaube*	vt	to believe
value	*Wert*	adj	valuable
to influence	*beeinflussen*	adj	influential
way of life	*Lebensart*	≈	lifestyle
skill	*Fertigkeit*	adj	skilful
experience	*Erfahrung*	vt	to experience
setting	*Umgebung*	≈	context
to encounter	*begegnen*	≈	to meet (with)
unfamiliar	*unbekannt*	≈	unknown
to adapt	*(sich) anpassen*	n	adaptation
to respond	*reagieren*	≈	to react
native	*Einheimische/r*	adj	native
perspective	*Perspektive*	≈	point of view
to challenge	*herausfordern*	≈	to call into question
to reconsider	*überdenken*	≈	to re-evaluate
to expand	*erweitern*	≈	to widen
world view	*Weltsicht*	≈	horizons
informed	*informiert, fundiert*	≈	well-informed
biased [ˈbaɪəst]	*einseitig*	n	bias
to break out of	*ausbrechen aus*	<>	to be constrained by
to enhance	*erhöhen, verbessern*	n	enhancement
employment	*Beschäftigung*	vt	to employ
globalized	*globalisiert*	n	globalization
self-motivated	*eigenmotiviert*	n	self-motivation
independent	*selbständig*	n	independence
to embrace	*annehmen*	<>	to avoid, to shun
to cope with	*fertig werden mit*	≈	to overcome, to deal with

What is a blended family?

In a blended family or stepfamily, one or both partners have been married before. Each has lost a spouse through divorce or death, and one or both of them have children from their previous marriage. They fall in love and decide to remarry, and in turn, form a new, blended family that includes children from one or both of their first households.

How common are blended families?

Today, at least one third of all children in the USA are expected to live in a blended family before they reach the age of 18. The blended family is becoming more of a norm than an aberration. Born of conflict and loss, newfound commitment, and often heart-wrenching transition, blended families face many lifestyle adjustments and challenges.

Fortunately, most blended families are able to work out their problems and live together successfully. But it takes careful planning, open discussions of feelings, positive attitudes, mutual respect and patience.

What role should the non-residential parent play in the blended family?

After a divorce, children usually adjust better to their new lives when the parent who has moved out of the family home maintains a good relationship with them. When parents remarry, the non-residential parent often begins to lose touch with the children. Fathers appear to be the worst offenders; on average, dads reduce their visits to their children by half within the first year of remarriage.

The less a parent visits, the more likely a child is to feel abandoned. The non-residential parent can remain in touch by developing special activities that involve only the children and him/herself.

It is not a good idea for parents to speak negatively about their ex-partners in front of their children. This undermines a child's self-esteem and may put him or her in the troubling position of defending that parent.

[http://www.helpguide.org/mental/blended_families_stepfamilies.htm]

3 Family and community

▸ **blended family**	*Patchworkfamilie*	cf	to blend – *mischen*
▸ **stepfamily**	*Stieffamilie*	cf	stepmother, etc.
▸ **spouse** [spaʊs] (formell)	*Ehepartner/in, Gemahl/in*	≈	husband/wife
▸ **divorce**	*Scheidung*	vt	to divorce
▸ **previous**	*früher*	≈	preceding
▸ **marriage** ['mærɪdʒ]	*Ehe*	vti	to marry
▸ **to fall in love**	*sich verlieben*		
▸ **to remarry**	*wieder heiraten*	n	remarriage
▸ **household**	*Haushalt*	≈	family unit
▸ **common**	*häufig*	<>	rare
▸ **norm**	*Norm(alfall)*	adj	normal
▸ **aberration** [ˌæbə'reɪʃn]	*Abweichung*	adj	aberrant [ə'berənt]
▸ **loss**	*Verlust*	vti	to lose
▸ **newfound**	*neu entdeckt*	≈	brand new
▸ **commitment**	*Bindung*	cf	to be committed to
▸ **heart-wrenching** ['hɑːt rentʃɪŋ]	*herzzerreißend*	≈	heart-breaking
▸ **transition**	*Übergang*	phr	period of ~
▸ **to face**	*sich gegenübersehen*	≈	to be confronted with
▸ **lifestyle**	*Lebensstil*	≈	way of life
▸ **adjustment**	*Anpassung*	≈	adaptation
▸ **challenge**	*Herausforderung*	vt	to challenge
▸ **to work out**	*lösen*	≈	to solve
▸ **attitude**	*Einstellung*	≈	mind-set, approach
▸ **mutual**	*gegenseitig*	≈	reciprocal
▸ **patience**	*Geduld*	<>	impatience
▸ **to play a role**	*eine Rolle spielen*	≈	to play a part
▸ **non-residential**	*ausgezogen*	cf	to reside (formal) – *wohnen*
▸ **to adjust to**	*sich anpassen an*	≈	to adapt to
▸ **to move out**	*ausziehen*	≈	to leave home
▸ **family home**	*Familienwohnung*	cf	parental home – *Elternhaus*
▸ **to maintain**	*aufrechterhalten*	≈	to continue
▸ **relationship**	*Beziehung*	phr	to have a good ~ with sb
▸ **to lose touch with**	*die Verbindung verlieren zu*	≈	to lose contact with
▸ **on average**	*im Durchschnitt*	adj	average
▸ **to reduce**	*reduzieren*	n	reduction
▸ **to abandon**	*verlassen*	n	abandonment
▸ **to involve**	*einschließen*	n	involvement
▸ **to undermine**	*untergraben*	≈	to weaken
▸ **self-esteem**	*Selbstwertgefühl*	≈	self-confidence
▸ **troubling**	*schwierig*	≈	disturbing
▸ **to defend**	*verteidigen*	<>	to attack

Urban and rural lifestyles

Thread: The countryside is soooo boring!!

Why do 'townies' all want to live in the country? I live in a small village in Cumbria in the north of England and I hate it. It's so boring here. There are no facilities: there's no leisure centre, no entertainment, no nightlife, not even adequate medical care. To go shopping you need to go to Kendal, the nearest big town, and to get there you're dependent on public transport if you're too young to drive. Only there are just two buses a day.

posted by: scarecrow

Reply *posted by:* townmouse

Scarecrow, I understand your frustration and boredom. I used to live in a small, isolated community like you, but when I was 14 my family moved to Manchester. It's nice having all the convenience of a big city nearby – the shopping malls, the cinemas, the cafés and clubs. But don't be fooled: life in the big city has its drawbacks, too.

Firstly, there's the traffic congestion. I only live five miles from the city centre, but it takes me more than half an hour to drive to college. If I take the tram and the bus I have to change twice, and if I cycle I'm breathing in all the exhaust fumes of thousands of vehicles.

Secondly, there's the lack of security and community spirit. People around here are scared – scared of the gangs, scared that their houses will be burgled, scared that their kids will be sold drugs in the school playground.

Reply *posted by:* greenie

I think you're lucky living in the country, scarecrow. You've got all that unspoilt nature around you. OK, so there are problems, and the government doesn't invest enough in rural communities. There are lots of recreational opportunities in the country though. Hiking, fishing, horseriding, etc. Maybe you'll appreciate these things more as you get older – from what you say I'm guessing you're about 15, right?

▸ **urban** ['ɜːbən]	*städtisch*	cf	suburban
▸ **rural**	*ländlich*	≈	country (attrib adj)
▸ **lifestyle**	*Lebensstil*	≈	way of life
▸ **countryside**	*Land(schaft)*	cf	landscape – *Landschaft*
▸ **townie** (coll)	*Städter/in*	<>	country bumpkin (coll)
▸ **country**	*Land*	<>	town
▸ **village**	*Dorf*	phr	~ life, the global ~
▸ **facilities**	*Einrichtungen*	≈	amenities
▸ **leisure centre**	*Freizeitzentrum*	≈	sports centre
▸ **entertainment**	*Unterhaltung*	vt	to entertain
▸ **nightlife**	*Nachtleben*	cf	social life
▸ **adequate**	*ausreichend*	<>	inadequate
▸ **medical care**	*ärztliche Versorgung*	cf	dental care
▸ **dependent on**	*abhängig von*	n	dependency
▸ **public transport**	*öffentliche Verkehrsmittel*	vt	to transport
▸ **frustration**	*Enttäuschung, Frust*	vt	to frustrate
▸ **boredom** ['bɔːdəm]	*Langeweile*	vt	to bore
▸ **isolated**	*isoliert*	≈	cut off
▸ **community**	*Gemeinde*	adj	communal
▸ **convenience**	*Komfort*	<>	inconvenience
▸ **nearby**	*nahe (gelegen)*	<>	far away
▸ **shopping mall**	*Einkaufszentrum*	≈	shopping centre
▸ **drawback**	*Nachteil*	≈	disadvantage
▸ **traffic congestion**	*Verkehrsstau*	adj	congested
▸ **city centre**	*Stadtzentrum*	AE	downtown
▸ **to change**	*umsteigen*	AE	to transfer
▸ **to cycle**	*mit dem Rad fahren*	n	bicycle, bike
▸ **to breathe in**	*einatmen*	≈	to inhale
▸ **exhaust fumes** [ɪg'zɔːst fjuːmz]	*Abgase*	cf	exhaust pipe – *Auspuff*
▸ **vehicle** ['viːəkl]	*Fahrzeug*	adj	vehicular
▸ **lack of**	*Fehlen von*		
▸ **security**	*Sicherheit*	adj	secure
▸ **community spirit**	*Gemeinschaftsgeist*		
▸ **scared**	*verängstigt*	≈	frightened
▸ **gang**	*Bande*	cf	~ warfare – *Bandenkrieg*
▸ **to burgle**	*einbrechen (in)*	n	burglary, burglar
▸ **drug**	*Droge*	cf	~ addict – *Drogenabhängige/r*
▸ **unspoilt**	*unberührt*	vt	to spoil – *verderben*
▸ **nature**	*Natur*	adj	natural
▸ **to invest**	*investieren*	n	investment
▸ **recreational**	*Freizeit-, Erholungs-*	n	recreation
▸ **opportunity**	*Möglichkeit*	adj	opportune
▸ **hiking**	*Wandern*	vi	to hike
▸ **to appreciate** [ə'priːʃieɪt]	*würdigen, schätzen*	n	appreciation

http://forum.newsonline.info/readerpoll.asp

The News – Online Forum

What's better for the UK: multiculturalism or integration?

The UK is one of the most multicultural nations on Earth. We are made up of four different countries. We are also made up of a variety of different cultures from all parts of the globe. For our future success we need to continue the great British tradition of tolerance.

Answers

Integration. If migrants want to live here, they need to make an effort to learn our language and respect our laws and customs. If they can't do that, they have no place in our country. **Ben, Glasgow, Scotland**

Ben, you seem to feel threatened by the idea of diversity – people having different beliefs and yes, speaking different languages! I think that's a very sad attitude. Diversity doesn't threaten our society, it enriches it.
Tara, Ontario, Canada

When you write 'integration', don't you really mean 'assimilation'?

Integration to me means that people acknowledge a common thread of British identity – but are free to have their own cultural beliefs as well. For example, you can be British but still be proud of your Scottish, Indian or Polish heritage.

Assimilation on the other hand suggests that all newcomers have to accept the 'dominant' British culture – to think the same way, to conform. A British government minister once suggested that people weren't really British unless they supported Great Britain in international sporting events! Do we really want that kind of homogeneous, conformist Britain?
Meera, London, England

'Multiculturalism' has become a codeword for sitting back passively and letting extremists and fundamentalists take over our country.

Look at the 2005 bombings in London: they were perpetrated by young British Muslims who felt hatred for the country they grew up in. They no longer identified with British society in any way. Instead, British people had become for them 'the enemy'.

Why are we allowing our young people to become radicalized like this? We must try harder to integrate them into our society. **Tariq, Leeds, England**

▸ **multiculturalism**	*Nebeneinander mehrerer Kulturen*	cf	pluralism
▸ **integration** [ˌɪntɪˈɡreɪʃn]	*Integration*	vti	to integrate (into)
▸ **multicultural**	*multikulturell*	<>	monocultural
▸ **to be made up of**	*bestehen aus*	≈	to consist of
▸ **variety**	*Vielzahl*	adj	varied
▸ **globe**	*Globus, Erdball*	adj	global
▸ **tolerance**	*Toleranz*	vt	to tolerate
▸ **migrant**	*Einwanderer/-rin*	vi	to migrate
▸ **to make an effort**	*sich Mühe geben*	≈	to try hard
▸ **to respect**	*respektieren, achten*	<>	to disrespect
▸ **law**	*Gesetz*	adj	lawful
▸ **custom**	*Brauch*	≈	tradition
▸ **to threaten**	*bedrohen*	n	threat
▸ **diversity**	*Vielfalt*	adj	diverse
▸ **belief**	*Glaube*	vt	to believe
▸ **attitude**	*Haltung, Einstellung*	≈	standpoint
▸ **to enrich**	*bereichern*	<>	to impoverish
▸ **assimilation**	*Assimilation*	vt	to assimilate
▸ **to acknowledge** [əkˈnɒlɪdʒ]	*anerkennen*	n	acknowledgement
▸ **common thread**	*gemeinsamer Faden*	≈	unifying element
▸ **identity**	*Identität*	v prep	to identify with
▸ **proud of**	*stolz auf*	n	pride
▸ **heritage**	*Herkunft, Erbe*	≈	legacy, birthright
▸ **newcomer**	*Ankömmling*	≈	new arrival
▸ **dominant**	*vorherrschend*	vt	to dominate
▸ **to conform**	*sich anpassen*	n	conformity
▸ **to support**	*unterstützen*	n	support
▸ **sporting event**	*sportlicher Wettkampf*	cf	cultural, social event
▸ **homogeneous** [ˌhɒməˈdʒiːniəs]	*homogen, gleichartig*	<>	heterogeneous
▸ **conformist**	*angepasst, konformistisch*	<>	non-conformist
▸ **codeword**	*verschleiernde Bezeichnung*	≈	euphemism
▸ **passively**	*passiv*	<>	actively
▸ **extremist**	*Extremist/in*	<>	moderate
▸ **fundamentalist**	*Fundamentalist/in*	n	fundamentalism
▸ **to take over**	*übernehmen*	≈	to seize control of
▸ **bombing**	*Bombenanschlag*	vt	to bomb
▸ **to perpetrate**	*verüben*	≈	to commit
▸ **hatred**	*Hass*	vt	to hate
▸ **to grow up**	*aufwachsen*	adj	grown up
▸ **to identify with**	*sich identifizieren mit*	cf	identity
▸ **enemy**	*Feind*	n	enmity
▸ **to radicalize**	*radikalisieren*	adj	radical
▸ **to integrate into**	*integrieren in*	n	integration

Racism

Racism is destructive. It disempowers people by devaluing their identity. It destroys community cohesion and creates divisions in society. It is the opposite of the democratic principle of equality and the right of all people to be treated fairly.

In Australia, journalist Michael Duffy is interviewing social commentator Andrew Norton.

Duffy Last December saw some appalling scenes in Sydney when an angry mob attacked people of Middle Eastern appearance. It raised the question of whether there's an underlying racism in Australia.

So when was the last time Australians were asked if they thought all races were equal, and what did they say?

Norton Well, that was back in 2001. There was a fairly small minority, under 15%, who could be classified as racist. That is, they believed that other races were inferior in some respect. But when asked whether they were in some way prejudiced against other races, a much higher number said 'yes'. About half the respondents admitted that they had some kind of prejudice against someone from another race. This might be minor stuff – they may not like the sound of their language or the smell of their cooking, but nevertheless it's still prejudice. If half our population feels this way, that's a cause for concern.

Duffy Do we know much about that 15%, what background they themselves have, for example?

Norton They tend to be older Australians of British origin. There's a clear pattern that younger people are generally more positive about racial diversity than older people.

Duffy What about immigrants or migrants themselves? Do we know how many of them have experienced prejudice?

Norton There was one survey which asked if people had ever experienced discrimination because of their ethnic origin in various situations. Under a quarter of the population had experienced any prejudice …

[Paragraph 1: http://www.racismnoway.com.au/library/understanding/index-What.html]
[http://www.abc.net.au/rn/counterpoint/stories/2006/1607107.htm]

racism ['reɪsɪzəm]	*Rassismus*	≈	xenophobia
destructive	*destruktiv*	<>	constructive
to disempower	*entmündigen*	cf	power – *Macht, Kraft*
to devalue	*abwerten*	cf	value – *Wert*
to destroy	*zerstören*	n	destruction
community	*Gemeinde*	adj	communal
cohesion	*Zusammenhalt*	adj	cohesive
division	*Teilung*	adj	divisive
democratic	*demokratisch*	n	democracy
principle	*Grundsatz, Prinzip*	≈	moral standard
equality	*Gleichheit*	<>	inequality
right	*Recht*	≈	entitlement
to treat	*behandeln*	n	treatment
fairly	*fair, gerecht*	n	fairness
appalling	*entsetzlich*	≈	awful, dreadful
scene	*Szene*	≈	sight
mob	*Menschenmenge*	≈	crowd
to attack	*angreifen*	n	attack
to raise	*aufwerfen*	≈	to prompt
underlying	*unterschwellig*	≈	hidden
race	*Rasse*	≈	ethnic group
equal	*gleich (berechtigt)*	<>	unequal
minority	*Minderheit*	<>	majority
to classify as	*einstufen als*	n	classification
racist ['reɪsɪst]	*rassistisch*	n	racist
inferior	*minderwertig*	n	inferiority
in some respect	*in gewisser Hinsicht*	≈	in some way
to be prejudiced against	*Vorurteile haben gegen(über)*	≈	to be biased against
to admit	*zugeben*	n	admission
prejudice	*Vorurteil*	≈	bias
population	*Bevölkerung*	≈	inhabitants
concern	*Sorge*	cf	to be concerned about
background	*Herkunft*	≈	personal circumstances
to tend to	*(dazu) neigen*	n	tendency
origin	*Herkunft*	v prep	to originate from
pattern	*Muster*	phr	to follow a ~
racial ['reɪʃl]	*Rassen-*	≈	ethnic
diversity	*Vielfalt*	adj	diverse
immigrant	*Einwanderer/-rin*	cf	immigration
migrant	*Einwanderer/-rin*	vi	to migrate
to experience	*erfahren, erleben*	n	experience
survey	*Umfrage*	vt	to survey
discrimination	*Diskriminierung*	v prep	to discriminate against
ethnic origin	*ethnische Herkunft*	≈	ethnicity

14,000 knife crime victims a year

Knife violence in Britain is far worse than official statistics suggest, with almost 14,000 people taken to hospital for injuries caused by knives and other sharp weapons last year. An average of 38 victims of stab wounds are admitted daily to accident and emergency departments across the country.

Assaults with sharp implements, including swords and daggers, resulted in 12,340 people being admitted last year – 446 of whom were no older than 14.

New figures highlight how the number of people prosecuted by courts for possessing knives has nearly doubled in 10 years. Most offenders were not jailed, with just 14 per cent ending up in prison.

London is the centre of a nationwide epidemic. Fatal stabbings of teenagers in London total 14 since the start of the year.

Hundreds of people attended a rally this morning in north London, where 16-year-old Ben Kinsella was stabbed to death last Sunday. The youngster had written a letter to the Prime Minister as part of his schoolwork, warning that knife violence was becoming 'part of our culture'.

Senior police officers want hospitals to notify police of all patients with stab wounds, in the same way that they do with gunshot victims. The police now want to use hospital records to identify knife-crime hotspots.

Campaigners calling for tough action were not impressed by the police announcement on Friday that just 75 officers will run a new taskforce against knife crime across London.

Lynn Costello, co-founder of Mothers Against Murder and Aggression, said: "We have to get tough. We've let our kids get away with murder for years."

[Slightly adapted: www.independent.co.uk]

4 Law and order

crime	*Verbrechen*	adj	criminal
victim	*Opfer*	<>	attacker
violence	*Gewalt*	adj	violent
statistics (pl)	*Statistik*		
to suggest	*andeuten*	n	suggestion
injury	*Verletzung*	vt	to injure
weapon ['wepən]	*Waffe*	phr	deadly ~
stab wound [wuːnd]	*Stichwunde*	vt	to stab, to wound
to admit to hospital	*ins Krankenhaus einliefern*	n	hospital admission
accident and emergency (A&E) department	*Unfall- und Notfallstation*	cf	casualty department – *Unfallstation*
assault	*Überfall*	vt	to assault
implement	*Gegenstand*	≈	instrument
sword [sɔːd]	*Schwert*		
dagger	*Dolch*		
to result in	*dazu führen*	n	result
to highlight	*deutlich machen*	≈	to emphasize
to prosecute	*strafrechtlich verfolgen*	n	prosecution
court	*Gericht*	cf	courtroom – *Gerichtssaal*
to possess	*besitzen*	n	possession
offender	*Straftäter/in*	cf	offence – *Delikt*
to jail	*einsperren*	n	jail
to end up	*landen*	≈	to find oneself
prison	*Gefängnis*	≈	jail, gaol
nationwide	*landesweit*	≈	countrywide
epidemic	*Epidemie*	adj	epidemic
fatal	*mit tödlichem Ausgang*	<>	non-fatal
stabbing	*Messerstecherei*	≈	knife attack
rally	*Kundgebung*	≈	demonstration
to stab to death	*totstechen*	cf	to knife – *stechen*
police officer	*Polizeibeamter/-tin*	≈	policeman/woman
to notify	*melden*	≈	to inform
gunshot	*Schusswaffen-*	cf	to shoot – *erschießen*
to identify	*identifizieren*	n	identification
hotspot	*Brennpunkt*	≈	trouble spot
campaigner	*Aktivist/in*	v prep	to campaign for/against
to call for	*fordern*	≈	to demand
taskforce	*Sonderkommission*	phr	to set up a ~
murder ['mɜːdə]	*Mord*	⚠	murderer – *Mörder/in*
aggression	*Aggression*	adj	agressive
to get tough	*durchgreifen*	≈	to take a hard line
to get away with	*(ungestraft) davonkommen mit*	≈	to escape punishment for

Talking Point: Cybercrime

Presenter With me in the studio is Nick Lane, a specialist in internet security. Nick, welcome to Talking Point. What is meant by cybercrime?

Nick It's a term which covers a huge range of illegal activities on the internet, including financial scams, computer hacking, online paedophile rings, virus attacks, e-mail stalking and websites that promote racial hatred or terrorism.

Presenter We hear a lot of alarming reports in the media about the growth of cybercrime. Should ordinary computer users be concerned by these reports, or are they really just for big businesses and governments to worry about?

Nick Ordinary computer users should be very concerned. If you buy a new computer today, take it home and connect it to the internet without any protection, the computer will be infected by malware within 30 minutes.

Presenter Sorry, what's malware?

Nick Malicious software. Any software that's designed to infiltrate or damage a computer system without the owner's informed consent.

Presenter And what might this malware do?

Nick It might be simply annoying – slowing your computer's performance or causing it to crash. Then again, it might include spyware to steal your personal details and use them in identity theft fraud – to get credit cards in your name, and so on. It might include a keystroke logger to capture your online passwords and enable thieves to gain control of your bank account. It might even recruit your computer to a botnet – a robot network – which can then be used to send out spam or even launch a large-scale attack on an organization's or country's computer network.

Presenter Wow! So shouldn't the government be doing something to track down the cybercriminals?

Nick Yes, and they are. But the problem for governments and law-enforcement agencies is that cybercrime isn't limited by national borders. An investigation that begins in one country may quickly lead to another, but without the co-operation of other nations, it's impossible to find the perpetrators and bring them to justice …

cybercrime	*Internetkriminalität*	≈	internet crime
security	*Sicherheit*	adj	secure
scam	*Betrug*	≈	fraud
computer hacking	*Computerknacken*	vt / v prep	to hack (into)
online	*im Internet*	≈	on the (inter)net
paedophile ring ['pi:dəʊfaɪl rɪŋ]	*Pädophilenring*	cf	paedophilia
virus attack	*Computervirusangriff*		
stalking	*Nachstellen*	vt	to stalk
to promote	*fördern*	≈	to encourage
racial hatred	*Rassenhass*	vt	to hate
alarming	*alarmierend*	n	alarm
growth	*Anwachsen*	vi	to grow
concerned	*besorgt*	n	concern
to connect	*anschließen*	n	connection
protection	*(Antiviren-)Schutz*	vt	to protect
to infect	*infizieren*	≈	to contaminate
malware	*infizierende Software*	abbr	mal(icious) (soft)ware
malicious [mə'lɪʃəs]	*böswillig*	<>	benign
to infiltrate	*eindringen in*	≈	to penetrate
to damage	*schädigen*	n	damage
consent	*Zustimmung*	≈	agreement
annoying	*lästig*	≈	irritating
performance	*Leistung*	vti	to perform
to crash	*abstürzen*	n	crash
personal details	*persönliche Daten*	≈	personal information
identity theft	*Identitätsdiebstahl*	≈	ID theft
fraud [frɔ:d]	*Betrug*	vt	defraud
keystroke logger	*Keylogger, Tasten-Rekorder*	vt	to log
to capture	*erbeuten*	n	capture
thief	*Dieb/in*	pl	thieves
to gain control of	*Zugriff erlangen für*	≈	to take over
to recruit	*rekrutieren*	n	recruitment
network	*Netz(werk)*	phr	telecommunications ~
to launch	*starten*	n	launch
large-scale	*Groß-*	<>	small-scale
to track down	*aufspüren*	≈	to trace
cybercriminal	*Internetkriminelle/r*	cf	hacker
law-enforcement agency	*Strafverfolgungsbehörde*	vt	to enforce
limited	*begrenzt*	n	limitation
national border	*Landesgrenze*	≈	national boundary
investigation	*Untersuchung*	vt	to investigate
co-operation	*Zusammenarbeit*	vi	to co-operate
perpetrator ['pɜ:pətreɪtə]	*Täter/in*	vt	to perpetrate
to bring to justice	*vor Gericht bringen*	≈	to prosecute

A look inside America's gun culture

The reaction to this latest massacre in the United States will be predictable. The first 24 hours will be full of shocked witnesses, traumatized victims and grieving families. Then, almost immediately, the discussion will switch to America's gun culture. Anti-gun campaigners will call on the President to restrict the availability of firearms. But the pro-gun lobby will cite the US Constitution's 'right to bear arms' and other familiar slogans such as 'guns don't kill people, people kill people'. Then the whole issue will disappear until the next, inevitable mass shooting.

Gun control is one of the most difficult issues in the USA. The right to own a gun and defend oneself is central to the American identity. Guns enabled settlers to protect themselves from Indians, animals and foreign armies. Citizens took responsibility for their self-defence. This 'Wild West' mentality is still evident in the US today. The importance of guns also comes from the role of hunting in American culture. In the nation's early years, hunting was essential for food and today it remains popular as both a sport and a way of life in many parts of the country.

Part of the reason this issue goes round in circles is that it is impossible to establish a causal link between guns and violence. Those advocating gun control point out that guns are involved in the vast majority of fatal violent crimes in the US. But they cannot prove that the guns cause the violence. There is no way of calculating the role the gun culture plays in comparison to poverty, education, mental illness, alcohol and unemployment.

Yet the impact of America's gun culture can be seen everywhere. When movies appear on television, sex is censored, but shootings are shown in graphic detail. Metal detectors are used in government buildings and even some schools.

There is no national gun register in the USA, so it is impossible to know exactly how many guns are in circulation or who has them. The FBI estimates there are more than 200 million guns in civilian hands.

[Adapted extracts: www.abc.net.au]

▸ **gun culture**	*Waffenkultur*	cf	drugs culture
▸ **massacre** ['mæsəkə]	*Massaker*	vt	to massacre
▸ **predictable**	*vorhersagbar*	vt	to predict
▸ **to shock**	*erschüttern*	n	shock
▸ **witness**	*Zeuge/-gin*	vt	to witness
▸ **to traumatize**	*traumatisieren*	adj	traumatic
▸ **victim**	*Opfer*	<>	attacker
▸ **to grieve**	*trauern*	n	grief
▸ **campaigner** [kæm'peɪnə]	*Aktivist/in*	v prep	to campaign for/against
▸ **to restrict**	*einschränken*	n	restriction
▸ **availability**	*Verfügbarkeit*	adj	available
▸ **firearm** ['faɪərɑːm]	*Schusswaffe*	≈	gun
▸ **constitution**	*Verfassung*	adj	constitutional
▸ **to bear arms**	*Waffen tragen*	≈	to carry weapons
▸ **slogan**	*Spruch*	≈	saying, catchphrase
▸ **issue**	*Thema*	≈	problem
▸ **inevitable**	*unvermeidlich*	<>	avoidable
▸ **mass shooting**	*Massenerschießung*	vt	to shoot
▸ **gun control**	*Waffenbesitz*	≈	firearms restrictions
▸ **to defend**	*verteidigen*	adj	defensive
▸ **to be central to**	*von zentraler Bedeutung sein*	<>	to be peripheral to
▸ **to protect**	*schützen*	n	protection
▸ **to take responsibility for**	*die Verantwortung übernehmen*	adj	responsible
▸ **self-defence**	*Selbstverteidigung*	<>	attack
▸ **Wild West**	*Wildwest-*	cf	Western (film)
▸ **mentality**	*Mentalität*	≈	mindset
▸ **hunting**	*Jagd*	vti	to hunt
▸ **way of life**	*Lebensweise*	≈	lifestyle
▸ **to go round in circles**	*sich im Kreise drehen*	≈	to be impossible to resolve
▸ **causal link**	*kausaler Zusammenhang*	cf	cause and effect
▸ **violence**	*Gewalt*	<>	non-violence
▸ **to advocate**	*befürworten*	n	advocacy
▸ **fatal**	*tödlich*	n	fatality
▸ **to prove**	*beweisen*	⚠	≠ *prüfen*
▸ **poverty**	*Armut*	adj	poor
▸ **mental illness**	*Geisteskrankheit*	≈	psychiatric disorder
▸ **unemployment**	*Arbeitslosigkeit*	cf	to be unemployed
▸ **impact**	*(Aus-)Wirkung*	≈	effect
▸ **to censor**	*zensieren*	n	censorship
▸ **shooting**	*Schießerei*	cf	gunshot – *Schuss*
▸ **graphic**	*bildlich*	adv	graphically
▸ **metal detector**	*Metalldetektor*	vt	to detect
▸ **to be in circulation**	*im Umlauf sein*	≈	to circulate
▸ **to estimate**	*schätzen*	n	estimate, estimation
▸ **civilian**	*Privat-*	<>	military

Web poll:

CCTV

In the UK, thousands of closed circuit TV cameras have been installed across the country in an attempt to reduce crime. London alone has 10,000 CCTV cameras. **Should other cities around the world follow London's example?**

YES 12029 **NO** 15341

Comments

Of course! It stands to reason that offenders will think twice about committing crimes if they know that the evidence will be recorded on video.
Jez, Sydney, Australia

Statistics show that there is no link between more CCTV cameras and more crimes being solved.
It is estimated that CCTV cameras have cost the British taxpayer about £200 million in the last 10 years, with no clear results. Maybe that money should have been spent recruiting and training more police officers. Better street lighting would also help. **Kev, Wandsworth, UK**

There probably is a deterrent effect, but it's difficult to prove, because you can't prove that someone was thinking of committing a crime but then changed their mind because of CCTV.
Also CCTV might just have the effect of moving crime to the suburbs where there is less surveillance. **R J Singh, Mumbai, India**

I think that there is a place for CCTV, but it depends on where and how it is used. It can be used in inner-city crime hotspots for example to catch drunken youths who assault people and vandalize property late at night. It's also reassuring to know that there is CCTV at train stations and other secluded places late at night. **KL, Cardiff, UK**

What about our right to privacy? The government is asking us to exchange our civil liberties for a false sense of security.
There are lots of cases of CCTV being misused by the operators, for example to spy on women in their bedrooms. **Sal, Leeds, UK**

They are turning our country into a police state. 10,000 cameras are just the beginning. Soon they'll want to track and record your every move.
Paula, Wimbledon, UK

4 Law and order

CCTV (closed-circuit television)	*Überwachungskameras*	phr	~ surveillance
to install	*installieren*	n	installation
attempt	*Versuch*	vt	to attempt
to reduce	*reduzieren*	n	reduction
crime	*Verbrechen*	adj	criminal
to stand to reason	*logisch sein*	≈	to be obvious
offender	*Straftäter/in*	vi	to offend
to think twice about	*es sich gut überlegen*	≈	to reconsider
to commit	*begehen*	≈	to perpetrate
evidence	*Beweis(e)*	phr	pieces of ~
to record	*aufzeichnen*	n	recording
link	*Zusammenhang*	≈	connection
to solve	*aufklären*	≈	to clear up
to estimate	*schätzen*	n	estimation
taxpayer	*Steuerzahler/in*	vt	to pay taxes
results	*Resultate*	v prep	to result in
to recruit	*anwerben*	n	recruitment
to train	*ausbilden*	n	training
police officer	*Polizeibeamter/-tin*	≈	policeman/woman
street lighting	*Straßenbeleuchtung*	cf	street light
deterrent [dɪ'terənt]	*abschreckend*	vt	to deter
to change one's mind	*es sich anders überlegen*	n	a change of mind
suburb	*Vorstadt*	adj	suburban
surveillance [sɜː'veɪləns]	*Überwachung*	phr	to keep sb under ~
inner-city	*innerstädtisch*	AE	downtown
hotspot	*Brennpunkt*		
drunken	*betrunken*	≈	intoxicated
to assault	*überfallen*	≈	to attack
to vandalize	*verwüsten*	n	vandalism
property	*Eigentum*	≈	belongings
reassuring	*beruhigend*	<>	worrying
secluded	*abgeschieden*	≈	lonely
right (to)	*Recht (auf)*	≈	entitlement
privacy	*Privatsphäre*	adj	private
civil liberties	*bürgerliche Freiheiten*	≈	human rights
sense	*Gefühl*	≈	feeling
security	*Sicherheit*	≈	safety
to misuse [ˌmɪs'juːz]	*missbrauchen*	n	misuse [ˌmɪs'juːs]
operator	*Betreiber/in*	vt	to operate
to spy on	*ausspionieren*	cf	peeping Tom – *Spanner*
police state	*Polizeistaat*	≈	authoritarian state
to track	*verfolgen*	≈	to trace, to follow

www.talkback.com/us_politics/crime

Is the death penalty a just and humane punishment?

In 2008, 37 criminals were executed in the USA, making a total of 1136 since the death penalty was reinstated in 1977. Over 3,200 prisoners were on death row.

Each year there are tens of thousands of homicides across the USA. If we abolish the death penalty, the problem will get worse – surely the possibility that you will lose your life if you are caught must be the ultimate deterrent? A murderer who is given a life sentence knows that there's a good chance he will be freed on parole within ten years. **Julia, California**

Crime statistics from countries which have abolished capital punishment show that the death penalty has little deterrent effect. Here in Canada the death penalty was abolished in 1975: the homicide rate fell, and has remained at a lower level ever since. **Ed, Toronto**

Society has to be protected against psychopaths and callous killers who have no respect for human life, no pity for their victims and no remorse for the suffering they inflict. The death penalty is cheaper and safer than keeping these people in prison. Why should we as tax-payers support these criminals for the rest of their lives? **Carlos, New York**

Capital punishment is the sign of a society which has no respect for the sanctity of life. Sentencing a fellow human being to death sends out the wrong message, leading to a more violent society. Killing is immoral, whether it is carried out by an individual or the state, and cannot be condoned. **Grant, New York**

We are executing innocent people along with the guilty. Fourteen states have reversed capital punishment decisions since 1975, and there have been many misconvictions which were discovered before it was too late. How many innocent people have been hanged, electrocuted, killed by lethal injection, and shot by firing squad in the name of justice? As long as there is police misconduct, unreliable testimony of witnesses and inadequate legal representation of defendants, we cannot risk a single execution. **Grace, Idaho**

Figures: US Department of Justice Bureau of Justice Statistics http://www.ojp.usdoj.gov/bjs/cp.htm

▸ **death penalty**	*Todesstrafe*	vt	to penalize – *bestrafen*
▸ **just**	*gerecht*	<>	unjust
▸ **humane** [hjuː'meɪn]	*human*	⚠	human – *menschlich*
▸ **punishment**	*Strafe*	vt	to punish
▸ **to execute**	*hinrichten*	n	execution
▸ **to reinstate** [ˌriːɪn'steɪt]	*wieder einsetzen*	≈	to bring back
▸ **on death row**	*im Todestrakt*		
▸ **homicide** (AE) ['hɒmɪsaɪd]	*Mord, Totschlag*	≈	murder (BE)
▸ **to abolish**	*abschaffen*	n	abolition
▸ **ultimate**	*äußerste(r, s)*		
▸ **deterrent** [dɪ'terənt]	*Abschreckung*	vt	to deter
▸ **life sentence**	*lebenslängliche Freiheitsstrafe*	≈	life imprisonment
▸ **to free on parole**	*auf Bewährung entlassen*		
▸ **capital punishment**	*Todesstrafe*		
▸ **callous** ['kæləs]	*gefühllos*	n	callousness
▸ **pity**	*Mitgefühl*	≈	compassion
▸ **victim**	*Opfer*		
▸ **remorse**	*Reue*	adj	remorseful
▸ **suffering**	*Leid*	vti	to suffer
▸ **to inflict**	*zufügen*		
▸ **to support**	*unterhalten*	n	support
▸ **sanctity**	*Unantastbarkeit*		
▸ **to sentence to death**	*zum Tode verurteilen*	n	sentence – *Strafe*
▸ **immoral**	*unmoralisch*	n	immorality
▸ **to condone**	*dulden*	≈	to tolerate
▸ **innocent**	*unschuldig*	n	innocence
▸ **guilty**	*schuldig*	n	guilt
▸ **to reverse**	*rückgängig machen*	n	reversal
▸ **misconviction**	*Fehlurteil*	vt	to misconvict
▸ **to hang**	*hängen*		
▸ **to electrocute**	*auf dem elektrischen Stuhl hinrichten*	cf	electric chair
▸ **lethal injection**	*tödliche Spritze*	vt	to inject sb with sth
▸ **firing squad**	*Exekutionskommando*		
▸ **justice**	*Gerechtigkeit*	<>	injustice
▸ **misconduct**	*Berufsvergehen*	cf	conduct – *Verhalten*
▸ **unreliable**	*unzuverlässig*	n	unreliability
▸ **testimony**	*Aussage(n)*	cf	to give testimony
▸ **witness**	*Zeuge, Zeugin*	vt	to witness
▸ **inadequate** [ɪn'ædɪkwət]	*unzulänglich*	n	inadequacy
▸ **legal representation**	*rechtliche Vertretung*	cf	lawyer – *Rechtsanwalt/wältin*
▸ **defendant**	*Angeklagte/r*	<>	plaintiff

B

The environment

1 The living planet

2 Climate change

3 Sustainability

Why is biodiversity important?

The natural environment is the source of all our resources for life. Environmental processes provide a wealth of services to the living world – air to breathe, water to drink and food to eat, as well as raw materials to use in our daily lives and natural beauty to enjoy.

Complex ecosystems with a wide variety of plants and animals tend to be more stable. A highly diverse ecosystem is a sign of a healthy system. Since all the living world – including humanity – is dependent on the natural environment, it is in our best interests and the interests of future generations to conserve biodiversity. At least 40 per cent of the world's economy and 80 per cent of the needs of the poor are derived from biological resources.

Some might argue that some species have become extinct with no obvious effect on the environment. But the Earth's systems are so complex that we still don't fully understand them. The careless loss of any part of the natural environment means that we may never know what its function was.

It is important to understand that environments are dynamic and constantly changing. A healthy, resilient environment evolves and adapts to naturally changing conditions and recovers from natural disasters such as floods and forest fires. It is fascinating to observe the far-reaching consequences even small changes can have and the importance of a large gene pool for species to adapt, survive and evolve.

Preservation of biodiversity is not necessarily about preserving everything currently in existence. It is more a question of 'walking lightly' on the Earth – a balance between respecting the natural changes that occur and protecting species and environments from wanton extinction and destruction.

Life on Earth would not be the same if our planet's biodiversity were to be radically affected.

[Adapted: www.eco-online.qld.edu.au]

1 The living planet

▸ **biodiversity**	*Artenvielfalt*	adj	biodiverse
▸ **natural**	*natürlich*	<>	artificial
▸ **environment**	*Umwelt*	≈	surroundings
▸ **source**	*Quelle*	≈	origin
▸ **resource** [rɪ'sɔːs]	*Ressource*	phr	natural ~s
▸ **environmental**	*Umwelt-*	cf	environmentalist
▸ **wealth** [welθ]	*Reichtum*	adj	wealthy
▸ **raw material**	*Rohstoff(e)*	<>	product
▸ **beauty**	*Schönheit*	adj	beautiful
▸ **ecosystem**	*Ökosystem*	≈	bionetwork
▸ **variety**	*Vielfalt*	adj	varied
▸ **stable**	*stabil*	n	stability
▸ **diverse**	*vielfältig*	n	diversity
▸ **sign**	*Zeichen*	≈	indication
▸ **humanity**	*Menschheit*	≈	humankind
▸ **dependent on**	*abhängig von*	n	dependence
▸ **to be in sb's best interests**	*in jds Interesse sein*	≈	to be beneficial to sb
▸ **to conserve**	*erhalten*	n	conservation
▸ **economy**	*Wirtschaft*	adj	economic
▸ **needs**	*Bedürfnisse*	≈	requirements
▸ **to be derived from**	*stammen von*	n	derivation
▸ **species** ['spiːʃiːz]	*Art(en)*		
▸ **to become extinct**	*aussterben*	≈	to die out
▸ **careless**	*leichtsinnig, sorglos*	n	carelessness
▸ **loss**	*Verlust*	vti	to lose
▸ **resilient** [rɪ'zɪliənt]	*robust*	n	resilience
▸ **to evolve**	*(sich) entwickeln*	n	evolution
▸ **to adapt to**	*sich anpassen an*	n	adaptation
▸ **conditions**	*Verhältnisse*	≈	circumstances
▸ **to recover from**	*sich erholen von*	n	recovery
▸ **disaster**	*Katastrophe*	≈	catastrophe
▸ **flood** [flʌd]	*Flut, Überschwemmung*	vti	to flood
▸ **far-reaching**	*weitreichend*	<>	limited
▸ **consequence**	*Folge, Konsequenz*	<>	cause
▸ **gene** [dʒiːn] **pool**	*Genpool*	adj	genetic
▸ **to survive**	*überleben*	n	survival
▸ **preservation**	*Erhalt, Schutz*	vt	to preserve
▸ **in existence**	*bestehend*	≈	existing
▸ **balance**	*Gleichgewicht*	≈	equilibrium
▸ **to respect**	*(be)achten*	<>	to disrespect
▸ **to protect**	*schützen*	n	protection
▸ **wanton**	*mutwillig*	≈	needless
▸ **extinction**	*Ausrottung*	phr	mass ~
▸ **destruction**	*Zerstörung*	adj	destructive
▸ **radically**	*radikal, grundlegend*	≈	drastically

www.eco-online.qld.edu.au

Threats to biodiversity

Overpopulation

The Earth's population is over six billion now. A thousand years ago, the Earth needed to support only 250 to 300 million people. The Earth's population has been growing at a faster and faster rate. Every day all these people are drawing on the Earth's resources, using more energy, land, water and natural resources (such as trees, fossil fuels, minerals, plants and animals).

Habitat loss

Humans continually encroach on the natural habitats of many species, as more and more land is taken over for housing, farming or mining. This fragments habitats, so that populations become isolated and less genetically diverse.

Global climate change

Climate change alters environments and can affect the species that live in those environments. Some may die out. Others, however, may flourish and expand their ranges. This may also have an adverse effect on the environment.

Pollution

Chemical use can have adverse effects on the environment. For example, pesticides used on crops can kill not only the pests they're intended for, but also bees and other beneficial insects. Acid rain damages the ecology of forests and lakes.

Overharvesting

If we use up the Earth's natural resources faster than they can be replaced, species can be seriously depleted or even become extinct. We need to use resources wisely and protect endangered species.

Introduced species

Sometimes, either accidentally or deliberately, new species are introduced into areas where they do not occur naturally. Some of these introductions are disastrous for the environment.

[Adapted and shortened: www.eco-online.qld.edu.au]

▸ **threat**	*Bedrohung*	vt	to threaten
▸ **overpopulation**	*Überbevölkerung*	vt	to overpopulate
▸ **to support**	*ernähren*	≈	to sustain
▸ **to draw on**	*in Anspruch nehmen*	≈	to make use of
▸ **resource**	*Ressource*	phr	natural ~
▸ **fossil fuel**	*fossiler Brennstoff*	vt	to fuel
▸ **mineral**	*Mineral*		
▸ **habitat**	*Lebensraum*	vt	to inhabit
▸ **loss**	*Verlust*	vti	to lose
▸ **to encroach on**	*vordringen in*	n	encroachment
▸ **species** ['spi:ʃi:z]	*Art(en)*		
▸ **housing**	*Hausbau*	≈	accommodation
▸ **farming**	*Landwirtschaft*	≈	agriculture
▸ **mining**	*Bergbau*	v prep	to mine for
▸ **to fragment** [fræg'ment]	*zerstückeln*	n	fragmentation
▸ **isolated**	*isoliert*	n	isolation
▸ **climate change**	*Klimawandel*	cf	global warming
▸ **to alter**	*verändern*	≈	to change
▸ **to die out**	*aussterben*	≈	to become extinct
▸ **to flourish**	*gedeihen*	≈	to thrive
▸ **to expand**	*ausdehnen*	<>	to contract
▸ **range**	*Lebensbereich*	vi	to range
▸ **adverse**	*nachteilig*	≈	detrimental
▸ **pollution**	*Umweltverschmutzung*	vt	to pollute
▸ **chemical**	*Chemikalien-*	cf	chemistry – *Chemie*
▸ **pesticide**	*Schädlingsbekämpfungsmittel*	cf	herbicide
▸ **crop**	*(Anbau-)Pflanzen*	phr	to grow ~s
▸ **pest**	*Schädling*	phr	~ control – *Schädlingsbekämpfung*
▸ **beneficial**	*nützlich*	vt	to benefit
▸ **acid rain**	*saurer Regen*	cf	acidity – *Säuregehalt*
▸ **to damage**	*schädigen*	n	damage
▸ **ecology** [i'kɒlədʒi]	*Ökologie*	adj	ecological [ˌi:kə'lɒdʒɪkl]
▸ **forest**	*Wald*	cf	forestry – *Forstwirtschaft*
▸ **lake**	*(Binnen-)See*	cf	pond – *Teich*
▸ **to overharvest**	*überbeanspruchen*	≈	to overexploit
▸ **to use up**	*aufbrauchen*	≈	to exhaust
▸ **to replace**	*ersetzen*	≈	to renew
▸ **to deplete**	*erschöpfen*	n	depletion
▸ **to become extinct**	*aussterben*	≈	to die out
▸ **wisely**	*weise*	n	wisdom
▸ **to endanger**	*gefährden*	≈	to put at risk
▸ **introduced species**	*eingeführte Arten*	<>	indigenous species
▸ **accidentally**	*zufällig*	≈	inadvertently
▸ **deliberately**	*absichtlich*	≈	intentionally
▸ **to occur**	*vorkommen*	n	occurrence (of)
▸ **disastrous**	*katastrophal*	≈	catastrophic

The environment

How the runaway greenhouse effect is causing climate change

The Earth has a natural temperature control system. Certain atmospheric gases are critical to this system and are known as greenhouse gases.

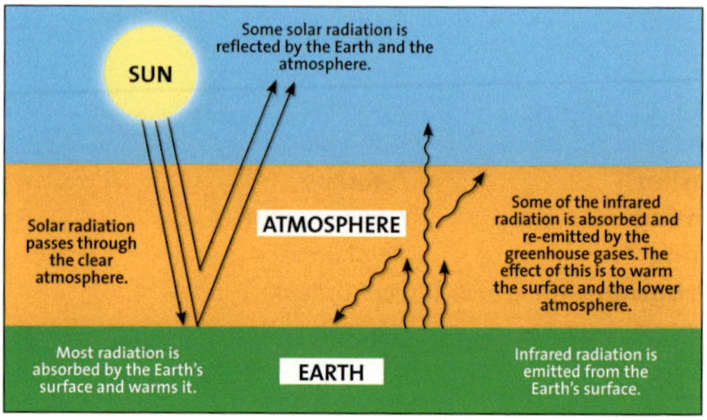

On average, about one third of the solar radiation that hits the Earth is reflected back into space. Of the remaining two thirds, some is absorbed by the atmosphere but most is absorbed by the land and oceans. The Earth's surface becomes warm and as a result emits infrared radiation.

Greenhouse gases in the atmosphere trap the infrared radiation, warming the atmosphere. Without the greenhouse effect the Earth's average global temperature would be -18° C, rather than 15° C as at present. The Earth would be a much less habitable place.

Greenhouse gases include water vapour, carbon dioxide, ozone, methane and nitrous oxide. All of these gases occur naturally in the atmosphere. However, in the last few centuries, the activities of humans have directly or indirectly caused the concentration of these gases to increase. These activities include industrial processes, deforestation and large-scale livestock farming. Scientists predict that this increase will enhance the greenhouse effect – making the planet warmer. This phenomenon is known as global warming.

In fact, climatologists estimate that the Earth's average global temperature has already increased by 0.3 to 0.6° Celsius since the beginning of the 20th century and attribute much of that change to human activities.

Predictions indicate that by the middle of the 21st century the Earth's global temperature may be 1 to 3° Celsius higher than today. This human-induced climate change has major implications for life on Earth.

▸ **runaway**	*unkontrollierbar*	≈	out of control
▸ **greenhouse**	*Treibhaus*	phr	~ effect, ~ gas
▸ **to cause**	*verursachen*	n	cause
▸ **climate change**	*Klimawandel*	adj	climatic
▸ **temperature control**	*Temperaturregelung*	adj	controllable
▸ **atmospheric**	*in der Atmosphäre*	≈	in the air
▸ **critical to**	*entscheidend für*	≈	vital
▸ **on average**	*im Durchschnitt*	phr	above/below ~
▸ **solar**	*Sonnen-*		
▸ **radiation**	*Strahlung*	vti	to radiate
▸ **to hit**	*auftreffen (auf)*	≈	to strike
▸ **to reflect**	*reflektieren*	n	reflection
▸ **space**	*(Welt-)Raum*	phr	outer ~
▸ **to absorb**	*absorbieren*	n	absorption
▸ **atmosphere**	*Atmosphäre*	cf	air – *Luft*
▸ **surface**	*Oberfläche*	phr	above/below the ~
▸ **to emit**	*ausstrahlen*	n	emission
▸ **infrared**	*infrarot*	cf	ultraviolet
▸ **to trap**	*speichern*	<>	to release
▸ **to warm**	*erwärmen*	<>	to cool
▸ **average**	*durchschnittlich*	≈	mean
▸ **habitable**	*bewohnbar*	<>	uninhabitable
▸ **water vapour**	*Wasserdampf*	vti	to vapourize
▸ **carbon dioxide**	*Kohlendioxid*		
▸ **ozone** ['əʊzəʊn]	*Ozon*		
▸ **methane** ['mi:θeɪn]	*Methan*		
▸ **nitrous oxide** [ˌnaɪtrəs 'ɒksaɪd]	*Distickstoffmonoxid, Lachgas*		
▸ **to occur**	*vorkommen*	≈	to be found
▸ **activity**	*Tätigkeit*	adj	active
▸ **industrial**	*industriell*	n	industry
▸ **deforestation**	*Abholzung*	vt	to deforest
▸ **large-scale**	*Massen-*	<>	small-scale
▸ **livestock**	*Vieh*	cf	cattle – *Vieh, Rinder*
▸ **scientist** ['saɪəntɪst]	*(Natur-)Wissenschaftler/in*	cf	science – *Naturwissenschaft(en)*
▸ **to predict**	*prophezeien*	≈	to forecast
▸ **to enhance**	*steigern*	n	enhancement
▸ **global warming**	*globale Erwärmung*	vti	to warm
▸ **climatologist** [ˌklaɪmə'tɒlədʒɪst]	*Klimaforscher/in*	cf	climate – *Klima*
▸ **to estimate**	*schätzen*	n	estimate
▸ **to attribute to**	*zuschreiben*	≈	to ascribe to
▸ **prediction**	*Vorhersage*	≈	forecast
▸ **to indicate**	*hinweisen auf*	n	indication
▸ **human-induced**	*durch Menschen verursacht*	≈	anthropogenic
▸ **implication**	*Auswirkung*	vt	to imply

Talking point: Is climate change real?

Presenter Here in the studio with me today are Green campaigner Claire South and climate change sceptic Dr Mike Roberts. Claire South, what would you say to sceptics like Dr Roberts?

South Firstly I would deny the need for any further debate about climate change. There is a broad consensus in the scientific community that human-induced climate change is real and is happening now. It's time to stop debating this issue and concentrate on finding solutions to the huge problem that faces us as a planet.

Presenter Dr Roberts, how do you respond to that?

Roberts First of all, I don't think it has been proven beyond reasonable doubt that we are experiencing a significant change in our climate. It's very difficult to achieve an accurate and reliable measurement of a global average temperature, and even more so to do that consistently over the course of a century or more. That sort of time-scale is needed to detect a major climate change, as opposed to a minor fluctuation. A number of respected scientists are concerned that the evidence may have been misinterpreted or the data may have been inaccurate in the first place.

South We've heard all this so many times. Dr Roberts' case sounds very reasonable, but what does it amount to? Simply an excuse for inaction. Climate change deniers want to carry on as normal and hope for the best. Even multinational oil companies acknowledge the reality of climate change! If we wait until there is definitive proof, it will be too late to act.

Roberts Please don't misrepresent my position. I'm not saying that we should do nothing. What I'm saying is that we should proceed with caution, rather than adopting hasty measures which will damage the world economy and endanger millions of jobs …

2 Climate change

▸ **climate change**	*Klimawandel*	vti	to change
▸ **campaigner** [kæm'peɪnə]	*Aktivist/in*	vt	to campaign (for, against)
▸ **sceptic**	*Skeptiker/in*	adj	sceptical
▸ **to deny**	*ablehnen, bestreiten*	n	denial
▸ **debate**	*Debatte, Diskussion*	≈	discussion
▸ **consensus**	*Konsens*	≈	agreement
▸ **scientific**	*wissenschaftlich*	n	science
▸ **human-induced**	*durch Menschen verursacht*	≈	anthropogenic
▸ **to debate**	*diskutieren über*	n	debate
▸ **issue**	*Thema, Frage*	cf	at ~ – *strittig*
▸ **to concentrate on**	*sich konzentrieren auf*	≈	to focus on
▸ **huge**	*riesig*	<>	tiny
▸ **to face**	*konfrontieren mit*	≈	to confront
▸ **reasonable**	*angemessen*	≈	sensible
▸ **doubt** [daʊt]	*Zweifel*	adj	doubtful
▸ **significant**	*significant, deutlich*	<>	insignificant
▸ **accurate**	*genau*	n	accuracy
▸ **reliable**	*zuverlässig*	n	reliability
▸ **measurement**	*Messung*	vt	to measure
▸ **consistently**	*ständig*	<>	inconsistently
▸ **time-scale**	*Zeitrahmen*	≈	time-frame
▸ **to detect**	*entdecken*	n	detection
▸ **fluctuation**	*Schwankung*	vi	to fluctuate
▸ **evidence**	*Beweis(e)*	≈	proof
▸ **to misinterpret**	*falsch interpretieren*	≈	to misunderstand
▸ **inaccurate**	*ungenau*	n	inaccuracy
▸ **excuse**	*Ausrede*	vt	to excuse
▸ **inaction**	*Nichtstun*	≈	lack of action
▸ **denier**	*Leugner/in*	<>	believer
▸ **to carry on**	*weitermachen*	≈	to continue
▸ **to hope for the best**	*das Beste hoffen*	cf	to fear the worst
▸ **oil company**	*Ölfirma*	≈	oil producer
▸ **to acknowledge**	*anerkennen*	<>	to deny
▸ **definitive**	*definitiv*	≈	authoritative
▸ **proof**	*Beweis(e)*	vt	to prove
▸ **to act**	*handeln*	n	action
▸ **to misrepresent**	*falsch darstellen*	n	misrepresentation
▸ **caution**	*Vorsicht*	adj	cautious
▸ **to adopt**	*ergreifen*	≈	to introduce
▸ **hasty**	*vorschnell*	≈	hurried
▸ **measure**	*Maßnahme*	≈	step
▸ **to damage**	*schaden*	n	damage
▸ **economy**	*Wirtschaft*	adj	economic
▸ **to endanger**	*gefährden*	≈	to put at risk

Practical steps against climate change

Campaigner What are you doing about climate change, sir?

Passer-by Me? What can I do about it?

Campaigner Well, there are a whole range of practical steps. You could cut back on your electricity consumption at home. You could also leave your car at home and cycle to work, or take public transport. That would reduce your carbon footprint …

Passer-by Come on, let's be realistic. Climate change is a global problem – cycling to work isn't going to make it go away! It's up to world leaders and big industry to agree a solution.

Campaigner Isn't that the kind of passive attitude that got us into this mess in the first place? 'Leave everything to the experts, they know what they're doing.' … Well it looks as if they didn't – the ice caps are melting, extreme weather events like droughts and flash floods are becoming more common, and there's a world food crisis. We have to take responsibility for our own actions. Now, here I've got a leaflet with ten easy steps to cut your personal carbon emissions …

Passer-by That's fine, and let's suppose I follow your ten easy steps. I buy some low-energy light bulbs and I install solar panels on the roof. What about the billions of people in emerging nations like China and India? They want cheap electricity, they want consumer goods and they want them now. It's no good us in the developed world telling them they need to worry about their carbon footprint.

Campaigner Ah, well, actually most emerging nations remain far below the energy consumption levels of the developed world. Here, take a look at this chart – the Indian economy for example is extremely energy efficient. The stereotype of inefficient Third World nations polluting the environment is a convenient myth to justify our own wasteful practices …

2 Climate change

▸ **practical**	*praktisch*	<>	impractical
▸ **step**	*Schritt*	≈	measure
▸ **climate change**	*Klimawandel*	vti	to change
▸ **to cut back on**	*einschränken*	≈	to reduce
▸ **electricity**	*Strom*	adj	electric(al)
▸ **consumption**	*Verbrauch*	vt	to consume
▸ **public transport**	*öffentlicher Nahverkehr*	AE	mass transit
▸ **to reduce**	*reduzieren*	n	reduction
▸ **carbon footprint**	*CO_2-Bilanz*	cf	ecological footprint
▸ **realistic**	*realistisch*	n	realism
▸ **to be up to**	*liegen an*	≈	to be down to
▸ **world leader**	*Weltführer/in*	vti	to lead
▸ **to agree**	*vereinbaren*	≈	to consent to
▸ **solution**	*Lösung*	vt	to solve
▸ **attitude**	*Haltung, Einstellung*	≈	point of view
▸ **mess**	*Schlamassel*	≈	difficult situation
▸ **to leave to**	*überlassen*	≈	to entrust to
▸ **ice cap**	*Polkappe*	cf	glacier – *Gletscher*
▸ **to melt**	*schmelzen*	<>	to freeze
▸ **extreme**	*extrem*	<>	moderate
▸ **weather**	*Wetter*	cf	climate – *Klima*
▸ **event**	*Ereignis*	≈	happening
▸ **drought** [draʊt]	*Dürre*	adj	drought-stricken
▸ **flash flood** ['flæʃ flʌd]	*plötzliche Überschwemmung*	vti	to flood
▸ **common**	*häufig, üblich*	<>	rare
▸ **crisis** ['kraɪsɪs]	*Krise*	pl	crises
▸ **responsibility**	*Verantwortung*	adj	responsible
▸ **action**	*Handlung*	vi	to act
▸ **leaflet**	*Flugblatt*	≈	flyer, pamphlet
▸ **to cut**	*einschränken*	≈	to reduce
▸ **carbon**	*Kohlenstoff*	cf	~ dioxide – CO_2
▸ **emission**	*Ausstoß*	vi	to emit
▸ **low-energy light bulb**	*Energiesparlampe*		
▸ **to install**	*montieren*	n	installation
▸ **solar panel**	*Sonnenkollektor*	cf	solar energy
▸ **emerging nation**	*Schwellenland*	vi	to emerge
▸ **consumer goods**	*Konsumgüter*	cf	to consume
▸ **the developed world**	*die Industrieländer*	<>	the developing world
▸ **consumption**	*Verbrauch*	≈	use
▸ **level**	*Niveau*	cf	a high/low ~ of
▸ **energy efficient** [ˌenədʒi ɪ'fɪʃnt]	*energiesparend*	n	energy efficiency
▸ **stereotype**	*Klischee*	adj	stereotypical
▸ **inefficient** [ˌɪnɪ'fɪʃnt]	*unwirtschaftlich*	n	inefficiency
▸ **to pollute**	*verschmutzen*	n	pollution
▸ **myth**	*Mythos*	≈	falsehood, fiction
▸ **to justify**	*rechtfertigen*	n	justification
▸ **wasteful**	*verschwenderisch*	n	waste
▸ **practice**	*Praxis*	≈	action, habit

Water wars

Water sustains every being on this planet. Without water, there would simply be no plants, no animals and no people. But the global water supply isn't just at risk, it's already in crisis.

Water covers 75% of the earth's surface. The total amount of water remains about the same from one year to the next as it circulates between the oceans, land and atmosphere in a cycle of evaporation and precipitation. This cycle is fundamental to the functioning of the Earth as it recycles water, and has a role in modifying and regulating the Earth's climate.

Fresh water makes up less than 3% of water on Earth, over two thirds of this is in polar ice caps and glaciers. Fresh water lakes and rivers make up only 0.009% of water on Earth and ground water makes up 0.28%.

All life forms require water. It makes up 60 to 70% of every living organism. The viability of all life on Earth depends on the availability of water.

In the discussion of the global food emergency, one underlying factor is barely mentioned: the world is running out of fresh water. Climate change, overconsumption and the inefficient use of this basic raw material are all to blame. Rivers are being sucked dry to irrigate food crops. Australia's only major river system, the Murray-Darling, no longer flows into the sea: all of the water evaporates, is used to provide drinking water to towns and cities or is used in farming.

'Water war' is a term devised by environmentalists for a conflict caused by an acute shortage of fresh water for drinking and irrigation. About 40% of the world's population is already affected by water shortages, with 20% lacking clean drinking water. Population growth and climate change will worsen the situation: the UN Environment Agency warns that almost 3 billion people will be severely short of water within 50 years. Possible flashpoints for water wars have been predicted in the Middle East, parts of Africa and in many of the world's major river systems, including the Danube.

[Adapted extracts: http://www.worldwaterwars.com]

2 Climate change

▸ **to sustain**	*aufrechterhalten*	adj	sustainable
▸ **being**	*Lebewesen*	≈	creature
▸ **supply**	*Vorrat*	vt	to supply
▸ **at risk**	*gefährdet*	≈	in danger
▸ **in crisis** ['kraɪsɪs]	*in der Krise*		
▸ **surface**	*Oberfläche*		
▸ **to circulate**	*zirkulieren*	n	circulation
▸ **cycle**	*Kreislauf*	adj	cyclical
▸ **evaporation**	*Verdunstung*	vti	to evaporate
▸ **precipitation**	*Niederschlag*	≈	rainfall
▸ **fundamental**	*wesentlich*	≈	essential
▸ **to modify**	*verändern*	≈	to alter
▸ **to regulate**	*regulieren*	≈	to control
▸ **climate**	*Klima*	cf	climatologist
▸ **fresh water**	*Süßwasser*	<>	salt water
▸ **ice cap**	*Polkappe*	cf	pole – *Pol*
▸ **glacier**	*Gletscher*	adj	glacial
▸ **groundwater**	*Grundwasser*		
▸ **life form**	*Lebensform*	adj	living
▸ **viability** [ˌvaɪə'bɪləti]	*Lebensfähigkeit*	adj	viable
▸ **to depend on**	*abhängen von*	adj	dependent
▸ **availability**	*Verfügbarkeit*	adj	available
▸ **emergency**	*Not*	≈	crisis
▸ **underlying**	*zugrunde liegend*	≈	fundamental
▸ **to run out of**	*nicht mehr haben, ausgehen*	cf	to run out – *alle werden*
▸ **climate change**	*Klimawandel*	cf	global warming
▸ **overconsumption**	*Überbeanspruchung*	cf	consumer – *Verbraucher/in*
▸ **inefficient** [ˌɪnɪ'fɪʃnt]	*unwirtschaftlich*	n	inefficiency
▸ **raw material**	*Rohstoff*	<>	product
▸ **to be to blame**	*schuld sein*	⚠	blame ≠ *blamieren*
▸ **to suck dry**	*trocken saugen*	≈	to drain
▸ **to irrigate**	*bewässern*	n	irrigation
▸ **food crops**	*Nahrungspflanzenanbau*	cf	harvest – *Ernte*
▸ **to flow**	*fließen*	≈	to run
▸ **to evaporate**	*verdunsten*	n	evaporation
▸ **drinking water**	*Trinkwasser*	≈	potable water (formal)
▸ **farming**	*Landwirtschaft*	≈	agriculture
▸ **environmentalist**	*Umweltschützer/in*	cf	environment – *Umwelt*
▸ **conflict** ['kɒnflɪkt]	*Konflikt*	≈	fight
▸ **shortage**	*Mangel, Knappheit*	≈	scarcity
▸ **irrigation**	*Bewässerung*	vt	to irrigate
▸ **population**	*Bevölkerung*	vt	to populate
▸ **growth**	*Wachstum*	<>	decline
▸ **to worsen** ['wɜːsn]	*verschlimmern*	<>	to improve
▸ **flashpoint**	*Brennpunkt*	≈	trouble spot
▸ **Middle East**	*Mittlerer Osten*	adj	Middle Eastern
▸ **Danube**	*Donau*		

What is sustainable development?

The past 20 years have seen a growing realization that the current model of development is unsustainable. In other words, we are living beyond our means. By clearing the rainforests and overfishing the oceans we are reducing biodiversity. Our industries are using up natural resources. Our consumption patterns are having a negative effect on the environment and the climate. In so many ways, our way of life is placing an increasing burden on the planet.

The increasing strain we put on resources and environmental systems such as water, land and air cannot go on forever. Especially as the world's population continues to increase and we already see a world where over a billion people live on less than a dollar a day.

A widely accepted definition of sustainable development is: 'development which meets the needs of the present without compromising the ability of future generations to meet their own needs'. Globally we are not even meeting the needs of the present let alone considering the needs of future generations.

Unless we start to make real progress towards reconciling these contradictions, we face a future that is less certain and less secure. We need to make a decisive move towards more sustainable development. Not just because it is the right thing to do, but also because it is in our own long-term best interests. It offers the best hope for the future. Whether at school, in the home or at work, we all have a part to play. Our small everyday actions add up to make a big difference.

For example, in the UK, households are responsible for around 25% of our total carbon emissions. Household energy demand continues to rise, which means we need to act now. Improvements in energy efficiency can usually be achieved for a small financial investment and soon pay for themselves. Energy conservation can be a simple matter of changing habits.

[Slightly adapted: http://www.sustainable-development.gov.uk/what/index.htm]

▸ **sustainable**	*nachhaltig*	n	sustainability
▸ **development**	*Entwicklung*	vti	to develop
▸ **realization**	*Erkenntnis*	≈	recognition
▸ **unsustainable**	*nicht nachhaltig*		
▸ **to live beyond one's means**	*über seine Verhältnisse leben*	<>	to live within one's means
▸ **to clear**	*abholzen*	n	clearing
▸ **rainforest**	*Regenwald*	cf	jungle – *Dschungel*
▸ **to overfish**	*überfischen*	n	overfishing
▸ **biodiversity**	*Artenvielfalt*	adj	biodiverse
▸ **to use up**	*aufbrauchen*	≈	to exhaust
▸ **natural resource**	*natürliche Ressource*		
▸ **consumption**	*Verbrauch*	vt	to consume
▸ **environment**	*Umwelt*	adj	environmental
▸ **way of life**	*Lebensweise*	≈	lifestyle
▸ **burden** ['bɜːdn]	*Last*	vt	to burden sb with
▸ **strain**	*Beanspruchung*	≈	pressure
▸ **population**	*Bevölkerung*	phr	~ explosion
▸ **to meet sb's needs**	*jds Bedürfnisse abdecken*	≈	to satisfy sb's needs
▸ **to compromise**	*schaden*	n	compromise
▸ **ability**	*Fähigkeit*	adj	able
▸ **to consider**	*berücksichtigen*	n	consideration
▸ **progress** ['prəʊgres]	*Fortschritt(e)*	vi	to progress [prə'gres]
▸ **to reconcile**	*ausgleichen*	n	reconciliation
▸ **contradiction**	*Widerspruch*	vt	to contradict
▸ **to face**	*sich gegenübersehen*	≈	to be confronted with
▸ **certain**	*gewiss*	n	certainty
▸ **secure**	*sicher*	<>	insecure
▸ **decisive**	*entscheidend*	<>	indecisive
▸ **move**	*Schritt*	≈	step
▸ **long-term**	*langfristig*	<>	short-term
▸ **hope**	*Hoffnung*	adj	hopeful
▸ **everyday**	*Alltags-*	≈	daily
▸ **action**	*Handlung*	adj	active
▸ **household**	*(privater) Haushalt*	cf	domestic – *häuslich*
▸ **responsible**	*verantwortlich*	n	responsibility
▸ **carbon**	*Kohlenstoff*	cf	~ dioxide – CO_2
▸ **emission**	*Ausstoß*	vt	to emit
▸ **demand**	*Bedarf, Nachfrage*	<>	supply
▸ **to act**	*handeln*	≈	to take action
▸ **improvement**	*Verbesserung*	<>	deterioration
▸ **efficiency**	*effiziente Nutzung*	adj	efficient
▸ **to achieve**	*erreichen*	n	achievement
▸ **investment**	*Investition*	vti	to invest
▸ **conservation**	*Einsparung*	vt	to conserve
▸ **habit**	*Gewohnheit*	adj	habitual

www.blogspot.de/annalytisch

my ethical blog

The ethical blogger goes organic

As an experiment I'm trying to live ethically for a year, but I'm taking it one step at a time. This week I'm focusing on what I eat. I was surprised by what I found out with a little research.

Did you know that our diet comprises almost a third of our carbon emissions? There is a great deal of energy used in food production.

So what is all that energy used for? Farm machinery requires power, of course, but industrialized farming also depends on fertilizers, pesticides and weedkillers. All of these are energy-intensive to produce.

Then, when the crop has been harvested, it has to be transported to centralized depots, sorted, packaged and distributed to supermarkets, often in refrigerated lorries, accumulating lots of 'food miles' along the way.

And that's just the fresh produce – processed food undergoes all kinds of additional processes in the factory, and all of them require energy.

The end result: for every kilojoule of nutrition in the food on your plate, 10 kilojoules of energy have been expended in producing it! That isn't just unsustainable, it's absurd.

So, what can we do about it? Well, buying organic food is a start. It doesn't solve the food miles problem, but it does mean that the food has been grown without the use of chemicals. What's more, organic farming methods can actually take carbon dioxide out of the air and trap it in the soil.

That's all very well, but it doesn't help my present dilemma. Here I am in the supermarket, trying to choose between the organic potatoes that have been flown all the way from Israel and the non-organic ones from 50 miles away in Norfolk …

Comments (2)

Posted by: Diane G
Go to the market instead. Buy local produce that hasn't been washed, sorted and packaged – and help local farmers.

Posted by: Veggie dude
Better still, dig up your lawn and grow your own vegetables. No transport costs, no energy costs and 100% organic. Plus you'll get a free workout. Better than driving to the gym, any day!

3 Sustainability

▸ **ethical**	*ethisch*	n	ethics (pl)
▸ **organic**	*organisch, biologisch*	adv	organically
▸ **to focus on**	*sich konzentrieren auf*	≈	to concentrate on
▸ **research**	*Nachforschung(en)*	vt	to research
▸ **diet** ['daɪət]	*Ernährung*	adj	dietary
▸ **to comprise**	*ausmachen*	≈	to make up
▸ **carbon**	*Kohlenstoff*	cf	~ dioxide – CO_2
▸ **emission**	*Ausstoß*	vt	to emit
▸ **production**	*Produktion*	vt	to produce
▸ **machinery** [mə'ʃiːnəri]	*Maschinen(park)*	≈	machines
▸ **to require**	*benötigen*	n	requirement
▸ **power**	*Energie*	≈	energy
▸ **industrialized**	*industrialisiert*	n	industry
▸ **farming**	*Landwirtschaft*	≈	agriculture
▸ **fertilizer**	*Dünger*	vt	to fertilize
▸ **pesticide**	*Schädlingsbekämpfungsmittel*	cf	pest – *Schädling*
▸ **weedkiller**	*Unkrautbekämpfungsmittel*	cf	weed – *Unkraut*
▸ **energy-intensive**	*energieintensiv*	<>	low-energy
▸ **crop**	*Ernte*	cf	to cultivate – *anbauen*
▸ **to harvest**	*ernten, einbringen*	vt	to harvest
▸ **to transport**	*transportieren*	n	transport(ation)
▸ **centralized**	*zentralisiert*	<>	decentralized
▸ **to sort**	*sortieren*	≈	to grade
▸ **to package**	*verpacken*	n	packaging
▸ **to distribute**	*verteilen*	n	distribution
▸ **to refrigerate** [rɪ'frɪdʒəreɪt]	*kühlen*	cf	refrigerator, fridge – *Kühlschrank*
▸ **to accumulate**	*ansammeln*	≈	to gather
▸ **food miles**	*Transportwege der Nahrungsmittel*	cf	carbon footprint
▸ **produce** ['prɒdjuːs]	*Produkt(e), Erzeugnis(se)*	≈	foodstuffs
▸ **processed**	*(weiter)verarbeitet*	n	processing
▸ **to undergo**	*unterliegen*		
▸ **factory**	*Fabrik*		
▸ **end result**	*Endergebnis*	≈	end effect
▸ **nutrition**	*Nahrung*	vt	nutritional
▸ **to expend**	*aufwenden*	≈	to use (up)
▸ **unsustainable**	*nicht nachhaltig*	cf	sustainability
▸ **chemical**	*Chemikalie*	adj	chemical
▸ **to trap**	*speichern*	≈	to catch
▸ **soil**	*(Erd-)Boden*	≈	earth
▸ **local**	*einheimisch*	<>	global
▸ **farmer**	*Landwirt/in*	vti	to farm
▸ **to dig up**	*umgraben*		
▸ **lawn**	*Rasen*	≈	grass
▸ **to grow**	*anbauen*		
▸ **workout**	*(Fitness-)Training*	≈	exercise session
▸ **gym**	*Fitnessstudio*	⚠	≠ *Gymnasium*

Biofuel use 'increasing poverty'

The replacement of traditional fuels with biofuels has dragged more than 30 million people worldwide into poverty, an aid agency report says. According to Oxfam, so-called green policies in developed countries are contributing to the world's soaring food prices, which hit the poor hardest. The group also says biofuels will do nothing to combat climate change. Its report urges the EU to scrap a target of making 10% of all transport run on renewable resources by 2020. Oxfam estimates the EU's target could increase carbon emissions 7000% by 2020 by changing land use. The report's author, Oxfam's biofuel policy adviser Rob Bailey, criticized rich countries for using subsidies to encourage the use of food crops to produce alternative energy sources like ethanol. 'If the fuel value for a crop exceeds its food value, then it will be used for fuel instead,' Bailey said. 'Rich countries … are making climate change worse, not better, they are stealing crops and land away from food production, and they are destroying millions of livelihoods in the process.'

Opportunity – or crime?

Biofuels are a divisive issue with strong arguments on both sides. Leaders such as Brazilian President Luiz Inacio Lula da Silva have suggested the biofuel boom provides developing nations with a great opportunity. In his opinion, it creates a profitable export for energy crop producers in Africa, Central America and the Caribbean that could enable them to climb out of poverty. But several aid agencies and analysts have warned of the possible downside of biofuel crop cultivation. One UN adviser went as far as describing biofuels as a 'crime against humanity'.

[Slightly adapted: news.bbc.co.uk]

▸ **biofuel**	*Biokraftstoff, Biosprit*	cf	fuel – *Treibstoff*
▸ **poverty**	*Armut*	adj	poor
▸ **replacement**	*Ersatz*	vt	to replace
▸ **aid agency**	*Hilfsorganisation*	vt	to aid
▸ **policy**	*Vorgehensweise*	≈	strategy
▸ **to contribute to**	*beitragen zu*	n	contribution
▸ **to soar** [sɔː]	*stark ansteigen*	<>	to plummet
▸ **to combat**	*bekämpfen*	≈	to fight (against)
▸ **to urge** [ɜːdʒ]	*drängen*	≈	to implore
▸ **to scrap**	*aufgeben*	≈	to get rid of
▸ **target**	*Ziel*	vt	to target
▸ **renewable**	*erneuerbar*	<>	non-renewable
▸ **to estimate**	*schätzen*	n	estimate
▸ **carbon**	*Kohlenstoff*	cf	~ dioxide – CO_2
▸ **emission**	*Ausstoß*	vt	to emit
▸ **land use**	*Landnutzung*	vt	to use
▸ **to criticize**	*kritisieren*	n	criticism
▸ **subsidy**	*Subvention*	vt	to subsidize
▸ **to encourage**	*fördern*	n	encouragement
▸ **food crop**	*Nahrungsmittelpflanzen*	cf	energy crop
▸ **source**	*Quelle*		
▸ **value**	*Wert*	adj	valuable
▸ **to exceed**	*übersteigen*	≈	to be greater than
▸ **to steal away from**	*stehlen von*	≈	to deprive of
▸ **production**	*Produktion*	vt	to produce
▸ **to destroy**	*vernichten*	n	destruction
▸ **livelihood** ['laɪvlihʊd]	*Lebensunterhalt*	≈	source of income
▸ **in the process**	*dadurch*	≈	thereby
▸ **opportunity**	*Chance*	≈	chance
▸ **crime**	*Verbrechen*	adj	criminal
▸ **divisive issue**	*strittige Frage*	vt	to divide
▸ **boom**	*Boom*	vi	to boom
▸ **developing nation**	*Entwicklungsland*	cf	development – *Entwicklung*
▸ **profitable**	*einträglich*	v prep	to profit from
▸ **export**	*Export*	<>	import
▸ **energy crop**	*Energiepflanzen*	≈	fuel crop
▸ **producer**	*Produzent/in*	adj	productive
▸ **to enable**	*(es) ermöglichen*	≈	to allow
▸ **downside**	*Nachteil*	<>	upside
▸ **cultivation**	*Anbau*	vt	to cultivate
▸ **humanity**	*Menschheit*	≈	humankind

www.greenpeace.org

Where does e-waste end up?

Many old electronic goods are waiting to be reused, recycled or thrown away. The US Environmental Protection Agency (EPA) estimates that as much as three quarters of the computers sold in the US are stockpiled in garages and cupboards. When thrown away, they end up in landfills or incinerators or, more recently, are exported to Asia.

Landfill: Toxic chemicals in electronics products can leach into the land over time or are released into the atmosphere, affecting nearby communities and the environment. In many European countries, regulations have been introduced to prevent electronic waste being dumped in landfills due to its hazardous content. However, this still continues in many countries.

Incineration: This releases heavy metals such as mercury into the air. Mercury released into the atmosphere can bioaccumulate in the food chain, particularly in fish. If the products contain PVC plastic, highly toxic chemicals are also released.

Reuse: A good way to increase a product's lifespan. Many old products are exported to developing countries. Although the benefits of reusing electronics in this way are clear, the old products are often dumped after a short period of use in areas that are unlikely to have hazardous waste facilities.

Recycling: Although recycling can be a good way to reuse the raw materials in a product, the hazardous chemicals in e-waste mean that electronics can harm workers in the recycling plants, as well as their neighbouring communities and environment.

In developed countries, electronics recycling takes place in purpose-built recycling plants under controlled conditions. In developing countries however, there are no such controls. Recycling is done by hand in scrapyards, often by children.

Export: E-waste is routinely exported by developed countries to developing ones, often in violation of international law. In developing countries, laws to protect workers and the environment are often inadequate or not enforced. It is also cheaper to recycle waste in developing countries; the cost of recycling a computer monitor in the US is ten times more than in China.

[Shortened: www.greenpeace.org]

▸ **e-waste** ['iː weɪst]	*Elektronikschrott*	cf	waste – *Abfall*
▸ **to end up**	*landen*	<>	to start out
▸ **electronic**	*elektronisch*	n	electronics
▸ **goods**	*Güter*		
▸ **to reuse** [ˌriːˈjuːz]	*wieder verwenden*	n	reuse
▸ **to recycle** [ˌriːˈsaɪkl]	*wieder verwerten*	n	recycling
▸ **to throw away**	*wegwerfen, entsorgen*	≈	to dispose of
▸ **environmental**	*Umwelt-*	n	environment
▸ **protection**	*Schutz*	vt	to protect
▸ **to stockpile**	*horten, lagern*	≈	to store
▸ **landfill**	*Mülldeponie*	≈	~ site
▸ **incinerator**	*Müllverbrennungsanlage*	vt	to incinerate
▸ **to export**	*exportieren*	n	export
▸ **toxic**	*giftig*	≈	poisonous
▸ **chemical**	*Chemikalie*	adj	chemical
▸ **to leach into**	*sickern in*	≈	to seep into
▸ **to release**	*freilassen, freisetzen*	n	release
▸ **atmosphere**	*Atmosphäre*	adj	atmospheric
▸ **regulation**	*Vorschrift*	vt	to regulate
▸ **to prevent**	*verhindern*	n	prevention
▸ **to dump**	*abladen*	n	dump
▸ **hazardous**	*gefährlich*	n	hazard
▸ **incineration**	*Verbrennung*	≈	burning
▸ **heavy metal**	*Schwermetall*	cf	lead [led] – *Blei*, copper – *Kupfer*
▸ **mercury**	*Quecksilber*		
▸ **to bioaccumulate**	*sich anreichern*	n	bioaccumulation
▸ **food chain**	*Nahrungskette*		
▸ **toxic**	*giftig*	n	toxin, toxicity
▸ **lifespan**	*Lebensdauer*	≈	lifetime
▸ **benefit**	*Vorteil*	adj	beneficial
▸ **facility**	*Einrichtung, Anlage*	phr	treatment ~ – *Aufbereitungsanlage*, storage ~ – *Lager*
▸ **raw material**	*Rohstoff*	<>	product
▸ **to harm**	*schädigen, schaden*	n	harm
▸ **recycling plant**	*Wiederverwertungsanlage*		
▸ **neighbouring**	*benachbart*	≈	nearby
▸ **to take place**	*stattfinden*	≈	to occur
▸ **purpose-built**	*eigens errichtet*	<>	converted
▸ **scrapyard**	*Schrottplatz*	vt	to scrap
▸ **routinely**	*routinemäßig*	n	routine
▸ **in violation of**	*unter Verletzung von*	vt	to violate
▸ **law**	*Gesetz, Recht*	adj	legal
▸ **inadequate**	*unzureichend*	n	inadequacy
▸ **to enforce**	*durchsetzen*	n	enforcement

C

Business

1 The global economy

2 The world of work

3 Consumerism

Forum

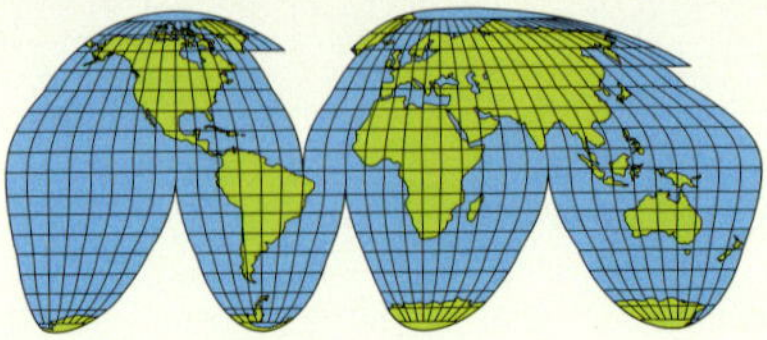

Thread: How does globalization affect me?

Help! My teacher gave me this essay title and I don't know what to write. It's such a huge topic, I don't know where to begin. Ideas, anyone?

Alexa, USA

Reply *Alain, Canada*

Think about the internet – and telecommunications in general. We live in a society where we can contact people on the other side of the world at the click of a mouse. You're benefiting from globalization by getting us to write your essay for you :)

Global telecommuniations enable the free exchange of ideas and information regardless of geographical location. On the other hand, it has become a lot easier to organize global terrorist or criminal networks, threatening global security.

Reply *uwesteffen*, Germany

Globalization is damaging cultural diversity. Whether you live in Thailand, Germany, Australia or Brazil, the chances are that you eat at McDonald's, drink Coke, wear Nike sneakers and watch The Simpsons on TV. It has led to the Americanization of the world and it's getting worse all the time.

Reply *brainy_beach_babe*, Australia

The main impact of globalization is economic. Globalization has resulted in free trade without import taxes and other restrictions. That has stimulated competition, leading to improved quality, variety and availability of goods, and at the same time creating new employment opportunities in both developed and developing countries.

Reply *Riccardino, Puerto Rico*

Free trade does not equal fair trade!

What we have seen with globalization is the rise of huge multinational corporations which wield more power than the average small country. Meanwhile Third World workers who produce raw materials and manufacture consumer goods for rich nations are being exploited, earning less in a month than the average European or American earns in a day.

1 The global economy

globalization	*Globalisierung*	adj	global, globalized
to affect	*sich auswirken auf*	n	effect
telecommunications	*Telekommunikation*	vti	to communicate (with)
to contact	*Kontakt aufnehmen zu*	n	contact
to benefit from	*profitieren von*	n	benefit
to enable	*ermöglichen*	≈	to make possible
exchange	*Austausch*	vt	to exchange
regardless of	*unabhängig von*	≈	irrespective of
location	*Ort*	vt	to locate
terrorist	*terroristisch*	n	terrorism
criminal	*kriminell*	n	crime
network	*Netz*	vti	to network
to threaten	*bedrohen*	n	threat
security	*Sicherheit*	adj	secure
to damage	*schaden*	n	damage
cultural	*kulturell*	n	culture
diversity	*Vielfalt*	adj	diverse
to lead to	*führen zu*	≈	to result in
Americanization	*Amerikanisierung*	cf	Anglicization
impact	*Auswirkung*	≈	effect
economic	*wirtschaftlich*	n	economy
to result in	*führen zu*	≈	to lead to
free trade	*Freihandel*	vti	to trade (with)
import tax	*Einfuhrzoll*	vt	to tax
restriction	*Beschränkung*	vt	to restrict
to stimulate	*stimulieren*	n	stimulation, stimulus
competition	*Wettbewerb*	vi	to compete (with)
quality	*Qualität*	cf	quantity – *Menge*
variety [vəˈraɪəti]	*Auswahl*	adj	varied
availability	*Verfügbarkeit*	adj	available
goods	*Waren*	cf	services – *Dienstleistungen*
employment	*Beschäftigung*	<>	unemployment
opportunity	*Möglichkeit*	≈	chance
developed country	*Industrieland*	vti	to develop
developing country	*Entwicklungsland*		
to equal	*gleichen*	≈	to be the same as
corporation	*Konzern*	adj	corporate
to wield	*ausüben*	≈	to exercise
power	*Macht*	adj	powerful
to manufacture	*herstellen*	n	manufacturing
consumer goods	*Konsumgüter*	cf	consumption – *Verbrauch*
to exploit	*ausbeuten*	n	exploitation

What kind of aid is best for Third World countries?

The kind of aid that is appropriate depends very much on the local situation in the country or region that is the recipient.

Humanitarian aid is often needed in emergency situations, e.g. when homes are destroyed and populations are displaced by natural catastrophes or war – medical supplies, food and shelter are needed. Refugee camps need to be set up quickly and the people in them provided with the basic necessities of life.

In times of crisis it's relatively easy to mobilize public opinion and get donations towards humanitarian aid, but the aid has to be distributed carefully so that it gets to the right people and is not lost to corruption and profiteering. Food aid may actually make the problem worse in the long term by depressing local prices and putting local producers out of business.

Development aid is help with building vital infrastructure such as clean water supplies, power supplies, schools and hospitals. This is really important long-term aid because it ultimately makes the local population more self-sufficient, because they are healthier and better educated. However, in countries with repressive regimes the scope for development aid is limited.

It's also important that local people are consulted so that the aid given is appropriate for their practical everyday needs and their cultural beliefs. Inappropriate infrastructure projects can actually be counterproductive. Generally speaking, small-scale, local projects are more likely to work. Best of all is when the initiative comes from local people themselves.

Fair trade is important to avoid exploitative trade relationships with poorer countries, so that producers get a fair share of the profits from their produce. So too are aspects of free trade – in particular the removal of barriers to imported goods from Third World countries.

aid	*Hilfe*	vt	to aid
appropriate	*angemessen*	<>	inappropriate
recipient	*Empfänger/in*	vt	to receive
humanitarian	*humanitär*	n	humanitarianism
emergency	*Not*	≈	crisis
population	*Bevölkerung*	cf	to depopulate – *entvölkern*
to displace	*verdrängen*	n	displacement
catastrophe [kə'tæstrəfi]	*Katastrophe*	≈	disaster
war	*Krieg*	cf	civil ~ – *Bürgerkrieg*
medical	*medizinisch*	n	medicine
supplies	*Versorgung*	vt	to supply
shelter	*Unterkunft*	vt	to shelter
refugee [ˌrefju'dʒiː] **camp**	*Flüchtlingslager*	cf	to seek refuge – *Zuflucht suchen*
basic	*Grund-*	≈	fundamental
necessity	*Bedürfnis*	adj	necessary
to mobilize	*mobilisieren*	n	mobilization
public opinion	*öffentliche Meinung*	cf	publicity
donation	*Spende*	vt	to donate
to distribute	*verteilen*	n	distribution
corruption	*Korruption*	adj	corrupt
profiteering	*Profitmacherei*	v prep	to profit from
in the long term	*langfristig*	<>	in the short term
to depress	*drücken*	<>	to inflate
to put sb out of business	*jdn aus dem Geschäft drängen*	cf	to go out of business – *Betrieb einstellen*
producer	*Produzent/in*	vt	to produce
development	*Entwicklung*	vti	to develop
vital	*lebenswichtig*	≈	crucial
infrastructure	*Infrastruktur*	≈	services and facilities
ultimately	*letzten Endes*	<>	initially
self-sufficient	*autark, unabhängig*	n	self-sufficiency
repressive	*repressiv*	n	repression
scope	*Spielraum*	≈	range
limited	*begrenzt*	n	limitation
to consult	*konsultieren*	n	consultation
counterproductive	*kontraproduktiv*	<>	productive
small-scale	*in kleinem Maßstab*	<>	large-scale
initiative [ɪ'nɪʃətɪv]	*Initiative*	phr	to take the ~ – *die Initiative ergreifen*
exploitative	*ausbeuterisch*	vt	to exploit
trade	*Handel*	vti	to trade
share	*Anteil*	vt	to share
produce ['prɒdjuːs]	*Erzeugnis(se)*	vt	to produce [prə'djuːs]
removal	*Abbau*	vt	to remove
barrier	*(Handels-)Schranke*	vt	to bar

Radio chat show: Celebrities and charity

DJ Signing up as an official ambassador for a well-known charity has almost become a routine part of the job for your average star. Celebrities like Bono, Oprah Winfrey and Steven Spielberg are putting millions of dollars into humanitarian projects such as Third-World schools, AIDS research and disaster relief. Does this mean that Hollywood has really developed a social conscience, or is it just a way for overpaid stars to feel good about themselves? What's your view?

Caller 1 I don't think it matters, frankly. Of course, the stars get something out of it themselves, whether in terms of tax deductions or increased media exposure. But they're also highlighting important issues – issues that ordinary people may not have thought about until they read in the celebrity gossip magazines that X has donated $1,000,000 to fighting AIDS in South Africa, or wherever.

Caller 2 Let's face it, these people get paid far more money than they should. I mean it's ridiculous that we pay an actor a thousand times more to pretend to be an AIDS doctor on screen than we actually pay the doctor in real life. So it's only fair that they should redistribute some of their wealth to people who really need it. They still keep plenty for themselves.

Caller 3 The other thing that concerns me is that a lot of this celebrity charity is well-meaning but not well-focused. Take Bob Geldof's work in Africa for example. Pumping huge amounts of cash into famine-stricken areas has just increased corruption and dependency on handouts, it hasn't actually addressed the root causes of poverty in sub-Saharan Africa. Apparently, since the original Band Aid concerts, the number of Africans living on overseas aid has increased by 500 per cent. That's no surprise, because you can't impose change from outside, you have to involve local grass-roots organizations.

▸ **celebrity**	*Promi(nente/r)*	≈	star
▸ **charity**	*Wohltätigkeit*	adj	charitable
▸ **to sign up**	*sich verpflichten*	n	signature
▸ **official**	*offiziell*	<>	informal, unofficial
▸ **ambassador**	*Botschafter/in*	cf	embassy – *Botschaft*
▸ **well-known**	*sehr bekannt*	<>	little-known
▸ **humanitarian**	*humanitär*	cf	humane – *human*
▸ **research**	*Forschung*	vt	to research
▸ **disaster relief**	*Katastrophenhilfe*	vt	to relieve
▸ **social conscience** [ˌsəʊʃl ˈkɒnʃəns]	*soziales Gewissen*	adj	conscientious [ˌkɒnʃiˈenʃəs]
▸ **overpaid**	*überbezahlt*	<>	underpaid
▸ **to feel good about**	*sich gut fühlen*	≈	to feel satisfied with
▸ **to get sth out of**	*Nutzen daraus ziehen*	≈	to benefit from
▸ **tax deduction**	*Steuerermäßigung*	vt	to deduct
▸ **media exposure** [ˌmiːdiə ɪkˈspəʊʒə]	*Medienpräsenz*	≈	media coverage
▸ **to highlight**	*hervorheben*	≈	to emphasize
▸ **issue**	*Thema*	≈	topic, problem
▸ **gossip**	*Klatsch*	vi	to gossip
▸ **to donate**	*spenden*	⚠	to spend ≠ *spenden*
▸ **ridiculous**	*lächerlich*	≈	absurd
▸ **actor**	*Schauspieler/in*	vi	to act
▸ **on screen**	*auf dem Bildschirm*	vt	to screen
▸ **to redistribute**	*umverteilen*	n	redistribution
▸ **wealth**	*Reichtum*	adj	wealthy
▸ **well-meaning**	*gut gemeint*	≈	well-intentioned
▸ **well-focused**	*zielgerichtet*	v prep	to focus on
▸ **to pump into**	*hineinpumpen*	≈	to inject into
▸ **cash**	*Geld*	≈	money, funds
▸ **famine-stricken**	*von Hunger bedroht*		
▸ **corruption**	*Korruption*	adj	corrupt
▸ **dependency**	*Abhängigkeit*	adj	dependent
▸ **handout**	*Almosen*	≈	aid, donation
▸ **to address**	*sich befassen mit*	<>	to ignore
▸ **root cause**	*eigentliche Ursache*	vt	to cause
▸ **poverty**	*Armut*	<>	wealth
▸ **overseas**	*ausländisch*	<>	domestic
▸ **to impose**	*erzwingen*	≈	to force (sth on sb)
▸ **change**	*Veränderung*	vti	to change
▸ **to involve**	*mit einbeziehen*	n	involvement
▸ **grass-roots**	*Basis*	≈	community-based

What is Fairtrade?

Fairtrade is about better prices, decent working conditions, local sustainability, and fair terms of trade for farmers and workers in the developing world. By requiring companies to pay sustainable prices, Fairtrade addresses the injustices of conventional trade, which traditionally discriminates against the poorest, weakest producers. It enables them to improve their position and have more control over their lives.

How much of the price we pay for Fairtrade products goes back to the producers?

Whatever the price of the product on the supermarket shelf, only the FAIRTRADE Mark ensures that the producers have received a fair price, as well as the social premiums to invest in the future of their communities. The Fairtrade price applies at the point where the producer sells to the next person in the supply chain (usually an exporter or importer). It is not calculated as a proportion of the final retail price, which is negotiated between the product manufacturer and the retailer.

Is buying Fairtrade products a good idea, given concerns about climate change?

Public concern about climate change and carbon emissions has been growing rapidly and there is no doubt that global action has to be taken now to deal with global warming. However if the debate becomes obsessed with the question of food miles, this could damage sustainable forms of agriculture.

Agriculture can play a critical role in the economic and social development of developing countries – up to one and a half million livelihoods in Africa alone are estimated to be dependent on UK consumption of agricultural produce. Increased agricultural growth is thought to be the most likely source of economic growth in Africa, given that 70% of the rural poor work on the land.

Can buying Fairtrade products help to fight climate change?

The Fairtrade system includes environmental standards which require producers to protect the natural environment. Producers are also encouraged to minimize the use of energy, especially energy from non-renewable sources.

In addition, by purchasing Fairtrade products, shoppers in the UK are ensuring that producer organisations receive a Fairtrade premium for investment in economic, social and environmental products of their own choice. These premiums can enable farmers to implement a range of environmental protection programmes which will contribute to the range of solutions needed to address climate change and ultimately benefit all of us.

[Adapted extracts: http://www.fairtrade.org.uk]

1 The global economy

▸ **trade**	*Handel*	vti	to trade (with)
▸ **decent** ['di:snt]	*anständig*	≈	adequate
▸ **conditions**	*Bedingungen*	≈	circumstances
▸ **local**	*lokal*	<>	global
▸ **sustainability**	*Nachhaltigkeit*	vt	to sustain
▸ **terms of trade**	*Handelsbedingungen*	≈	conditions of trade
▸ **sustainable**	*zukunftsfähig*	<>	unsustainable
▸ **injustice**	*Ungerechtigkeit*	adj	unjust
▸ **conventional**	*traditionell, üblich*	≈	normal
▸ **to discriminate against**	*benachteiligen*	adj	discriminatory
▸ **producer**	*Produzent/in*	<>	consumer
▸ **to ensure**	*sicherstellen*	≈	to make sure
▸ **social premium**	*Sozialbeitrag*		
▸ **to invest in**	*investieren in*	n	investment
▸ **community**	*Gemeinde*	adj	communal
▸ **supply chain**	*Versorgungskette*	cf	supply and demand
▸ **exporter**	*Exporteur*	vt	to export
▸ **importer**	*Importeur*	vt	to import
▸ **retail** ['ri:teɪl]	*Einzelhandels-*	cf	wholesale – *Großhandels-*
▸ **to negotiate**	*aushandeln*	n	negotiation
▸ **manufacturer**	*Hersteller*	vt	to manufacture
▸ **retailer** ['ri:teɪlə]	*Einzelhändler*	≈	shopkeeper
▸ **given concerns**	*angesichts der Sorgen*	vt	to concern
▸ **climate change**	*Klimawandel*	adj	climatic
▸ **carbon**	*Kohlenstoff*	cf	~ dioxide – CO_2
▸ **emission**	*Ausstoß*	vt	to emit
▸ **global warming**	*Erderwärmung*	vti	to warm
▸ **food miles**	*Transportwege der Nahrungsmittel*	cf	carbon footprint
▸ **to damage**	*schaden*	≈	to harm
▸ **agriculture**	*Landwirtschaft*	adj	agricultural
▸ **economic**	*wirtschaftlich*	n	economics (pl)
▸ **social**	*gesellschaftlich*	n	society
▸ **development**	*Entwicklung*	vti	to develop
▸ **livelihood**	*Lebensunterhalt*	≈	source of income
▸ **dependent on**	*abhängig von*	<>	independent of
▸ **consumption**	*Verbrauch*	vt	to consume
▸ **agricultural**	*landwirtschaftlich*	≈	farm (attrib adj)
▸ **produce**	*Produkt(e)*	adj	productive
▸ **growth**	*Wachstum*	<>	shrinkage, decline
▸ **rural**	*ländlich*	<>	urban
▸ **environmental**	*Umweltschutz-*	n	environment
▸ **to protect**	*schützen*	n	protection
▸ **to encourage**	*(dazu) anhalten*	<>	to discourage
▸ **to minimize**	*verringern*	<>	to maximize
▸ **non-renewable**	*nicht erneuerbar*	vt	to renew

Here's where we deal with questions that our readers ask.

Question I'm finishing school next year. How can I find a job?
JK, 17, Newcastle

Answer Of course, this depends very much on your individual circumstances: educational background, work experience, etc. Here are some of the common ways that people find work:

Careers adviser. If you're still at school or college, your institution's careers adviser should be able to give you general careers guidance as well as practical suggestions about how to go about finding a job.

Training provider. If you're doing some sort of vocational training, your training provider may be able to recommend you to a local employer.

Classified advertisements in newspapers. This is still a good way of finding a job, particularly in your local area.

Job search websites. These offer thousands of jobs nationally and even internationally. You can search by profession and often by job title. Often you will have to register with the website to apply for the jobs.

Word of mouth. Sometimes people hear about job vacancies in particular firms from friends and relations who are already working there. They may also be able to give you a personal recommendation.

Speculative applications. It's always worth a try sending letters of application and CVs to prospective employers. However to be successful you really need to research the company (e.g. via its website) and tailor your application to the employer, rather than sending out hundreds of identical applications.

Voluntary internship. In some industries you can get a 'foot on the ladder' by working for a few months on a voluntary basis. If a vacancy for a paid position comes up, you'll be in a good position to apply for it.

Employment agencies. These are private companies that match up workers with companies, particularly for temporary positions to cover holiday periods, etc. This is a good way of increasing your work experience and making you more employable.

Recruitment firms are like employment agencies but specialize more in permanent positions, often of an executive or a professional nature.

Jobcentre/Employment office. If you're receiving unemployment benefit, your local jobcentre (UK) or government employment office should be helping you to look for a job or training course.

▸ **circumstances**	*Umstände*	≈	situation
▸ **educational background**	*Bildungshintergrund*	n	education
▸ **work experience**	*Berufserfahrung*	vt	to experience
▸ **careers adviser**	*Berufsberater/in*	vt	to advise
▸ **careers guidance** [kəˈrɪəz ɡaɪdəns]	*Berufsberatung*	vt	to guide
▸ **training provider**	*Ausbildungsinstitut*	vt	to provide
▸ **vocational training**	*Berufsausbildung*	n	vocation
▸ **to recommend to**	*empfehlen an*	n	recommendation
▸ **employer**	*Arbeitgeber/in*	<>	employee
▸ **classified advertisement**	*Kleinanzeige*	abbr	classified ad
▸ **profession**	*Beruf*	adj	professional
▸ **job title**	*Berufsbezeichnung*	cf	job description – *Aufgabengebiet*
▸ **to register**	*(sich) anmelden*	n	registration
▸ **to apply for**	*sich bewerben um*	n	applicant
▸ **word of mouth**	*Mundpropaganda*	phr	by ~
▸ **job vacancy**	*freie Stelle*	adj	vacant
▸ **recommendation**	*Empfehlung*	≈	reference
▸ **speculative**	*unaufgefordert*	≈	on spec (coll)
▸ **application**	*Bewerbung*	cf	letter of ~
▸ **worth a try**	*einen Versuch wert*		
▸ **letter of application**	*Bewerbungsschreiben*	v prep	to apply for
▸ **CV**	*Lebenslauf*	AE	résumé
▸ **prospective**	*potentiell*	≈	potential
▸ **to research**	*Nachforschungen anstellen (über)*	n	research
▸ **to tailor to**	*maßschneidern nach*	adj	tailor-made
▸ **voluntary internship**	*Volontariat*	cf	intern – *Voluntär/in*
▸ **to get a foot on the ladder**	*einen Fuß auf die Leiter setzen*	≈	to get a foot in the door
▸ **on a voluntary basis**	*auf freiwilliger Basis*	≈	voluntarily
▸ **to come up**	*sich ergeben*	≈	to become available
▸ **employment agency**	*Stellenvermittlung*	vt	to employ
▸ **to match up**	*zuordnen*	≈	to pair
▸ **temporary**	*befristet*	cf	temp (coll) – *Aushilfskraft*
▸ **to cover**	*abdecken*	≈	to bridge
▸ **employable**	*einsetzbar*	<>	unemployable
▸ **recruitment firm**	*Anwerbefirma*	vt	to recruit
▸ **to specialize in**	*sich spezialisieren auf*	n	specialization
▸ **permanent**	*fest, dauerhaft*	<>	temporary
▸ **executive**	*leitend, Manager-*	≈	managerial
▸ **professional**	*fachlich*	n	profession
▸ **jobcentre**	*Jobcenter*	AE	labor exchange
▸ **unemployment benefit**	*Arbeitslosengeld*	AE	unemployment aid
▸ **training course**	*Ausbildungslehrgang, Umschulung*	cf	trainee – *Auszubildende/r*

Gender bias still exists within the executive workplace

Half of all managers at US companies are female, yet when it comes to senior posts, men outnumber the women by almost 6 to 1. Gender bias is still a factor in the American workplace.

The glass ceiling

According to a recent survey by TheLadders.com, the 'glass ceiling' is still a major problem for female executives. When asked whether men and women were paid the same for similar positions, a 71.5% majority said, 'no'. Likewise, 66.3% of executives surveyed said that women do not have as many opportunities as men to become company CEOs. Meanwhile, 54.1% of the survey respondents – representing both sexes – said that men and women are equally good at managing employees.

Working mothers

Despite the obstacles many working women still face, few want to trade in their suits for an apron. When asked whether they would continue to work after giving birth, 47% said they would continue to work part-time, even if they didn't need the second income. Twenty-seven per cent said they would continue to work full-time. Yet 55% of executives said that employees with young children are more likely to experience workplace discrimination.
As for family-friendly office environments, 63% of executives responding to the survey said that their workplace offers no assistance in the form of day care, on-site nursing facilities or time off for children's school events.

Sexual harassment

In one particularly disturbing statistic, 51.2% of female executives responding to the survey said they have experienced some form of sexual harassment. Twenty-six per cent said that they hadn't personally but knew of someone who had experienced harassment.

Parental leave

In the USA there is no automatic entitlement to paid maternity leave. This compares with one year's paid leave (at 90% of salary) in the UK, of which the last six months can be transferred to the father. In Germany mothers are entitled to up to 14 months paid leave, with some restrictions.

▸ **gender bias**	*geschlechtsspezifisches Vorurteil*	adj	biased
▸ **executive**	*leitend, Manager-*	≈	managerial
▸ **workplace**	*Arbeitsplatz*	≈	place of work
▸ **female**	*weiblich*	<>	male
▸ **senior**	*vorgesetzt, ranghoch*	<>	junior
▸ **post**	*Posten*	≈	position
▸ **to outnumber**	*übertreffen*	≈	to exceed
▸ **glass ceiling** [ˌglɑːs ˈsiːlɪŋ]	*unsichtbare Beförderungssperre*		
▸ **survey** [ˈsɜːveɪ]	*(Meinungs-)Umfrage, Untersuchung*	≈	opinion poll
▸ **major**	*von großer Bedeutung*	<>	minor
▸ **majority**	*Mehrheit*	<>	minority
▸ **to survey** [ˈsɜːveɪ]	*befragen*	≈	to poll
▸ **opportunity**	*Chance, Möglichkeit*	≈	chance
▸ **CEO** (abbr)	*Geschäftsführer/in*	=	Chief Executive Officer
▸ **respondent**	*Befragte/r*	v prep	to respond to
▸ **sex**	*Geschlecht*	≈	gender
▸ **to manage**	*leiten*	n	management
▸ **employee**	*Angestellte/r*	<>	employer
▸ **obstacle**	*Hindernis*	cf	to overcome an ~
▸ **to face**	*sich gegenübersehen*	≈	to be confronted with
▸ **to trade in for**	*eintauschen gegen*	≈	to exchange, to swap
▸ **suit**	*Anzug*		
▸ **apron**	*Schürze*		
▸ **to give birth**	*entbinden*	≈	to have a baby
▸ **part-time**	*Teilzeit-*	cf	to work ~
▸ **income**	*Einkommen*	≈	earnings
▸ **full-time**	*Vollzeit-*	cf	to work ~
▸ **to experience**	*erleben*	n	experience
▸ **discrimination**	*Diskriminierung*	v prep	to discriminate against
▸ **family-friendly**	*familienfreundlich*	≈	family-oriented
▸ **office environment**	*Büroumfeld*		
▸ **assistance**	*Unterstützung*	≈	help
▸ **day care**	*Tagespflege, Kindertagesstätte*	cf	crêche – *Kinderkrippe*
▸ **nursing facilities**	*Räume zu Stillen von Babys*	vt	to nurse
▸ **time off**	*Beurlaubung*	cf	to take ~
▸ **sexual harassment**	*sexuelle Belästigung*	vt	to harass
▸ **disturbing**	*alarmierend*	≈	worrying
▸ **parental leave**	*Elternzeit*	phr	to take ~
▸ **entitlement**	*Anspruch*	≈	right
▸ **maternity leave**	*Mutterschaftsurlaub*	cf	paternity leave
▸ **salary**	*Gehalt*	≈	pay
▸ **to transfer**	*übertragen*	n	transfer
▸ **to be entitled to**	*Anspruch haben auf*	≈	to have a right to
▸ **restriction**	*Einschränkung*	vt	to restrict

Bullying in the workplace

Bullying at work is when someone tries to intimidate another worker, often in front of colleagues. It's often, though not always, done to someone in a less senior position.

It's similar to harassment, which is where someone's behaviour is offensive – for example, making sexual comments, or abusing someone's race, religion or sexual orientation.

Examples of bullying behaviour

Bullying includes abuse, physical or verbal violence, humiliation and undermining someone's confidence. You are probably being bullied if, for example, you're constantly picked on or humiliated in front of colleagues, physically or verbally abused or regularly blamed for problems caused by others. Another form of bullying is when you're always given too much to do, so that you regularly fail in your work, or are unfairly passed over for promotion or denied training opportunities.

Bullying can be face-to-face, in writing, over the phone or by email.

What to do if you're bullied at work

Employers have a 'duty of care' to their employees and this includes dealing with bullying at work. There are measures you can take if you're being bullied.

Get advice

Speak to someone about how you might deal with the problem informally. This might be a trade union representative, someone in the firm's human resources department or your supervisor.

Talk to the bully

The bullying may not be deliberate. If you can, talk to the person in question. Work out what to say beforehand. Describe what's been happening and why you object to it. Stay calm and be polite. If you don't want to talk to them yourself, ask someone else to do so for you.

Keep a written record or diary

Write down details of every incident and keep copies of any relevant documents.

Make a formal complaint

This is the next step if you can't solve the problem informally. To do this you must follow your employer's grievance procedure.

[Shortened: http://www.direct.gov.uk/en/Employment/DiscriminationAtWork/DG_10026670]

▸ **bullying**	*Mobbing, Tyrannisieren*	cf	bully – *Tyrann*
▸ **to intimidate**	*einschüchtern*	n	intimidation
▸ **colleague**	*Kollege/-gin*	≈	co-worker
▸ **senior position**	*leitende Stellung*	<>	junior position
▸ **harassment**	*Belästigung*	vt	to harass
▸ **behaviour**	*Benehmen*	vi	to behave
▸ **offensive**	*beleidigend*	vt	to offend
▸ **comment**	*Bemerkung*	v prep	to comment on
▸ **to abuse** [ə'bju:z]	*beschimpfen*	≈	to insult
▸ **race**	*Rasse*	adj	racial
▸ **sexual orientation**	*sexuelle Orientierung*	cf	gay – *schwul*, lesbian – *lesbisch*
▸ **abuse** [ə'bju:s]	*Beschimpfung*	≈	insult(s)
▸ **physical**	*körperlich*	<>	mental
▸ **violence**	*Gewalt*	adj	violent
▸ **humiliation**	*Demütigung*	≈	shame
▸ **to undermine**	*untergraben*	<>	to bolster
▸ **confidence**	*(Selbst-)Vertrauen*	adj	confident
▸ **to pick on**	*herumhacken auf*	≈	to victimize
▸ **to humiliate**	*demütigen*	≈	to shame
▸ **to blame**	*jdm die Schuld geben*		
▸ **to fail**	*versagen*	n	failure
▸ **unfairly**	*ungerecht*	n	(un)fairness
▸ **to pass over**	*übergehen*	≈	to disregard
▸ **promotion**	*Beförderung*	vt	to promote
▸ **to deny** [dɪ'naɪ]	*verweigern*	n	denial
▸ **training**	*(Fort-)Bildung*	vti	to train
▸ **opportunity**	*Möglichkeit*	≈	chance
▸ **face-to-face**	*von Angesicht zu Angesicht*	≈	in person
▸ **duty**	*Pflicht*	≈	obligation
▸ **care**	*Fürsorge, Sorgfalt*	<>	carelessness
▸ **measure** ['meʒə]	*Maßnahme*	≈	step
▸ **advice**	*Rat*	vt	to advise
▸ **informally**	*inoffiziell*	<>	formally, officially
▸ **trade union**	*Gewerkschaft*	phr	to belong to a ~
▸ **representative**	*Vertreter/in*	≈	official
▸ **human resources**	*Personal(abteilung)*	abbr	HR
▸ **supervisor**	*Vorgesetzte/r*	vt	to supervise
▸ **deliberate** [dɪ'lɪbərət]	*absichtlich, bewusst*	<>	unintentional
▸ **to object to**	*ablehnen*	n	objection
▸ **record**	*Aufzeichnung*	vt	to record
▸ **diary** ['daɪəri]	*Tagebuch*	≈	journal
▸ **incident**	*Vorfall, Ereignis*	≈	case, occurrence
▸ **complaint**	*Beschwerde*	vi	to complain (about)
▸ **grievance**	*Klage*	≈	complaint

Radio show: Fat cat salaries

Presenter Today on 'This is money' we have a question from Maxine Baretta from Christchurch:

Maxine How do companies justify paying their bosses six-figure salaries? I earn little more than the minimum wage working on the shop floor, but the boss of my company gets £2 million a year. Surely these fat cat salaries are unfair, aren't they?

Panellist 1 The usual argument used to justify high boardroom pay is that to recruit and retain the best managers, a company needs to offer a competitive salary – one that's on a par with other similar companies. In fact, your boss's pay is relatively modest – the average chief executive of a top company takes home nearly £3 million annually.

And remember, shareholders can vote against a big salary increase if they don't believe the boss is worth it. Shouldn't exceptional performance be rewarded?

Another point is that a lot of the pay package may be made up of performance bonuses and share option schemes – the boss only earns a lot if the company does well.

Panellist 2 Well, I'd dispute that. Often there is no credible link between a company's performance and the pay of its top executives – just look at 'golden parachute' deals to persuade incompetent bosses to resign quietly.

More importantly, companies have lost touch with reality if they think it's OK to pay bosses salaries that are out of all proportion to what their employees get. After all, if a company is doing well, surely that's a reflection on the productivity of the employees, not just the senior managers. Did you know that UK bosses now take home 98 times more than their employees? That salary gap hits workforce morale and threatens social cohesion.

Panellist 3 The worst of it is, the majority of the super-rich avoid paying income tax through various tax breaks.

Presenter But that's another issue. Maxine, I don't think we've given a full answer to your question, but it's a complex matter …

▸ **fat cat** (coll)	*jd mit viel Geld und Einfluss, großes Tier*	≈	big boss
▸ **salary**	*Gehalt*	≈	pay
▸ **to justify**	*rechtfertigen*	n	justification
▸ **six-figure**	*sechsstellig*	≈	(multi-)million-dollar
▸ **minimum wage**	*Mindestlohn*	cf	to earn the ~
▸ **shop floor**	*Produktion(sbereich)*	≈	ordinary workers
▸ **boardroom**	*Vorstandsebene*	≈	director's level
▸ **pay**	*Gehalt*	≈	remuneration
▸ **to recruit**	*einstellen*	n	recruitment
▸ **to retain**	*halten*	n	retention
▸ **competitive**	*konkurrenzfähig*	v prep	to compete with
▸ **on a par with**	*vergleichbar mit*	≈	comparable with
▸ **modest**	*bescheiden*	<>	extravagant
▸ **chief executive**	*Geschäftsführer/in*	abbr	CEO
▸ **annually**	*jährlich*	≈	each year
▸ **shareholder**	*Aktionär/in*	≈	stockholder
▸ **to vote against**	*stimmen gegen*	n	vote
▸ **exceptional**	*außergewöhnlich*	n	exception
▸ **performance**	*Leistung(en)*	vi	to perform
▸ **to reward**	*entlohnen*	n	reward
▸ **pay package**	*Gehaltszahlung*		
▸ **share**	*Aktie*	≈	stock
▸ **to dispute**	*bestreiten*	n	dispute
▸ **credible**	*glaubwürdig*	<>	incredible
▸ **link**	*Verbindung*	≈	connection
▸ **golden parachute**	*goldener Fallschirm*	≈	golden handshake
▸ **incompetent**	*inkompetent*	n	incompetence
▸ **to resign**	*zurücktreten*	≈	to hand in one's resignation
▸ **to lose touch with**	*die Verbindung verlieren zu*	<>	to keep in touch with
▸ **to be out of all proportion to**	*in keinem Verhältnis stehen zu*	≈	to bear no relation to
▸ **reflection on**	*Folge von*	v prep	to reflect on
▸ **productivity**	*Produktivität*	adj	productive
▸ **salary gap**	*Gehaltslücke, -kluft*	≈	pay difference
▸ **workforce**	*arbeitende Bevölkerung*	≈	the workers
▸ **morale**	*Arbeitsmoral*	≈	spirits
▸ **to threaten**	*bedrohen*	n	threat
▸ **social cohesion**	*sozialer Zusammenhalt*	adj	cohesive
▸ **income tax**	*Einkommenssteuer*	vt	to tax
▸ **tax break**	*Steuervergünstigung*	cf	tax evasion – *Steuerhinterziehung*

What is ethical fashion?

Ethical fashion takes into consideration the people behind the clothes we wear, as well as the environment. When you buy a piece of clothing, you may not think twice about where it was made, by whom and under what conditions. The clothing industry is a complex one: all the clothes we wear have a story behind them.

The journey of a pair of jeans from cotton plant to landfill site

Growing the cotton. Cotton is often seen as a natural, eco-friendly fabric. In fact it uses nearly 25% of the world's insecticides. These are harmful both to the farmers growing the cotton and to the environment.

Processing the fabric. Chemicals are an important part of making your jeans look and feel the way they do. Many of them are toxic to people and to the environment.

Sewing the jeans. Because labour costs are lower, clothing is often made in some of the poorest parts of the world. Although this can bring benefits to communities through providing work and steady incomes, it often means unfair and unsafe working conditions, long hours, and pay which is too low to pay for food, healthcare and other basic needs.

Transporting the jeans to Europe. Most clothing travels thousands of miles to consumers. This involves travel by sea, by road and even by air, using a lot of fuel. This pollutes the environment we live in and is responsible for global warming.

Buying the jeans. You can probably buy a pair of jeans for as little as €10 in some highstreet stores. Prices this low mean that less money goes to the people who make the clothes on the other side of the world.

Disposing of the jeans. When you throw away a worn-out pair of jeans, it will probably end up in a landfill site. While the denim will decompose, being organic, chemicals used as part of the manufacturing process will find their way into the earth.

An ethical fashion industry

The fashion industry does not need to be this way. Many companies produce clothes in an ethical way which benefits people and does not damage the environment. You can do a lot by supporting these companies, by customizing your own clothes and buying second hand.

[http://www.bbc.co.uk/blast/art/articles/what_is_ethical_fashion.shtml]

3 Consumerism

▸ **ethical**	*ethisch*	n	ethics
▸ **fashion**	*Mode*	adj	fashionable
▸ **to take into consideration**	*berücksichtigen*	≈	to consider
▸ **environment**	*Umwelt*	adj	environmental
▸ **piece of clothing** [piːs əv 'kləʊðɪŋ]	*Kleidungsstück*		
▸ **to think twice about**	*es sich gut überlegen*	≈	to reflect carefully upon
▸ **conditions**	*Bedingungen*	≈	circumstances
▸ **clothing industry**	*Bekleidungsindustrie*		
▸ **cotton**	*Baumwolle*	cf	wool – *Wolle*
▸ **landfill site**	*Mülldeponie*	≈	dump
▸ **to grow**	*anbauen*	n	growth
▸ **eco-friendly**	*umweltfreundlich*	≈	environmentally friendly
▸ **fabric**	*Stoff*	⚠	≠ Fabrik
▸ **insecticide**	*Insektenbekämpfungsmittel*	≈	pesticide
▸ **harmful**	*schädlich*	<>	harmless
▸ **to process**	*(weiter) verarbeiten*	≈	to prepare
▸ **chemical**	*Chemikalie*	adj	chemical
▸ **toxic**	*giftig*	n	toxicity
▸ **to sew** [səʊ]	*nähen*	≈	to stitch
▸ **labour** ['leɪbə]	*Arbeit*	≈	work
▸ **benefit**	*Vorteil*	<>	detriment
▸ **community**	*Gemeinde*	adj	communal
▸ **steady**	*fest, regelmäßig*	≈	reliable
▸ **income**	*Einkommen*	≈	earnings
▸ **working conditions**	*Arbeitsbedingungen*		
▸ **healthcare**	*medizinische Versorgung*	≈	medical care
▸ **basic needs**	*Grundbedürfnisse*	≈	fundamental needs
▸ **to transport**	*transportieren*	n	transport(ation)
▸ **consumer**	*Verbraucher/in*	vt	to consume
▸ **fuel**	*Treibstoff*	vt	to fuel
▸ **to pollute**	*verschmutzen*	n	pollution
▸ **responsible for**	*verantwortlich für*	n	responsibilty
▸ **global warming**	*Erderwärmung*		
▸ **highstreet store** (BE)	*Kaufhaus*	≈	major retailer
▸ **to dispose of**	*entsorgen*	n	disposal
▸ **to throw away**	*wegwerfen*	≈	to put in the rubbish
▸ **worn-out**	*abgenutzt, abgetragen*	<>	new
▸ **to end up**	*enden, landen*	<>	to start out
▸ **to decompose**	*(sich) zersetzen*	≈	to rot
▸ **manufacturing process**	*Herstellungsprozess*	vt	to manufacture
▸ **to benefit**	*nützen*	<>	to be detrimental to
▸ **to damage**	*schaden*	n	damage
▸ **to support**	*unterstützen*	n	support
▸ **to customize**	*individuell gestalten*	adj	custom(ized)
▸ **second hand**	*aus zweiter Hand, gebraucht(e Kleidung)*	<>	new

Belinda's Blog

1.2.2010

Search

Comment

Buy Less Stuff!

I've always been a bit of a shopaholic. I get a thrill from online shopping – just click on items and in your shopping basket they go. Then it's off to the checkout, type in your credit card details and that's that. Then there's the pleasurable anticipation of waiting for the shiny new things to arrive at your door.

Recently, though, I've had to rethink my spending habits. For one thing, I can no longer pay off my credit card bill every month, so I'm in debt. For another, I've moved to a new, smaller flat. I'm surrounded by all these possessions I don't need and don't have room for, and they're cluttering up my life.

Credit card companies encourage us to spend irresponsibly by giving us lots of spending power, but sooner or later we've still got to pay the bills. The same principle applies to individuals as to national economies: runaway consumerism always ends in depression!

So now I've decided to Buy Less Stuff. I've drawn up a seven-point plan to help me achieve this:

1 Maintain. If I take care of the stuff I already have, e.g. service my bike regularly, it will last longer.

2 Repair. If something is broken, I'll fix it instead of throwing it away.

3 Make do. My laptop will last another year. I don't need to upgrade it just yet, even though the latest model looks sleek and stylish and has 20 times more memory.

4 Borrow. I only need a car about once a month, so my brother will lend me his. Rather than buying books and DVDs from Amazon, I can borrow them for free from my local library.

5 Buy second hand. The possibilities are endless: charity shops, eBay, freecycle.com …

6 Do without. Do I really need that tempting new kitchen gadget, e.g. that espresso maker I saw the other day? I've managed without one up to now, so clearly I don't.

7 Buy quality. When I really need things, I can spend a little more on high-quality goods that will last longer.

3 Consumerism

▸ **shopaholic**	*Kunde/Kundin im Kaufrausch*	cf	alcoholic
▸ **to get a thrill from**	*es aufregend finden*	adj	thrilling
▸ **shopping basket**	*Warenkorb*	cf	shopping trolley – *Einkaufswagen*
▸ **checkout**	*Kasse*	≈	cash register
▸ **pleasurable** ['pleʒərəbl]	*angenehm*	vt	to please
▸ **anticipation**	*Erwartung, Vorfreude*	vt	to anticipate
▸ **shiny**	*glänzend*	≈	glossy
▸ **to rethink**	*überdenken*	≈	to reconsider
▸ **spending**	*Ausgaben*	≈	expenditure
▸ **habit**	*Gewohnheit*	adj	habitual
▸ **to pay off**	*abbezahlen*	≈	to pay in full
▸ **credit card bill**	*Kreditkartenabrechnung*	≈	credit card statement
▸ **to be in debt**	*Schulden haben*	<>	to be out of debt
▸ **possession(s)**	*Besitz*	vt	to possess
▸ **to clutter up**	*verstopfen*	n	clutter
▸ **to encourage to**	*dazu verleiten*	<>	to discourage from
▸ **irresponsibly**	*unverantwortlich*	<>	responsibly
▸ **spending power**	*Kaufkraft*	≈	buying power
▸ **principle**	*Prinzip*	≈	rule
▸ **economy**	*Wirtschaft*	adj	economic
▸ **runaway**	*unkontrollierbar*	≈	uncontrolled
▸ **consumerism**	*Konsumismus*	vt	to consume
▸ **depression**	*Depression*	vt	to depress
▸ **to maintain**	*pflegen*	n	maintenance
▸ **to service**	*warten*	n	service
▸ **to last**	*halten, dauern*	adj	lasting
▸ **to repair**	*reparieren*	≈	to mend
▸ **to fix**	*instand setzen*	<>	to break
▸ **to make do**	*sich begnügen*		
▸ **to upgrade** [ˌʌp'greɪd]	*aufrüsten*	n	upgrade ['ʌpgreɪd]
▸ **sleek**	*schnittig, elegant*	n	sleekness
▸ **stylish**	*modisch*	≈	fashionable
▸ **to borrow (from)**	*ausborgen*	n	borrowing
▸ **to lend (to)**	*(ver)leihen*	n	lending
▸ **for free**	*umsonst, gratis*	≈	free of charge
▸ **charity shop**	*Wohltätigkeitsladen*	adj	charitable
▸ **to do without**	*auskommen ohne*	≈	to forego
▸ **tempting**	*verlockend*	n	temptation
▸ **gadget**	*Gerät*	≈	appliance
▸ **to manage**	*auskommen*	≈	to cope
▸ **high-quality**	*hochwertig*	<>	low-quality
▸ **goods**	*Waren, Güter*	≈	items

D

The arts

1 Literature

2 Performing arts

3 Art

Figurative language

Even when they express extremes, such as 'beautiful' and 'ugly', everyday words rarely appeal to the imagination. Thus authors seek new ways to convey thoughts, perceptions and feelings – ways which are more striking and effective, which attract the reader's attention, excite his or her imagination and maybe arouse strong feelings.

One such method is figurative language, i.e. a use of language which departs from the literal meaning of the words. Classical rhetoric identified several hundred such 'figures of speech', but here are some of the more common:

A simile occurs when one thing is expressly compared to another which, taken literally, is fundamentally dissimilar to it, e.g. 'My blood, it is like light'[1]. Logic tells us that blood cannot possibly be like light, but we understand that the writer is alluding to certain attributes or characteristics of light – it is bright, swift and weightless. Applying these characteristics to 'blood' creates a forceful expression of joy and energy.

If the writer does not state that a comparison is being made – i.e. does not use a word such as 'like' or 'as' – a simile becomes a metaphor, e.g. 'Once my heart was a summer rose'[2]. Sometimes the object of comparison is implied rather than stated, e.g. 'Faith in their hands shall snap in two'[3] – where the implied image is that of breaking a stick.

Figurative language often makes an impact by comparing an abstract concept – such as faith in the last example – to something concrete, i.e. something which can be perceived by the senses. This has the effect of making the concept much more immediate. When figurative language is used to evoke pictures in the reader's mind, it is also called 'imagery'.

The literary symbol may be defined as something which means itself and something more as well, i.e. it is to be understood in both a literal and a metaphorical sense. Thus when 'man and shadow meet'[4], the shadow is both the man's literal shadow, meeting him as he falls to the ground, and a symbol of death. Often, a symbol is not clear-cut, but is open to various interpretations, which can make it very subtle and complex.

[1] *Thom Gunn, 'Rites of passage'*
[2] *Edith Sitwell, 'Song'*
[3] *Dylan Thomas, 'And death shall have no dominion'*
[4] *Keith Douglas, 'How to kill'*

figurative ['fɪgərətɪv]	*bildlich*	<>	literal
to express	*ausdrücken*	adj	expressive
extreme	*Extrem*	adj	extreme
everyday	*alltäglich*	≈	commonplace
to appeal to	*ansprechen*	n	appeal
imagination	*Vorstellungskraft, Phantasie*	adj	imaginative
to convey	*vermitteln*	≈	to express
perception	*Wahrnehmung*	vt	to perceive
striking	*eindrucksvoll*	vt	to strike
effective	*wirkungsvoll*	n	effect
to attract sb's attention	*jds Aufmerksamkeit erregen*		
to excite	*anregen*	≈	to cause
to arouse	*erwecken*	≈	to evoke
to depart from	*abweichen von*	n	departure
literal	*wörtlich*	<>	figurative
figure of speech	*Redewendung*		
simile ['sɪməli]	*Gleichnis*	cf	metaphor
expressly	*ausdrücklich*	≈	explicitly
fundamentally	*grundlegend*	<>	superficially
to allude to	*anspielen auf*	n	allusion
attribute	*Merkmal*	vt	to attribute sth to sb
characteristic	*Eigenschaft*	adj	characteristic
to apply to	*verwenden für*	adj	applicable
forceful	*kraftvoll, eindringlich*	n	forcefulness
metaphor	*Metapher*	cf	simile
to imply	*implizieren, andeuten*	adj	implicit
image	*Bild*	≈	picture
to make an impact	*eine Wirkung erzielen*	≈	to have an effect
abstract	*abstrakt*	n	abstraction
concept	*Vorstellung*	≈	idea
concrete	*konkret*	≈	tangible
to perceive	*wahrnehmen*	cf	perceptive – *scharfsinnig*
immediate	*unmittelbar, direkt*	<>	remote
to evoke	*hervorrufen*	adj	evocative
imagery	*Metaphorik*		
literary	*literarisch*	<>	factual
metaphorical [ˌmetə'fɒrɪkl]	*metaphorisch, bildlich*	<>	literal
clear-cut	*klar, eindeutig*	<>	vague [veɪg]
subtle ['sʌtl]	*subtil, hintergründig*	n	subtlety
complex	*komplex*	n	complexity

The British novel post-1945

After World War II, a new generation of British novelists focused on humanity's more sinister qualities. In novels such as *Lord of the Flies* (1954), William Golding placed individuals or small groups in extreme situations: as the rules of civilized society become weaker, his characters quickly degenerate into violence and brutality. George Orwell presented a similiarly pessimistic view of humanity in his satirical fable *Animal Farm* (1945) and in his futuristic novel *1984* (1949).

In *The Prime of Miss Jean Brodie* (1961) Muriel Spark portrayed a schoolteacher whose control of her pupils is really fascism on a small scale. The small, enclosed world created in each of these works can be seen as an allegory of society in general, or a parable of human nature.

In contrast to these symbolic novels was a new type of social realism: novels about contemporary life in Britain, written in an accessible style and focusing on the lives of young working-class people whom a wide readership could recognize and identify with. Two famous works of this type were John Braine's *Room at the Top* (1957) and Alan Sillitoe's *Saturday Night and Sunday Morning* (1958). The anti-Establishment tone of this type of writing caused its authors to be known as the Angry Young Men. Iris Murdoch began in this realist tradition but she quickly found her own style in works such as *A Severed Head* (1961), in which character study is combined with complicated plots and supernatural incidents. Her novels have been described as psychological detective stories.

Britain found its ex-Empire a rich topic for narrative fiction. Paul Scott in his *Raj Quartet* (1966–1975) portrayed Anglo-Indian relationships and the personal, political, racial and religious conflicts which arise from them, presenting events from various viewpoints which only gradually reveal the whole picture.

Indian independence was given a far more lively treatment by Salman Rushdie in novels such as *Midnight's Children* (1981), written in the style known as Magic Realism, in which realistic characters and events mingle with the fantastic and the allegorical. The Anglo-Caribbean writer V. S. Naipaul explored problems of nationality and identity in novels such as *In a Free State* (1971) and short stories such as those in the collection *A Flag on the Island* (1967).

novelist	*Romanschriftsteller/in*	cf	novel – *Roman*
to focus on	*sich konzentrieren auf*	≈	to concentrate on
sinister ['sɪnɪstə]	*düster*	≈	dark
extreme	*extrem*	≈	exceptional
to degenerate into	*ausarten zu*	adj	degenerate
to present [prɪ'zent]	*bieten*	n	presentation
pessimistic	*pessimistisch*	n	pessimism
view	*Sicht*	≈	opinion
satirical	*satirisch*	n	satire
fable	*Fabel*		
futuristic	*futuristisch*	<>	historical
to portray	*darstellen*	n	portrayal
allegory ['æləgəri]	*Allegorie*	adj	allegorical
parable	*Parabel*		
symbolic	*symbolisch*	n	symbolism
social realism	*sozialer Realismus*		
contemporary [kən'temprəri]	*zeitgenössisch*	n	contemporary – *Zeitgenosse/genossin*
accessible [ək'sesəbl]	*zugänglich*	<>	obscure, difficult
readership	*Leserschaft*	≈	readers
to identify with	*sich identifizieren mit*	n	identification with
tone	*Ton*	≈	tenor
character study	*Charakterstudie*	vt	to characterize
plot	*Handlung*	≈	storyline
supernatural	*übernatürlich*	n	the supernatural
incident	*Ereignis*	≈	event, happening
psychological [ˌsaɪkə'lɒdʒɪkl]	*psychologisch*	n	psychology
detective story	*Kriminalroman*	≈	whodunnit (coll)
topic	*Thema*	≈	subject
narrative fiction	*Erzählliteratur*	vt	to narrate
relationship	*Beziehung*		
racial	*rassisch, Rassen-*	n	race – *Rasse*
to arise from	*entstehen aus*	⚠	arise–arose–arisen
event	*Ereignis*	≈	incident, happening
to reveal	*erkennen lassen*	<>	to conceal
lively	*lebendig*	<>	dull, staid
treatment	*Behandlung, Bearbeitung*	vt	to treat
to mingle with	*sich (ver)mischen mit*	≈	to be mixed with
fantastic	*phantastisch*	<>	realistic
allegorical [ˌælə'gɒrɪkl]	*allegorisch*	vt	to allegorize
identity	*Identität*	v prep	to identify with
short story	*Kurzgeschichte*	cf	novella – *Novelle*
collection	*Sammlung*	≈	anthology

What is poetry?

Ben How would you define poetry?

Lisa How about: a piece of writing that rhymes?

Ben But rhyme isn't an essential part of poetry – look at Shakespeare's blank verse, for example, or a lot of modern poetry.

Lisa But a regular rhythm or metre is essential – a regular pattern of stressed and unstressed syllables, which you don't get in prose. There may also be other sound patterns, such as rhyme, alliteration or assonance.

Hazel But political speeches and other kinds of writing intended to be persuasive sometimes use these things as rhetorical devices. Does that make them poetry?

Lisa I suppose not ... OK, how about this? Poetry is written in lines – the line breaks are important, and you can't just change them arbitrarily to fit the width of the page. Prose is organized into sentences according to rules of grammar, and into paragraphs according to its content. But poetry is organized into lines and stanzas – that is to say, it has a sound structure.

Ben So poetry is meant to be read aloud.

Hazel But so are political speeches. And so are plays, which may be in verse or in prose. So that doesn't get us far. Also, if you wrote out a poem as prose – without line breaks – would it then be prose or still poetry?

Lisa Hmm, I'm not sure ... Another characteristic of poetry is that it need not follow the normal rules of syntax.

Hazel These are all just formal criteria. Isn't the important thing the content? Poems are much more concise than prose and much more intense in their emotional appeal, expressing in a few lines what might take a whole essay or a whole novel to express in prose.

Lisa That's a very subjective definition. Also, what about epic poetry, which can be as long as a novel? Or verse drama?

Ben OK, OK. Maybe there's no single criterion. But if a text is organized into lines and contains regular patterns of sound, if it is emotionally intense, if it uses a lot of imagery, if it uses unusual syntax – then it's clearly poetry. If none of these things is true, then it's clearly prose.

Lisa And if only some are true, then it may be poetic prose – or prosaic poetry!

▸ **poetry**	*Lyrik, Poesie*	cf	poet – *Dichter/in*
▸ **to define**	*definieren*	n	definition
▸ **to rhyme**	*(sich) reimen*		
▸ **rhyme**	*Reim*	adj	rhyming
▸ **essential**	*wesentlich*	<>	non-essential
▸ **blank verse**	*Blankvers*		
▸ **regular**	*regelmäßig*	<>	irregular
▸ **rhythm** ['rɪðəm]	*Rhythmus*	adj	rhythmic
▸ **metre**	*Metrum*	adj	metrical
▸ **pattern**	*Schema, Muster*	phr	to arrange in a ~
▸ **syllable**	*Silbe*		
▸ **prose**	*Prosa*		
▸ **alliteration**	*Alliteration, Stabreim*	adj	alliterative
▸ **assonance**	*Assonanz*		
▸ **intended**	*gedacht*	n	intent(ion)
▸ **persuasive**	*überzeugend*	n	persuasion
▸ **rhetorical device**	*rhetorisches Mittel*	cf	rhetoric – *Rhetorik*
▸ **line break**	*Zeilenumbruch*		
▸ **arbitrarily** ['ɑːbətrerɪli]	*willkürlich*	adj	arbitrary
▸ **to organize into**	*einteilen in*	n	organization
▸ **according to**	*entsprechend*	≈	in accordance with
▸ **stanza**	*Strophe*		
▸ **structure**	*Aufbau*	adj	structural
▸ **play**	*Theaterstück, Drama*	cf	playwright – *Dramatiker/in*
▸ **in verse**	*in Versform*	<>	in prose
▸ **characteristic**	*Merkmal*	adj	characteristic
▸ **criterion**	*Kriterium*	pl	criteria
▸ **concise**	*knapp*	<>	verbose
▸ **intense**	*intensiv*	n	intensity
▸ **emotional appeal**	*emotionale Anziehungskraft*	v prep	to appeal to
▸ **to express**	*ausdrücken*	adj	expressive
▸ **subjective**	*subjektiv*	<>	objective
▸ **epic poetry**	*Epik*	cf	heroic epic – *Heldenepos*
▸ **imagery**	*Metaphorik*	≈	figurative language
▸ **poetic**	*poetisch*	n	poetry
▸ **prosaic** [prə'zeɪɪk]	*prosaisch*	≈	unimaginative

Ted Hughes and the poetry of violence

There is a stark contrast between the poetry of Ted Hughes (1930–1998) and that of older contemporaries such as Philip Larkin (1922–1985) and John Betjeman (1906–1984). They are witty and ironic – he is intensely serious; they depict the attitudes of middle-class society – he concerns himself with nature and myth; their tone is conversational, understated – he freely expresses his awe and horror.

Hughes' most accessible poems take as their subjects commonplace features of the English countryside: garden birds; thistles growing in a field; a pond. Written in free verse (without the artificial structure of rhyme and metre), his poetry appeals powerfully to our senses, is always dynamic, full of strong verbs and nouns with few adjectives. His 'nature poems' are never purely descriptive, and certainly never the gentle, idyllic images we traditionally associate with this subject matter. To Hughes, garden birds can be more terrifying than any monster:

Terrifying are the attent sleek thrushes on the lawn More coiled steel than living … *

Where we are used to seeing a small brown bird, Hughes sees a ruthless killing machine. This vision could seem exaggerated, even ridiculous, and some have found Hughes' preoccupation with death and violence to be excessive and morbid. Yet Hughes is a convincing, accurate observer of animal behaviour. With his farming background, he knows that nature is a fight for survival – automatic, unquestioning, without our human doubts and excuses. As Hughes' hawk says:

… the one path of my flight is direct
Through the bones of the living.
No arguments assert my right … *

This implicit contrast between nature's directness and its weak, selfdoubting human observer is a central theme of Hughes' poetry. We sense that Hughes admires and even envies animals for their honesty, their inability to be self-conscious or hypocritical.

* *'Thrushes' and 'Hawk Roosting', both from Lupercal, 1960*

▸ **stark contrast**	*krasser Gegensatz*	vt	to contrast
▸ **contemporary**	*Zeitgenosse/genossin*	adj	contemporary
▸ **witty**	*geistreich*	n	wit
▸ **ironic**	*ironisch*	n	irony
▸ **intensely**	*äußerst*	n	intensity
▸ **attitude**	*Haltung*	≈	viewpoint
▸ **to concern oneself with**	*sich beschäftigen mit*	n	concern
▸ **myth**	*Mythos*	adj	mythical
▸ **conversational**	*leger, informell*	<>	formal
▸ **understated**	*subtil, unaufdringlich*	<>	overstated
▸ **awe** [ɔː]	*Ehrfurcht*	adj	awesome – *Ehrfurcht gebietend*
▸ **horror**	*Entsetzen*	vt	to horrify – *entsetzen*
▸ **accessible** [ək'sesəbl]	*zugänglich*	<>	obscure
▸ **commonplace**	*alltäglich, banal*	≈	banal
▸ **free verse**	*freier Vers*		
▸ **artificial**	*künstlich*	<>	natural
▸ **to appeal to**	*ansprechen*	n	appeal
▸ **powerfully**	*stark*	n	power
▸ **senses**	*Sinne*	cf	sensuous – *sinnlich*
▸ **dynamic**	*dynamisch*	<>	static
▸ **descriptive**	*beschreibend*	cf	narrative – *erzählend*
▸ **idyllic**	*idyllisch*	n	idyll
▸ **image**	*Bild, Vorstellung*	cf	imagery – *Metaphorik*
▸ **to associate with**	*assoziieren mit*	n	association
▸ **subject matter**	*Stoff, Thema*		
▸ **terrifying**	*furchterregend*	vt	to terrify
▸ **ruthless**	*unbarmherzig*	n	ruthlessness
▸ **vision**	*Vorstellung*		
▸ **exaggerated**	*übertrieben*	n	exaggeration
▸ **ridiculous** [rɪ'dɪkjələs]	*lächerlich*	≈	laughable
▸ **preoccupation**	*(ständige) Beschäftigung*	≈	obsession
▸ **excessive**	*übertrieben*	<>	moderate
▸ **morbid**	*krankhaft, morbid*	<>	healthy
▸ **convincing**	*überzeugend*	n	conviction
▸ **accurate**	*genau*	<>	inaccurate
▸ **observer**	*Beobachter/in*	cf	observation – *Beobachtung*
▸ **survival**	*Überleben*	vti	to survive
▸ **doubt**	*Zweifel*	vt	to doubt
▸ **to admire**	*bewundern*	n	admiration
▸ **to envy**	*beneiden*	adj	envious
▸ **honesty**	*Ehrlichkeit*	adj	honest
▸ **self-conscious** [ˌself 'kɒnʃəs]	*befangen*	n	self-consciousness
▸ **hypocritical** [ˌhɪpə'krɪtɪkl]	*heuchlerisch*	n	hypocrisy [hɪ'pɒkrəsi]

Comedy

Throughout the history of the theatre there have been many attempts to define comedy. Many different types of play fall within this broad category.

In his *Poetics*, Aristotle claimed that comedy depicts human beings as worse than they are in reality, tragedy as better; comedy concerned the domestic lives of ordinary people, whereas tragedy concerned great events and noble characters. Some modern writers (such as Henri Bergson) have emphasized comedy's role in ridiculing and so correcting antisocial behaviour. Others emphasize the superiority which the audience feels when laughing at a comic character. A general definition might be that a comedy is a play which has a happy ending, in which the difficulties experienced by the protagonist(s) are resolved; such a play need not be humorous in the sense of trying to make the audience laugh.

Classical Greek and Roman comedy often used quite coarse language and dealt frankly with sexual themes. The plays of Aristophanes are satirical, mocking philosophers and parodying tragic drama. In the comedies of Terence and Plautius, young lovers have to outwit wicked or stupid characters who are obstacles to their happiness. Most classical comedy has stock characters who represent social types, with little individualization.

William Shakespeare's comedies (e.g. *As You Like It* and *A Midsummer Night's Dream*) often combine romantic plots with serious themes and exploration of the darker side of human nature; several of his plays do not fit conventional definitions of comedy or tragedy and so are called tragicomedies. In plays such as *The Winter's Tale*, tragic errors are made and tragic suffering endured, but there is an unexpected (often artificial or improbable) resolution and a happy ending.

Modern comedy does not follow any particular pattern. The farces of numerous British writers feature slapstick, improbable situations and exaggerated characters. Oscar Wilde wrote light-hearted social satire of the type called comedy of manners. Samuel Beckett and Harold Pinter combined comedy and tragedy in plays which show the absurdity of life, portraying the breakdown of relationships and communication with black humour. In much modern drama, comedy is blended with realism in exploring the problems of daily life.

▸ **comedy**	*Komödie*		
▸ **to depict**	*darstellen*	≈	to portray
▸ **tragedy**	*Tragödie*	adj	tragic
▸ **domestic life**	*häusliches Leben*	≈	everyday life
▸ **noble**	*edel; adlig*	n	nobility
▸ **to ridicule**	*verspotten, verlachen*	adj	ridiculous – *lächerlich*
▸ **antisocial**	*unsozial*	<>	socially acceptable
▸ **superiority** [suːˌpɪəriˈɒrəti]	*Überlegenheit*	<>	inferiority
▸ **comic**	*komisch*	≈	comical
▸ **to resolve**	*(auf)lösen*	n	resolution
▸ **humorous**	*lustig, komisch*	n	humour
▸ **coarse**	*derb*	<>	refined
▸ **to deal with**	*behandeln*	≈	to handle
▸ **frankly**	*offen*	≈	openly
▸ **satirical**	*satirisch*	n	satire
▸ **to mock**	*verspotten*	n	mockery
▸ **to parody**	*parodieren*	n	parody
▸ **to outwit**	*überlisten*	≈	to outsmart
▸ **to be an obstacle to sth**	*einer Sache im Wege stehen*	≈	to stand in the way of sth
▸ **stock character**	*Typ*	≈	stereotypical character
▸ **to represent**	*darstellen*	n	representation
▸ **individualization**	*Individualisierung*	cf	individual – *Individuum*
▸ **plot**	*Handlung*	≈	storyline
▸ **exploration**	*Erforschung*	vti	to explore
▸ **human nature**	*menschliche Natur*		
▸ **tragicomedy**	*Tragikomödie*	adj	tragicomic
▸ **tragic**	*tragisch*		
▸ **error**	*Fehler*	≈	mistake
▸ **suffering**	*Leiden, Leid*	vti	to suffer
▸ **to endure**	*ertragen*	≈	to bear
▸ **artificial**	*künstlich*	≈	contrived
▸ **improbable**	*unwahrscheinlich*	≈	unlikely
▸ **resolution**	*Auflösung*	≈	outcome
▸ **slapstick**	*Klamauk*	phr	~ comedy, humour
▸ **exaggerated**	*übertrieben*	n	exaggeration
▸ **light-hearted**	*leicht, vergnüglich*	<>	serious
▸ **social satire**	*Gesellschaftssatire*	cf	satirist – *Satiriker/in*
▸ **comedy of manners**	*Sittenkomödie*		
▸ **absurdity**	*Absurdität*	adj	absurd
▸ **breakdown**	*Zusammenbruch*	vti	to break down
▸ **relationship**	*Beziehung*	v prep	to relate to
▸ **realism**	*Realismus*	adj	realistic

Tragedy

A tragedy may be loosely defined as a play in which a sequence of events leads to a catastrophic conclusion.

The first definition of tragedy was given by Aristotle in his *Poetics*: a unified action which is serious and deals with events of importance, concerning the downfall of a person whose character is fundamentally good but not perfect: his or her downfall is caused by some flaw or error of judgement. The events arouse pity and fear in the audience.

Greek tragedy used familiar myths such as those found in Homer's works as its subject matter. As in Sophocles' *Oedipus the King*, their plots generally traced a development by which the hero or heroine becomes involved in a situation which is inescapable but intolerable, leading inevitably to disaster. In this suffering, the protagonist shows the most admirable aspects of his or her character, enduring his or her fate with courage and dignity.

In England around 1600, writers such as Christopher Marlowe and William Shakespeare made important developments in tragedy. In Shakespeare's great tragedies, the heroes are figures of high rank and great ability and virtue. They have many opportunities to choose paths which will not lead to disaster, but relentlessly make the wrong choices because of character flaws (e.g. Macbeth's ambition, Othello's jealousy) and the influence of evil, whether human or supernatural. The main plot is set in a context which involves many major and minor characters with their own viewpoints and motivations. There are subplots which mirror or contrast with the main plot.

French drama of the seventeenth century produced tragedies according to strict principles taken from Aristotle, adhering to the unities of time (the whole plot development to take no more than 24 hours), place (only one setting) and action (no subplots), and took their subject matter also from classical legend.

German tragic drama of the late eighteenth and early nineteenth century drew upon both the neoclassical and the English traditions. In northern and eastern Europe in the nineteenth century, Henrik Ibsen, August Strindberg and Anton Chekhov developed a new kind of tragedy which explored contemporary problems concerning how the individual relates to society.

▸ **tragedy**	*Tragödie*	adj	tragic
▸ **sequence**	*Abfolge*		
▸ **catastrophic**	*verhängnisvoll*	n	catastrophe [kə'tæstrəfi]
▸ **conclusion**	*Schluss*	vti	to conclude
▸ **unified**	*einheitlich*		
▸ **downfall**	*Niedergang*	≈	demise
▸ **fundamentally**	*im Wesentlichen*	<>	superficially
▸ **flaw**	*(Charakter)Schwäche*	adj	flawed
▸ **error of judgement**	*Fehlurteil*		
▸ **to arouse**	*erwecken*	≈	to evoke
▸ **pity**	*Mitleid*	vt	to pity
▸ **subject matter**	*Stoff*		
▸ **to trace**	*verfolgen*	≈	to follow
▸ **development**	*Entwicklung*	vti	to develop
▸ **hero/heroine** [hɪərəʊ; 'herəʊɪn]	*Held/Heldin*	adj	heroic
▸ **inescapable** [ɪnɪ'skeɪpəbl]	*unausweichlich*		
▸ **intolerable**	*unerträglich*	≈	unbearable
▸ **inevitably** [ɪn'evɪtəbli]	*zwangsläufig*	n	inevitability
▸ **disaster**	*Katastrophe*	adj	disastrous
▸ **admirable**	*bewundernswert*	<>	contemptible
▸ **fate**	*Schicksal*		
▸ **courage** ['kʌrɪdʒ]	*Mut*	adj	courageous [kə'reɪdʒəs]
▸ **dignity**	*Würde*	adj	dignified
▸ **rank**	*Stand*	≈	social position
▸ **ability**	*Fähigkeit*	≈	capability
▸ **virtue**	*Tugend*	adj	virtuous
▸ **relentlessly** [rɪ'lentləsli]	*unaufhörlich*		
▸ **ambition**	*Ehrgeiz*	adj	ambitious
▸ **jealousy** ['dʒeləsi]	*Eifersucht*	adj	jealous
▸ **influence**	*Einfluss*	vt	to influence
▸ **evil**	*Böse(s)*	<>	good(ness)
▸ **supernatural**	*übernatürlich*		
▸ **major**	*Haupt-*		
▸ **minor**	*Neben-*		
▸ **viewpoint**	*Standpunkt*	≈	point of view
▸ **subplot**	*Nebenhandlung*		
▸ **to mirror**	*(wider)spiegeln*	≈	to reflect
▸ **principle**	*Prinzip, Grundsatz*		
▸ **to adhere to** [əd'hɪə]	*sich halten an*	n	adherence to
▸ **unities of time, place and action**	*Einheit von Zeit, Ort und Handlung*		
▸ **legend**	*Sage*	adj	legendary
▸ **to explore**	*erforschen*	n	exploration
▸ **contemporary**	*zeitgenössisch*		

Modern Theatre Classics

A Raisin in the Sun*

A Raisin in the Sun is a play by Lorraine Hansberry that debuted on Broadway in 1959. The story is partly autobiographical, being based upon the author's family's own experiences. It was the first play written by a black woman to be produced on Broadway, as well as the first play with a black director (Lloyd Richards) on Broadway.

Waiting for the curtain to rise on opening night, Hansberry did not expect the play to be a success, as it had received mixed reviews from a preview audience the night before. Half a century later, the play is considered one of the classics of contemporary theatre and has been adapted for TV or film three times as well as being made into a musical.

The play is set in the 1950s on the Southside of Chicago. The Younger family is a poor black family living in an old run-down apartment in a black neighbourhood. When Lena, the mother of Walter and Beneatha, receives insurance money from the death of her husband, everyone argues over what to do with it. The money is a catalyst for conflict and confrontation, but also for personal development. Walter, in particular, undergoes a journey from self-delusion to painful self-knowledge when his business partner betrays him and disappears with the money, finally achieving a new pride in his identity as a black American.

Central themes of the play include a person's need for dreams and aspirations, particularly in hard times and difficult circumstances, the power of money to create divisions within a family and the fragility of material wealth, which can vanish in an instant. These themes give the play as much relevance today as when it was first performed.

[Some info from http://en.wikipedia.org/wiki/A_Raisin_in_the_Sun (first three paragraphs)]

**Deutscher Titel: Ein Fleck in der Sonne; raisin = Rosine*

2 Performing arts

▸ **theatre**	*Theater*	adj	theatrical
▸ **classic**	*Klassiker*		
▸ **play**	*Theaterstück*	cf	playwright – *Dramatiker/in*
▸ **to debut** ['deɪbjuː]	*debütieren*	n	debut
▸ **autobiographical**	*autobiografisch*	n	autobiography
▸ **to be based upon**	*basieren auf*		
▸ **experience**	*Erlebnis*	vt	to experience
▸ **to produce**	*produzieren*	n	production
▸ **director**	*Regisseur/in*	vt	to direct
▸ **curtain** ['kɜːtn]	*Vorhang*	phr	the ~ rises/falls
▸ **opening night**	*Premiere(abend)*	≈	first night, premiere
▸ **to be a success**	*Erfolg haben*	<>	to be a failure
▸ **to receive mixed reviews**	*gemischte Kritiken erhalten*		
▸ **audience** ['ɔːdiəns]	*Publikum*		
▸ **to consider sth sth**	*etw als etw ansehen*	≈	to regard sth as sth
▸ **contemporary**	*zeitgenössisch*	≈	modern-day
▸ **to adapt**	*bearbeiten*	n	adaptation
▸ **to be set in**	*spielen in*	n	setting
▸ **to argue over**	*sich streiten um*	n	argument
▸ **catalyst for**	*Auslöser für*	vt	to catalyze
▸ **conflict**	*Konflikt*	v prep	to conflict with
▸ **confrontation**	*Konfrontation*	vt	to confront
▸ **personal development**	*persönliche Entwicklung*	vti	to develop
▸ **to undergo**	*durchmachen*	≈	to experience
▸ **journey**	*Reise, Weg*		
▸ **self-delusion**	*Selbsttäuschung*	vt	to delude
▸ **painful**	*schmerzlich*	n	pain
▸ **self-knowledge**	*Selbsterkenntnis*	≈	self-awareness
▸ **to betray**	*betrügen*	n	betrayal
▸ **to achieve**	*gewinnen*	n	achievement
▸ **pride**	*Stolz*	adj	proud
▸ **identity**	*Identität*	v prep	to identify with
▸ **central**	*zentral*	<>	minor
▸ **theme**	*Thema*	adj	thematic
▸ **dream**	*Traum*	vi, v prep	to dream (of)
▸ **aspiration**	*Ambition*	v prep	to aspire to
▸ **hard times**	*schwere Zeiten*	<>	good times
▸ **circumstances**	*Umstände*	≈	situation
▸ **power**	*Macht*	adj	powerful
▸ **division**	*Spaltung*	adj	divisive
▸ **fragility** [frə'dʒɪləti]	*Brüchigkeit*	adj	fragile ['frædʒaɪl]
▸ **wealth**	*Reichtum*	<>	poverty
▸ **to vanish**	*verschwinden*	≈	to disappear
▸ **in an instant**	*im Handumdrehen*	≈	suddenly
▸ **relevance**	*Bedeutung*	adj	relevant
▸ **to perform**	*aufführen*	n	performance

Film review

Dark Side of the Street, 18

Bruce Norris stars as tough LA lawyer and karate champion Chuck Lee in this uninspiring action movie, and also makes his debut as a director. The fight scenes are staged with enthusiasm and the special effects are really spectacular, but that can't disguise a predictable plot and wooden acting. The film contains a high – and sometimes shocking – level of violence. **

Dancing at Enniskillen, PG

This is a powerful, sombre drama, portraying the harsh realities of life in Ireland in the 1890s without sentimentality. Director Alan Beith coaxes moving performances from an inexperienced cast, particularly the young leads Kate (played by Cathy Riordan) and Fergal (played by Michael Keane), who are well supported by David Regan and Meg McCormack as Fergal's parents. ****

Kisses for You, PG

This quirky, bittersweet romantic comedy looks likely to be the box office hit of the summer. Katherine Turner is perfectly cast in the role of single mother Jenny Kelly, while Ken Bacon is excellent as her boyfriend. The script is imaginative and the dialogue is often very witty. ****

The Fourth Level, 15

This tense psychological thriller is set in a nightclub in London's Soho. It focuses on the interaction between four key characters (played by Jack Thorpe, Meg Pryan, Mel Gee and Jon Jones). The direction is imaginative but sometimes confused. Fortunately John Houseman's screenplay, adapted from his own novel, is full of dark humour. The result is a modern film noir, flawed, but still a masterpiece. ***

▸ **review**	*Kritik*	vt	to review
▸ **to star in**	*die Hauptrolle spielen in*	cf	the film stars Chuck Lee
▸ **uninspiring**	*nicht gerade aufregend*	n	inspiration
▸ **to make one's debut** ['deɪbjuː]	*sein Debüt geben*	v prep	to debut in
▸ **director**	*Regisseur/in*	vt	to direct
▸ **fight scene** ['faɪt siːn]	*Kampfszene*	cf	love scene
▸ **to stage**	*inszenieren*	cf	stage – *Bühne*
▸ **special effects**	*Spezialeffekte*	cf	sound effects
▸ **spectacular**	*sensationell*	cf	impressive
▸ **to disguise** [dɪs'gaɪz]	*verschleiern*	≈	to gloss over
▸ **predictable**	*berechenbar*	vt	to predict
▸ **plot**	*Handlung*	≈	storyline
▸ **wooden**	*hölzern*	<>	natural
▸ **acting**	*Schauspielerei*	n	actor
▸ **a high level of**	*ein hohes Maß an*	<>	a low level of
▸ **violence**	*Gewalt(tätigkeit)*	adj	violent
▸ **powerful**	*ausdrucksvoll*	n	power
▸ **sombre**	*düster*	<>	cheerful
▸ **to portray**	*schildern, darstellen*	n	portrayal
▸ **sentimentality**	*Sentimentalität*	adj	sentimental
▸ **moving**	*ergreifend*	cf	to be moved by
▸ **performance**	*Darstellung*	vti	to perform
▸ **cast**	*Besetzung, Mitwirkende*	phr	~ list
▸ **lead** [liːd]	*Hauptdarsteller/in*	≈	~ing man, lady
▸ **to support**	*unterstützen*	phr	~ing role – *Nebenrolle*
▸ **quirky**	*schrullig*	≈	eccentric
▸ **bittersweet**	*bittersüß*		
▸ **comedy**	*Komödie*	<>	tragedy
▸ **box office hit**	*Kassenschlager*	<>	box office flop
▸ **perfectly**	*vollkommen*	n	perfection
▸ **to cast**	*besetzen*		
▸ **script**	*Drehbuch*	cf	scriptwriter
▸ **imaginative**	*fantasievoll*	n	imagination
▸ **dialogue**	*Dialog*		
▸ **witty**	*geistreich*	n	wit
▸ **tense**	*spannungsgeladen*	n	tension
▸ **psychological thriller**	*Psychothriller*	cf	thrill – *Nervenkitzel*
▸ **to be set**	*spielen*	n	setting
▸ **to focus on**	*sich konzentrieren auf*	n	focus on
▸ **interaction**	*Interaktion*	vi, v prep	to interact (with)
▸ **direction**	*Regie*		
▸ **confused**	*verworren, konfus*	≈	muddled
▸ **screenplay**	*Drehbuch*	≈	script
▸ **to adapt**	*bearbeiten, adaptieren*	n	adaptation
▸ **dark humour**	*schwarzer Humor*	≈	black humour
▸ **flawed** [flɔːd]	*mit Mängeln*	n	flaw
▸ **masterpiece**	*Meisterstück*	≈	masterwork

Describing and analysing an image

This picture is used to campaign against the destruction of the world's forests. It is intended to surprise and challenge the viewer.

The viewer's first impression is that this is an image of two burning trees. However, on closer viewing, we realize that it shows the '9/11' attack, when terrorists crashed airliners into the World Trade Building and other buildings. The artist has created a composite image, replacing the World Trade Building with tree trunks.

The caption interprets this strange and unsettling image for us, telling us: 'Nature's 9/11 24/7'. The message is that the natural environment is being destroyed every day. There is perhaps also an implication that environmental catastrophes are not reported sufficiently in the news. By using a confronting image, the artist is trying to bring home to us the damage that is being done to our environment.

In conclusion, through a visual metaphor using a reference to an emotive event from recent history, this image tries to shock us into caring more about the environment. Although it conveys its message quite effectively, some people may find the image quite disturbing, and even be offended by this use of the 9/11 theme. Others may find it too exaggerated to be persuasive.

▸ **to describe**	*beschreiben*	n	description
▸ **to analyse**	*analysieren*	n	analysis
▸ **image**	*Bild*	≈	picture
▸ **to campaign against**	*kämpfen gegen*	n	campaign
▸ **to be intended to**	*sollen*	n	intention
▸ **to surprise**	*überraschen*	n	surprise
▸ **to challenge**	*herausfordern*	n	challenge
▸ **viewer**	*Betrachter/in*		
▸ **impression**	*Eindruck*	phr	to give/receive the ~ that …
▸ **on closer viewing**	*bei näherer Betrachtung*	≈	on closer inspection
▸ **to realize**	*feststellen*	n	realization
▸ **to show**	*zeigen*	≈	to depict
▸ **artist**	*Künstler/in*	adj	artistic
▸ **to create**	*(er)schaffen*	≈	to make
▸ **composite**	*zusammengesetzt*	n	composition
▸ **to replace with**	*ersetzen durch*	n	replacement
▸ **caption**	*Bildzeile, -unterschrift*		
▸ **to interpret**	*interpretieren*	n	interpretation
▸ **strange**	*fremdartig*	≈	bizarre
▸ **unsettling**	*beunruhigend*	≈	worrying
▸ **message**	*Botschaft*		
▸ **implication**	*Andeutung*	vt	to imply
▸ **confronting**	*konfrontierend*		
▸ **to bring home to**	*vor Augen führen*	≈	to make clear to
▸ **in conclusion**	*zusammenfassend*	≈	to sum up
▸ **visual**	*bildlich, visuell*		
▸ **metaphor**	*Metapher*	adj	metaphorical
▸ **reference**	*Bezug*	v prep	to refer to
▸ **emotive**	*emotional*		
▸ **to shock into**	*durch Schockieren dazu bringen*	n	shock
▸ **to care about**	*sich kümmern um*	adj	caring
▸ **to convey**	*vermitteln*	≈	to get across
▸ **effectively**	*wirkungsvoll*	n	effectiveness
▸ **disturbing**	*verstörend*	vt	to disturb
▸ **to offend**	*beleidigen*	adj	offensive
▸ **exaggerated**	*übertrieben*	n	exaggeration
▸ **persuasive**	*überzeugend*	vt	to persuade

E

The media

1 Broadcasting

2 The press

3 Online

4 Censorship and control

The best and worst of TV

In our reader survey, we asked what were the best and worst aspects of television today. Here are some of your replies:

Emma Smythe

Best: Documentaries which find ways of making specialized subjects like archaeology and astrophysics intelligible to the general public without being patronizing.

Worst: Dull, high-brow arts programmes with conceited 'experts' who discuss awful paintings and horrible music.

Melissa Clayton

Best: Soap operas like EastEnders with superb acting and the courage to explore sensitive and difficult issues.

Worst: Popular science programmes with unnecessary special effects and 'artistic' camerawork.

Jarvis Barnes

Best: Current affairs programmes with intelligent interviewers like Jeremy Paxman. He asks searching questions, and insists on getting proper answers from his interviewees.

Worst: Horrible reality TV shows like Big Brother that humiliate participants, and talent shows for contestants with no talent.

Nawaz Malik

Best: Stand-up comedians who have something original to say – who can be outrageous but get away with it because of their charm and wit.

Worst: Celebrity panel games populated by has-beens from sport and pop music. Most of the so-called 'spontaneous' humour is rehearsed before the show.

Will Davies

Best: Comedy dramas with strong casts, clever scripts and a subtle sense of humour.

Worst: Bland, contrived sitcoms with exaggerated studio laughter to signal even the weakest jokes. Apparently, the producers don't trust us to recognize a joke unless we hear a burst of hysterical laughter.

Kayleigh Howell

Best: Recent cinema releases and film classics on cable TV.

Worst: Home improvement and gardening shows. I can't stand the smug presenters!

▸ **documentary**	*Dokumentarfilm*		
▸ **specialized**	*spezialisiert*	<>	general
▸ **intelligible** [ɪn'telɪdʒəbl]	*verständlich*	<>	unintelligible
▸ **patronizing**	*herablassend*	vt	to patronize
▸ **high-brow**	*intellektuell*	<>	low-brow
▸ **arts programme**	*Kultursendung*	cf	the arts – *die Künste*
▸ **conceited** [kən'siːtɪd]	*eingebildet*	n	conceit
▸ **soap opera**	*Seifenoper, TV-Serie*	coll	soap
▸ **acting**	*schauspielerische Leistung*	n	actor – *Schauspieler/in*
▸ **courage**	*Mut*	adj	courageous
▸ **sensitive**	*heikel*	cf	insensitive – *taktlos*
▸ **issue**	*Thema*	≈	topic
▸ **popular science programme**	*populärwissenschaftliche Sendung*	⚠	≠ *Programm*
▸ **artistic**	*künstlerisch*	cf	artist – *Künstler/in*
▸ **camerawork**	*Kameraführung*	cf	cameraman/woman
▸ **current affairs programme**	*Info-Magazin zu aktuellen Themen*	≈	news programme
▸ **searching**	*bohrend*	n	search – *Suche*
▸ **to insist on**	*bestehen auf*	adj	insistent
▸ **interviewee**	*Interviewpartner/in*	vt	to interview
▸ **reality TV show**	*Reality-Fernsehshow*		
▸ **to humiliate**	*demütigen*	n	humiliation
▸ **participant**	*Teilnehmer/in*	v prep	to participate in
▸ **talent show**	*Talent-Show*	adj	talented
▸ **contestant**	*Kandidat/in*		
▸ **talent**	*Talent*	≈	ability
▸ **stand-up comedian**	*Alleinunterhalter/in*	cf	stand-up comedy
▸ **outrageous** [ˌaʊt'reɪdʒəs]	*unverschämt*	cf	cheeky – *frech*
▸ **to get away with**	*sich erlauben können*		
▸ **wit**	*Witz*	adj	witty – *geistreich*
▸ **celebrity** [sə'lebrəti]	*Prominente/r*		
▸ **panel game**	*Ratespiel*	cf	panel – *Rateteam*
▸ **has-been**	*vergessene Berühmtheit*	<>	wannabe *(coll)* – *Möchtegern*
▸ **spontaneous** [spɒn'teɪniəs]	*spontan*	n	spontaneity
▸ **to rehearse** [rɪ'hɜːs]	*einstudieren*	n	rehearsal
▸ **comedy drama**	*TV-Komödie*		
▸ **cast**	*Besetzung*	vt	to cast
▸ **subtle** ['sʌtl]	*subtil, fein*	n	subtlety
▸ **bland**	*fade*	≈	tame
▸ **contrived**	*gekünstelt, gestellt*	≈	artificial
▸ **sitcom**	*Situationskomödie*		
▸ **classic**	*Klassiker*	adj	classic
▸ **home improvement**	*Heimverschönerungs-*	≈	DIY
▸ **smug**	*selbstgefällig*	n	smugness
▸ **presenter**	*Moderator/in*	vt	to present

Should we ban advertising on children's TV?

Recent surveys appear to show that a majority of parents in the UK are in favour of a complete ban on advertising during and after programmes designed to appeal to under-16s. The reasons given by respondents include frustration with incessant pestering by children who want treats that they see advertised on TV. Around 58 per cent of parents admit their children have pressured them into buying goods they saw on TV.

The UK already has strict regulations on advertising which targets children. This includes a ban on the advertising of junk food during children's TV. The ban covers children's shows, dedicated children's channels, as well as youth-oriented and adult programmes that could appeal to children.

Parenting experts are not sure that prohibiting all advertising to children would achieve anything. 'We live in a consumer society,' says one expert, 'so children are going to be exposed to advertising. That's inevitable. Parents have to learn to say 'no' to their children.'

Child psychologist Dr Pat Spungin says: 'Children are impressionable and susceptible to advertising; I think the TV companies should take a responsible approach to advertising during programmes that are popular with children. For their part, parents who talk to their children about advertising can help them become more media literate.'

TV companies and the advertising industry are strongly against any further restrictions on advertising. As a marketing industry spokesman pointed out: 'The ban on fast food advertising has cost TV channels up to £39 million yearly in lost advertising revenue. But research suggests that the restrictions are having little or no impact on childhood obesity.'

A TV company executive commented: 'Ofcom's own research shows that 70 per cent of children's viewing takes place outside of children's airtime, so the advertising ban is pointless. All that it has achieved is to take money away from the makers of quality children's programmes, leading to more cheap US imports. A total ban on advertising during children's programming would mean the end of commercial TV for children. Is that really what the public wants?'

1 Broadcasting

▸ **to ban**	*verbieten*	≈	to prohibit
▸ **advertising**	*Werbung*	cf	advertisement
▸ **survey** ['sɜːveɪ]	*Umfrage*	vt	to survey ['sɜːveɪ]
▸ **to be in favour of**	*befürworten*	<>	to be against
▸ **complete**	*vollständig*	<>	partial
▸ **ban**	*Verbot*	≈	prohibition
▸ **programme**	*Sendung*	⚠	≠ *Programm*
▸ **to appeal to**	*sich richten an*	n	appeal
▸ **respondent**	*Befragte/r*	v prep	to respond to
▸ **frustration**	*Frust, Verärgerung*	adj	frustrated
▸ **incessant** [ɪn'sesnt]	*unaufhörlich*	≈	continual
▸ **to pester**	*belästigen*	≈	to annoy
▸ **to advertise**	*werben (für)*	≈	to promote
▸ **to pressure into**	*drängen zu*	n	pressure
▸ **goods**	*Waren*	phr	consumer ~
▸ **regulation**	*Vorschrift(en)*	vt	to regulate
▸ **to target**	*sich richten an*	≈	to be aimed at
▸ **junk food**	*minderwertige Nahrung*	≈	fast food
▸ **to cover**	*umfassen*	≈	to include
▸ **dedicated**	*speziell*	phr	to be ~ to sth
▸ **channel**	*Kanal, Programm*	≈	(TV) station
▸ **youth-oriented**	*an Jugendliche gerichtet*	n	orientation
▸ **adult**	*Erwachsenen-*	<>	children's
▸ **to prohibit**	*verbieten*	n	prohibition
▸ **to achieve**	*erreichen*	n	achievement
▸ **consumer society**	*Konsumgesellschaft*	cf	consumerism
▸ **to be exposed to**	*ausgesetzt sein*	n	exposure
▸ **inevitable**	*unausweichlich*	<>	avoidable
▸ **impressionable**	*beeinflussbar*	≈	easily influenced
▸ **susceptible to** [sə'septəbl]	*empfänglich für*	n	susceptibility
▸ **responsible**	*verantwortlich*	n	responsibility
▸ **approach**	*Vorgehen(sweise)*	vti	to approach
▸ **popular with**	*beliebt bei*	n	popularity
▸ **media literate**	*medienkritisch*	n	media literacy
▸ **restriction**	*Einschränkung*	vt	to restrict
▸ **revenue**	*Einnahmen*	≈	income
▸ **impact**	*Auswirkung*	≈	effect
▸ **childhood**	*Kindheit*	<>	adulthood
▸ **obesity**	*Fettleibigkeit*	adj	obese
▸ **viewing**	*Fernsehen*	cf	viewer
▸ **airtime**	*Sendezeit*	≈	broadcasting time
▸ **pointless**	*sinnlos*	<>	useful
▸ **import**	*Import*	vt	to import
▸ **commercial TV**	*kommerzielles Fernsehen*	<>	public service TV
▸ **public**	*(die) Zuschauer*	adj	public

New mail

Send Chat Attach Addresses Fonts Save

From: Jo Edmundson
To: Rudi Böttcher
Subject: The British press

Hi Rudi,

Here's the info you wanted for your assignment.

We divide our newspapers into broadsheets and tabloids. This distinction refers to their format (tabloids being half the size of broadsheets), but is also a quality judgement. 'Tabloid journalism' has come to mean a type of reporting which is populist, unreliable and sensationalist – although some tabloids really aren't too bad. The downmarket tabloids are sometimes given the derogatory label 'gutter press'. Although some of them pride themselves on their investigative journalism, they tend to distort the facts or exaggerate for the sake of a good story.

Of the tabloid dailies, *The Sun* has the highest circulation, with 3 million copies sold every day. The *News of the World* is the most popular tabloid weekly, again with a readership of around 3 million. The tabloids are highly competitive, and try to come up with exclusives – interviews or reports which no other newspaper has. The ingredients of tabloid style include attention-grabbing headlines (involving very bad puns), short, moralizing articles written in a strange jargon (suspects are 'quizzed' by the police instead of being questioned; good-looking women are 'stunners'); gossip and supposition rather than fact; and soft-porn photos.

Broadsheets are often referred to as the 'quality' or 'serious' press and generally have a high standard of writing, including comprehensive coverage of the latest news, analysis of issues of long-term interest, and essays in which the writer expresses a point of view. They deal with serious issues in an authoritative way, but a dry, slightly facetious humour is valued as part of good journalistic style.

Broadsheet journalists often have greater freedom to express their opinions, even if these don't coincide with the editor's and the proprietor's political stance.

If you need more info on any of our papers, let me know. Alternatively, you can always take a look at their websites. :-) Jo

▸ **broadsheet**	*großformatige Zeitung*		
▸ **tabloid**	*kleinformatige Zeitung*		
▸ **distinction**	*Unterscheidung*	vt	to distinguish
▸ **quality judgement**	*Qualitätsbewertung*	vt	to judge
▸ **journalism**	*Journalismus*	cf	journalist
▸ **reporting**	*Berichterstattung*	cf	reporter
▸ **populist**	*populistisch*	n	populism
▸ **unreliable**	*unzuverlässig*	≈	untrustworthy
▸ **sensationalist**	*reißerisch*	n	sensationalism
▸ **downmarket**	*Massen-*	<>	upmarket
▸ **derogatory**	*abfällig*	≈	pejorative
▸ **gutter press**	*Skandalpresse*	cf	gutter – *Gosse*
▸ **investigative** [ɪn'vestɪgətɪv]	*Enthüllungs-*	vti	to investigate
▸ **to distort**	*verzerren*	n	distortion
▸ **to exaggerate**	*übertreiben*	n	exaggeration
▸ **daily**	*Tageszeitung*		
▸ **circulation**	*Auflage*		
▸ **weekly**	*Wochenzeitung*		
▸ **readership**	*Leserschaft*		
▸ **competitive** [kəm'petətɪv]	*wettbewerbsorientiert*	vi	to compete
▸ **exclusive**	*Exklusivbericht*	≈	scoop
▸ **report**	*Bericht*	vti	to report
▸ **attention-grabbing**	*Aufmerksamkeit heischend*	vt	to grab – *packen*
▸ **headline**	*Schlagzeile*	cf	to hit the ~s – *Schlagzeilen machen*
▸ **pun**	*Wortspiel*	≈	play on words
▸ **moralizing**	*moralisierend*	≈	moralistic
▸ **article**	*Artikel*	≈	piece
▸ **gossip**	*Klatsch*	vi	to gossip
▸ **supposition**	*Mutmaßung*	≈	speculation
▸ **comprehensive** [ˌkɒmprɪ'hensɪv]	*umfassend*	<>	partial ['pɑ:ʃl]
▸ **coverage**	*Berichterstattung*	vt	to cover
▸ **analysis**	*Analyse*	vt	to analyse
▸ **issue**	*Frage, Angelegenheit*	≈	topic
▸ **long-term**	*langfristig*	<>	short-term
▸ **authoritative** [ɔ:'θɒrətətɪv]	*zuverlässig*	n	authority – *Authorität*
▸ **facetious** [fə'si:ʃəs]	*spöttisch, witzelnd*	n	facetiousness
▸ **to value**	*schätzen*	n	value – *Wert*
▸ **journalistic**	*journalistisch*	n	journalism
▸ **to coincide with**	*übereinstimmen mit*	≈	to match
▸ **editor**	*Chefredakteur/in*	vt	to edit – *redigieren*
▸ **proprietor** [prə'praɪətə]	*Eigentümer/in*	≈	owner
▸ **stance** [stæns]	*Einstellung*	≈	attitude, standpoint

THE NEWSPAPER

Here's what our readers say about us:

"The Newspaper keeps me up to date with current affairs. The news coverage is balanced and reliable. It's factual, not judgemental. The 'News in Brief' column is a useful synopsis of the very latest news."
L.G., Leicester

"The Newspaper employs some of the best columnists in the business. Their in-depth commentary and analysis is thought-provoking and perceptive. The Newspaper is never afraid to challenge popular prejudices and stereotypes."
E.F., Barnsley

"On Thursdays I always turn to the Society section for Carolyn Barnes' provocative and witty pieces. She's controversial, opinionated but very clever – I rarely agree with a word she writes, but at least she's never predictable."
J.S., Gravesend

"What I like best are your special features. The Newspaper really explains the background to events and puts the news in context. You don't make assumptions about your readers' knowledge, but you're never patronizing."
L.M., Morecambe

"To be honest, we mainly buy The Newspaper for the television listings. Your critic Barry Skinner's reviews are great – a reliable guide to what's worth watching and what's not."
E.J. and N.J., Exeter

"The Newspaper's satirical cartoonist Steve Belling is brilliant. His wicked caricatures of public figures are a hilarious send-up of the pompous world of politics."
R.G., Harlech

"Your 'Leisure' supplement on Saturdays is one of the best – just the right balance between entertaining trivia and serious articles."
S.H., Hampstead

But don't take their word for it

THE NEWSPAPER

– because there are two sides to every story

up to date	*auf dem Laufenden*	<>	out of touch
current affairs	*aktuelle Themen*	≈	topical issues
balanced	*ausgewogen*	<>	one-sided, biased
factual	*sachlich*	n	fact – *Tatsache*
judgemental [dʒʌdʒ'mentl]	*wertend, kritisch*	n	judgement – *Urteil*
in brief	*Kurz-*	adj	brief – *kurz*
column ['kɒləm]	*Kolumne*	cf	columnist
synopsis	*Zusammenfassung*	≈	summary
in-depth	*eingehend, tief schürfend*	<>	superficial
commentary	*Kommentar*	v prep	to comment on
thought-provoking	*zum Nachdenken anregend*	cf	provocative – *provokativ*
perceptive	*scharfsinnig*	cf	to perceive – *erkennen*
to challenge	*in Frage stellen*	≈	to question
popular	*weit verbreitet*	n	popularity
prejudice	*Vorurteil*	adj	prejudiced
stereotype	*Klischee(vorstellung)*	adj	stereotypical
provocative [prə'vɒkətɪv]	*provokativ*	n	provocation
witty	*geistreich*	n	wit
piece	*Artikel*	≈	article
controversial [ˌkɒntrə'vɜːʃl]	*kontrovers*	n	controversy [kən'trɒvəsi]
opinionated	*rechthaberisch*	≈	dogmatic
predictable	*berechenbar*	n	predictability
special feature	*Sonderbeitrag*		
background to	*Hintergründe von*		
context	*Zusammenhang*	phr	in ~, out of ~
to make assumptions	*Vermutungen anstellen*	vt	to assume – *annehmen*
patronizing	*herablassend*	vt	to patronize
television listings	*Fernsehprogrammübersicht*	vt	to list – *auflisten*
critic	*Kritiker/in*	cf	to criticize – *kritisieren*
review	*Rezension, Kritik*	vt	to review
guide to	*Führer für*	vt	to guide
satirical	*satirisch*	n	satire
wicked	*boshaft*	≈	cutting
caricature	*Karikatur*	vt	to caricature
public figure	*öffentliche Persönlichkeit*		
hilarious [hɪ'leəriəs]	*urkomisch*		
send-up	*Veralberung*	vt	to send up
pompous	*wichtigtuerisch*	n	pomposity
supplement	*Beilage*	adj	supplementary
entertaining	*unterhaltend*	n	entertainment
trivia	*Trivialitäten*	adj	trivial

LETTERS TO THE EDITOR

The Editor
The Newspaper
London

A gross intrusion

How dare your paper publish intimate photos of Laura Jarrod on holiday with her boyfriend? ('Saucy Laura reveals all', May 21) The photos were taken without her permission and knowledge after the official photo shoot. This is a gross intrusion into her privacy. Clearly, your paper is prepared to flout the voluntary code of practice in a most blatant and cynical way. There is no question of these photos being 'in the public interest', and there is no way the public has a 'right to know' about Ms Jarrod's taste in swimwear. It is high time that effective legislation is introduced to prevent unscrupulous so-called NEWSpapers from hounding people in this way, excusing their actions with the fact that their victims are in the public eye for one reason or another.
M. Merton, Warwick

The British press is not bound by any legislation to respect the privacy of individuals or their families. However, like other British newspapers, we abide by a voluntary code of practice drawn up by the Press Complaints Commission (PCC). This states that an individual's family life, home, health and correspondence should be respected, unless intrusions can be justified. The code also forbids the use of telephoto lenses to take pictures of individuals in places "where there is a reasonable expectation of privacy". In the case of Laura Jarrod, no laws or voluntary codes have been broken.
– Editor

Fair game

How hypocritical of Laura Jarrod to protest about the photos recently published in your paper. Far from being an innocent victim of press persecution, Laura Jarrod has systematically courted press attention to further her career and earn a great deal of money – far more than her talents as an actress deserve. This means that she is 'fair game' as far as media attention is concerned. The photos were not particularly revealing, and not in bad taste. Furthermore, they were taken in a spot which is visible from a public beach. Ms Jarrod's libel action against your newspaper is one more example of her greed.
S. Singh, Leeds

2 The press

▸ **gross** [grəʊs]	*grob, ungeheuerlich*	≈	outrageous
▸ **intrusion**	*Verletzung*	vi	to intrude (on/upon)
▸ **to publish**	*veröffentlichen*	n	publication
▸ **intimate** ['ɪntɪmət]	*intim*	n	intimacy
▸ **permission**	*Erlaubnis*	vt	to permit
▸ **photo shoot**	*Fotosession*	cf	photographer – *Fotograf/in*
▸ **privacy**	*Privatsphäre*	adj	private
▸ **to flout**	*missachten*	≈	to ignore, to disregard
▸ **code of practice**	*Verhaltenskodex*	cf	in practice – *in der Praxis*
▸ **blatant**	*unverfroren*	≈	barefaced
▸ **cynical** ['sɪnɪkl]	*zynisch*	n	cynicism
▸ **in the public interest**	*von öffentlichem Interesse*		
▸ **it is high time**	*es wird höchste Zeit*		
▸ **effective**	*wirksam*	n	effectiveness
▸ **unscrupulous**	*skrupellos*	≈	unprincipled
▸ **to hound**	*jagen*	≈	to persecute
▸ **to excuse** [ɪk'skjuːz]	*entschuldigen*	n	excuse [ɪk'skjuːs]
▸ **victim**	*Opfer*	vt	to victimize
▸ **in the public eye**	*im Blickpunkt der Öffentlichkeit*		
▸ **to be bound by**	*verpflichtet sein durch*	≈	to be constrained by
▸ **to respect**	*respektieren*	n	respect
▸ **to abide by**	*sich halten an*	≈	to adhere to
▸ **to draw up**	*entwerfen, aufstellen*	≈	to draft
▸ **correspondence**	*Korrespondenz*	vi	to correspond (with)
▸ **to justify**	*rechtfertigen*	n	justification
▸ **to forbid**	*verbieten*	⚠	forbid–forbade–forbidden
▸ **telephoto lens**	*Teleobjektiv*	≈	zoom lens
▸ **reasonable**	*vernünftig*	≈	sensible
▸ **expectation**	*Erwartung*	vt	to expect
▸ **fair game**	*Freiwild*	phr	to be ~
▸ **hypocritical** [ˌhɪpə'krɪtɪkl]	*heuchlerisch*	n	hypocrisy [hɪ'pɒkrəsi]
▸ **to protest about**	*protestieren wegen*	n	protest
▸ **innocent**	*unschuldig*	<>	guilty
▸ **persecution**	*Verfolgung*	vt	to persecute
▸ **systematically**	*systematisch*	<>	at random
▸ **to court**	*buhlen um*	≈	to seek
▸ **attention**	*Aufmerksamkeit*	adj	attentive
▸ **to further**	*fördern*	<>	to hinder
▸ **revealing**	*enthüllend*	n	revelation
▸ **in bad taste**	*geschmacklos*	≈	in poor taste
▸ **libel action** ['laɪbl]	*Verleumdungsklage*	adj	libellous

The evolving web

The early World Wide Web of the 1990s was democratic in that anyone with a little computer expertise could set up a website, but the entertainment and information value of most websites was very low. Websites were largely static: you could view them in a browser but interaction with the website was very limited. Most websites were basically advertising.

In the 2000s we saw the emergence of a new approach to website design, often referred to as Web 2.0. The term Web 2.0 doesn't refer to any particular technological advances, but rather a shift in how the web is used by software developers and end users.

With Web 2.0 we've seen a rise in user-created content, through wikis where people pool their knowledge, blogs where they express themselves freely on any topic that interests them, social networking sites where they can 'meet' and interact with new friends, and even virtual worlds like Second Life that offer a parallel existence which is in some ways almost as complex as the real world.

A wiki is a website which allows anyone who accesses it to contribute or edit content. In other words, it is a collaborative online information source. Users can modify any page or create new pages within the site, using simple tools which are provided as part of the interface. Some wikis operate entirely on trust, others require users to register and log in to prevent abuse of the site, such as posting illegal or misleading content, or vandalizing the site by deleting or changing content maliciously.

The best known example of a wiki is Wikipedia, the online encyclopedia. Anyone can contribute to it, but the quality of contributions is monitored. For many people, it's the first place they look when they want to find out about a topic.

It's interesting to compare Wikipedia with Encyclopædia Britannica online, a 'conventional' online encyclopedia, written by experts and reviewed and updated systematically. Britannica may be more reliable, but the articles in Wikipedia cover a wider range of topics, often in greater depth. Wikipedia is constantly evolving and responds very quickly to recent events, so that it is usually up to date. Perhaps most importantly Wikipedia is free, whereas Britannica requires a subscription for full access.

Web 2.0 is an exciting development in how the internet is used. What can we look forward to from Web 3.0?

▸ **to evolve**	*sich entwickeln*	n	evolution
▸ **expertise** [ˌekspɜːˈtiːz]	*Fachkenntnis(se)*	adj	expert
▸ **entertainment value**	*Unterhaltungswert*	vt	to entertain
▸ **static**	*gleich bleibend*	<>	animated
▸ **to view**	*betrachten*	≈	to look at
▸ **interaction**	*Interaktion*	adj	interactive
▸ **limited**	*begrenzt*	≈	restricted
▸ **advertising**	*Werbung*	vti	to advertise
▸ **emergence**	*Entstehung*	adj	emergent
▸ **approach**	*Herangehen(sweise)*	vt	to approach
▸ **advance**	*Fortschritt*	vti	to advance
▸ **software developer**	*Softwareentwickler/in*	vti	to develop
▸ **end user**	*Endnutzer/in*		
▸ **user-created**	*durch Nutzer erstellt*	n	creation
▸ **content**	*Inhalt(e)*	vt	to contain
▸ **to pool**	*sammeln, vereinigen*	≈	to combine
▸ **knowledge**	*Wissen*	vt	to know
▸ **to express oneself**	*sich aussprechen*	n	self-expression
▸ **social networking site**	*soziales Netzwerk*	vti	to network
▸ **to interact with**	*interagieren mit*	n	interaction
▸ **parallel existence**	*Paralleluniversum*	≈	alternative existence
▸ **to access** [ˈækses]	*aufrufen*	n	access
▸ **to contribute**	*beitragen*		
▸ **to edit**	*bearbeiten*	n	editing
▸ **collaborative**	*gemeinschaftlich*	n	collaboration
▸ **source**	*Quelle*	≈	resource
▸ **to modify**	*verändern*	n	modification
▸ **to create**	*erstellen*	adj	creative
▸ **tool**	*Werkzeug*	cf	toolkit
▸ **interface**	*Schaltfläche, Schnittstelle*	phr	user ~
▸ **on trust**	*auf Vertrauensbasis*	vt	to trust
▸ **to register**	*anmelden*	n	registration
▸ **to log in**	*sich einloggen*	<>	to log out/off
▸ **abuse** [əˈbjuːs]	*Missbrauch*	vt	to abuse [əˈbjuːz]
▸ **to post**	*ins Internet stellen*	n	post
▸ **misleading**	*irreführend*	vt	to mislead
▸ **to vandalize**	*(mutwillig) beschädigen*	n	vandalism
▸ **to delete**	*löschen*	n	deletion
▸ **maliciously**	*böswillig*	<>	innocently
▸ **contribution**	*Beitrag*		
▸ **to monitor**	*überwachen*	≈	to check
▸ **to review**	*überprüfen, -arbeiten*	≈	to revise
▸ **to update**	*aktualisieren*	n	update
▸ **systematically**	*systematisch*	<>	ad hoc
▸ **reliable**	*zuverlässig*	n	reliabilty
▸ **in depth**	*gründlich*	≈	thoroughly
▸ **up to date**	*auf dem neuesten Stand*	<>	out of date
▸ **subscription**	*Gebühr*	v prep	to subscribe to

www.symantec.com

Social networking sites – not just for kids

According to recent research, one adult in five has visited a social networking site.

Social networking sites can serve a variety of purposes.
You can easily share lots of things on these sites: pictures and videos, messages, web links, events, etc. They are a great way of keeping in touch with friends and family as well as making new social or professional acquaintances. They have become a commonly used tool for promoting politicians and campaigns, as well as music bands and new movies. They are a great support for viral marketing. Professional networking sites, such as LinkedIn, allow you to meet virtual colleagues and are also useful for attracting the attention of employers, as well as documenting your career history. Companies use social networking sites to deepen relationships with their customers. For example, the myNBC site lets users create profiles, read blogs, and chat with people who love (or hate) the same shows on NBC TV.

Take good care of your online image.
Remember that anything you post on a website will be accessible to anyone in the world, forever. You may have difficulty removing your personal information from a site even if you cancel your account. Think before posting anything you might regret in a few years. Make sure you set your privacy preferences when you first register on the site. Social networking sites may broadcast information about you to everyone in your group or, more specifically, reveal your plans for the weekend or the fact that you've just bought a new CD or book.

Proceed with caution.
In addition to concerns about privacy, the use of social networking sites also raises security issues. Don't disclose too many personal details and don't believe everything people write about themselves. Cybercriminals may exploit the trust they build up on a social networking site to involve victims in a fraud. Identity thieves may steal your employment history or other personal information. 'Regular' thieves may also check your online diary to find out when you will be away on vacation.

Conclusion
Social networking sites are a great way for all kinds of people to meet online and share their common interests. But be careful what information you post on sites like these.

[Shortened: www.symantec.com/content/en/au/clubsymantec/socialnetsites/article.html]

▸ **social networking site**	*soziales Netzwerk*	vti	to network
▸ **message**	*Nachricht*	phr	to send sb a ~
▸ **web link**	*Link im Internet*	≈	hyperlink
▸ **to keep in touch with**	*in Verbindung bleiben mit*	<>	to lose touch with
▸ **professional**	*beruflich*	n	profession
▸ **acquaintance**	*Bekanntschaft*	cf	to be acquainted with
▸ **to promote**	*unterstützen*	n	promotion
▸ **politician** [ˌpɒləˈtɪʃn]	*Politiker/in*	adj	political
▸ **campaign** [kæmˈpeɪn]	*Kampagne*	v prep	to campaign for/against
▸ **support**	*Unterstützung, Hilfe*	vt	to support
▸ **colleague** [ˈkɒliːg]	*Kollege/-gin*	≈	co-worker
▸ **to attract sb's attention**	*jds Aufmerksamkeit erregen*	≈	to get sb's attention
▸ **employer**	*Arbeitgeber/in*	<>	employee
▸ **to document** [ˈdɒkjument]	*dokumentieren*	≈	to provide evidence of
▸ **career history**	*berufliche Laufbahn*	≈	professional history
▸ **to deepen**	*vertiefen*	≈	to intensify
▸ **relationship**	*Beziehung*	≈	connection
▸ **profile**	*Profil*	vt	to profile
▸ **to post**	*ins Netz stellen*	n	post(ing)
▸ **accessible**	*zugänglich*	n	accessibility
▸ **to cancel**	*stornieren*	n	cancellation
▸ **to regret**	*bedauern*	adv	regretfully
▸ **to set a preference**	*eine Präferenz festsetzen*	vt	to prefer
▸ **privacy** [ˈprɪvəsi]	*Privatsphäre*	adj	private
▸ **to register**	*sich anmelden*	n	registration
▸ **to broadcast**	*senden, verbreiten*	≈	to send
▸ **to reveal**	*enthüllen*	<>	to conceal
▸ **caution**	*Vorsicht*	adj	cautious
▸ **concern**	*Bedenken*	≈	worry
▸ **to raise an issue**	*eine Frage aufwerfen*	≈	to throw up an issue
▸ **security**	*Sicherheit*	adj	secure
▸ **to disclose**	*offen legen*	≈	to reveal
▸ **cybercriminal** [ˌsaɪbəˈkrɪmɪnl]	*Internet-Kriminelle/r*	cf	cybercrime [ˈsaɪbəkraɪm]
▸ **to exploit**	*ausnutzen*	n	exploitation
▸ **trust**	*Vertrauen*	vt	to trust
▸ **to involve in**	*verwickeln*	n	involvement
▸ **victim**	*Opfer*	vt	to victimize
▸ **fraud**	*Betrug*	cf	fraudster
▸ **identity thief**	*Identitätsdieb/in*	cf	theft
▸ **employment history**	*Berufsweg*	≈	job history
▸ **diary**	*Tagebuch*	≈	journal
▸ **common**	*gemeinsam*	≈	shared

Forum

Computer game addiction

I think my son is addicted to a computer game. He plays for hours every evening and seems quite obsessed with this game. As a result he's neglecting his schoolwork and he doesn't want to go out with his friends any more – he used to be quite outgoing, now he seems very withdrawn, even secretive. I've tried to talk to him about it but he denies that there's a problem. If I insist, he gets very angry and defensive.

I'm very worried for him. He's 17 and he should be working hard to get good grades as he wants to go to college next year. I don't want him to sacrifice his career for a game!

I don't know much about the game he plays. I understand that it's called 'Age of Magic' and it's an online multiplayer game. Does anyone know anything about this game? Is it addictive?

Worried Mom *May 2* *21:45*

Reply *ex gamer* *May 2* *23:06*

I know the game you mean. I don't think it's any more (or less) addictive than any other role-playing game. It's in the nature of these games that you have to immerse yourself in them and invest a lot of time in your character.

Your son may well grow out of this obsession (if that's what it is). I know I did. But I don't think it's advisable to confront him or try to force him to give up the game. Maybe though you can negotiate some 'ground rules' with him, e.g. a number of hours a week to play the game?

The most important thing is: don't worry, it's probably just a harmless craze that he'll soon get tired of.

Reply *Dr Al* *May 3* *08:06*

I wouldn't dismiss your son's game playing as a harmless teenage obsession. There is no doubt that some people do find computer games addictive, just as others become addicted to gambling. There may also be an underlying mental health issue that needs professional attention. On the other hand, he may simply be stressed because of his exams and using this virtual world to escape from reality for a while.

I think it's very important that you sit down with your son and discuss your concerns with him calmly and objectively.

▸ **addiction**	*Sucht*	cf	addict
▸ **to be addicted to**	*süchtig sein auf*	≈	to be hooked on (coll)
▸ **obsessed with**	*besessen von*	≈	preoccupied with
▸ **to neglect**	*vernachlässigen*	n	neglect
▸ **outgoing**	*kontaktfreudig*	≈	extrovert(ed)
▸ **withdrawn**	*verschlossen*	≈	introvert(ed)
▸ **secretive** ['si:krətɪv]	*verschwiegen*	n	secretiveness
▸ **to deny**	*abstreiten*	n	denial
▸ **to get defensive**	*in die Defensive gehen*	n	defensiveness
▸ **to be worried for**	*sich Sorgen machen um*	≈	to be concerned for
▸ **to sacrifice**	*verzichten auf*	n	sacrifice
▸ **multiplayer**	*mit mehreren Mitspielern*	<>	single-player
▸ **addictive**	*süchtig machend*	n	addictiveness – *Suchtpotential*
▸ **role-playing game**	*Rollenspiel*	cf	to play a role
▸ **to immerse oneself in**	*sich vertiefen in*	n	immersion
▸ **to invest**	*investieren*	n	investment
▸ **to grow out of**	*herauswachsen aus*	≈	to outgrow
▸ **obsession**	*Besessenheit*	adj	obsessive
▸ **advisable**	*ratsam*	n	advice
▸ **to confront**	*(damit) konfrontieren*	n	confrontation
▸ **to force**	*zwingen*	≈	to compel
▸ **to give up**	*aufgeben*	≈	to quit
▸ **to negotiate** [nɪ'gəʊʃieɪt]	*aushandeln*	n	negotiation
▸ **ground rules**	*Grundregeln*	≈	basic rules
▸ **harmless**	*harmlos*	<>	harmful
▸ **craze**	*Manie*	≈	trend, fashion
▸ **to get tired of**	*(einer Sache) überdrüssig werden*	≈	to get fed up with
▸ **to dismiss**	*abtun*	adj	dismissive
▸ **gambling**	*Glücksspiel*	vti	to gamble
▸ **underlying**	*grundlegend*		
▸ **mental health**	*Geisteszustand*	cf	mental illness
▸ **issue**	*Frage, Problem*	≈	problem
▸ **stressed**	*gestresst, unter Druck*	n	stress
▸ **exam**	*Examen, Prüfung*	phr	~ grade, school leaving ~
▸ **virtual**	*virtuell*	phr	~ reality
▸ **to escape from**	*fliehen aus*	n	escape
▸ **reality**	*Realität*	adj	real
▸ **concern**	*Sorge*	≈	worry
▸ **calmly**	*in Ruhe*	<>	hysterically
▸ **objectively**	*objektiv*	<>	subjectively

Forum

What's the point of Second Life?

I don't understand what attracts people to virtual worlds like Second Life. I can see why companies advertise or set up virtual stores in Second Life, because they can make real-life profit. But what do ordinary users gain from it? It seems weird to spend real money on intangible things in a made-up world.

Dipa *Aug 21* *20:06*

Reply *ElenaY* *Aug 22* *07:32*

Allow me to answer your question with another question: what do people gain by watching a movie or TV show? If you have ever bought a DVD or a book, then you believe that entertainment and recreation have an economic value.

Reply *jj* *Aug 22* *11:57*

The point of Second Life is fantasy: trying something new that you can't do in your own life. In a sense, you actually are that person, it isn't just role-playing. One life isn't always enough for all our wishes and dreams.

Reply *Dante* *Aug 22* *12:42*

Most people start playing out of curiosity. They keep playing because they want to keep in touch with their new friends. It's about joining, exploring and bonding with a new social group.

Reply *pixel* *Aug 25* *01:29*

There are also material incentives to spend time in virtual worlds. Did you know that many employers conduct interviews in Second Life? If you want to get noticed and make influential contacts, Second Life is a great professional arena.

Reply *Doc* *Sep 1* *09:05*

For people who attend virtual lectures by world-famous professors, Second Life is an educational opportunity. For many reasons, learning in an avatar-based environment can be much more stimulating than in a real-life classroom.

Reply ¡carmen! Sep 4 10:55

The point of Second Life? New friendships. The excitement of creating clothes, buildings, landscapes just by thinking them up. The fun of becoming someone else, or expressing yourself more fully. Games. Socializing. Activism. Being able to wander through someone else's artwork ...

▸ **point**	*Sinn*	≈	purpose
▸ **to attract sb to sth**	*jdn zu etw anziehen*	n	attraction
▸ **virtual**	*virtuell*	<>	real-life
▸ **to advertise**	*werben*	n	advertisement
▸ **real-life**	*im realen Leben*	<>	virtual
▸ **profit**	*Profit, Gewinn*	v prep	to profit from
▸ **to gain (from)**	*gewinnen (durch)*	<>	to lose
▸ **weird** [wɪəd]	*merkwürdig*	≈	strange
▸ **intangible** [ɪn'tændʒəbl]	*immateriell, nicht greifbar*	<>	tangible
▸ **made-up**	*erfunden, vorgestellt*	≈	fictitious
▸ **entertainment**	*Unterhaltung*	vt	to entertain
▸ **recreation**	*Erholung*	adj	recreational
▸ **economic value**	*wirtschaftlicher Wert*		
▸ **fantasy**	*Phantasie*	vi	to fantasize (about)
▸ **role-playing**	*Rollenspiel*	cf	to play a role
▸ **wish**	*Wunsch*	≈	desire
▸ **dream**	*Traum*	vi	to dream (about/of)
▸ **curiosity** [ˌkjʊəri'ɒsəti]	*Neugier*	adj	curious
▸ **to keep in touch**	*in Kontakt bleiben*	<>	to lose touch
▸ **to join**	*sich anschließen*	<>	to leave
▸ **to explore**	*erkunden*	n	exploration
▸ **to bond with**	*sich verbünden mit*	n	bond
▸ **material**	*materiell*	<>	immaterial
▸ **incentive**	*Anreiz*	≈	motivation
▸ **employer**	*Arbeitgeber/in*	<>	employee
▸ **to conduct**	*durchführen*	≈	to carry out
▸ **interview**	*Vorstellungsgespräch*	vt	to interview
▸ **influential** [ˌɪnflu'enʃl]	*einflussreich*	n	influence
▸ **contact** ['kɒntækt]	*Kontakt*	vt	to contact
▸ **professional**	*beruflich*	n	profession
▸ **to attend**	*teilnehmen (an)*	⚠	≠ to visit
▸ **lecture**	*Vorlesung*	≈	talk
▸ **educational**	*Bildungs-*	vt	to educate
▸ **opportunity**	*Möglichkeit*	≈	chance
▸ **environment**	*Umgebung*	adj	environmental
▸ **stimulating**	*stimulierend*	n	stimulation
▸ **friendship**	*Freundschaft*		
▸ **excitement**	*Begeisterung, Spannung*	adj	exciting
▸ **to create**	*entwerfen*	adj	creative
▸ **to think up**	*sich ausdenken, vorstellen*	≈	to invent
▸ **to express oneself**	*sich ausdrücken*	adj	expressive
▸ **to socialize**	*geselligen Umgang pflegen*	adj	social
▸ **artwork**	*Kunstwerk*	adj	artistic

Researchers link computer games and violence

A study published this month looks at how violence in computer games influences young adults. The findings are worrying. The researchers found that there's a clear link between the violence portrayed in computer games and violent and antisocial behaviour.

Researchers randomly divided a group of 100 male students aged 18–21 into two groups.

One group played a game with only low-level violence (The Simpsons). The other group played a game with frequent high-level violence (Grand Theft Auto).

Before and after playing the game, both groups filled in a questionnaire that tested their attitudes towards acts of violence and their attitude towards risky pastimes – alcohol and marijuana use and unprotected sex. Their blood pressure was measured during play.

Men who played Grand Theft Auto had greater increases in blood pressure, more negative moods, more uncooperative behaviour, more conflict in their social interaction with others, and more permissive attitudes toward using alcohol and marijuana, compared to those who played The Simpsons.

Their socioeconomic background and the levels of violence they had experienced in the past made no difference.

Are these effects transitory, or are they lasting? That's the big question. To date there hasn't been a lot of research into the long-term effects of computer game violence because computer games are a recent phenomenon.

But there is plenty of evidence that shows a link between TV violence and long-term antisocial and violent behaviour, say the researchers. Exposure to TV and media violence in childhood increases aggressive behaviour and criminality well into young adulthood, even after taking into account things like early aggressive behaviour, family socioeconomic status, parenting characteristics, and the safety of their particular community, say the researchers.

How does violence have this effect? Repeated acts of violence desensitize the natural aversion to violence that the child would otherwise have. And if the game rewards violent acts, but not non-violent ones, the child begins to think violence is not only acceptable, but desirable. The longer a child is exposed to violence, the more ingrained these attitudes become.

There's a widespread but false belief that violent games are healthy because they allow kids a way of venting their aggression. They don't.

[Shortened and slightly adapted: http://www.abc.net.au]

▸ **researcher**	*Forscher/in*	vt	to research
▸ **to link**	*eine Verbindung sehen zwischen*	≈	to connect
▸ **violence**	*Gewalt*	<>	non-violence
▸ **to influence**	*beeinflussen*	≈	to affect
▸ **worrying**	*beunruhigend*	n	worry
▸ **to portray**	*darstellen*	n	portrayal
▸ **violent**	*gewalttätig*	<>	non-violent
▸ **antisocial** [ˌænti'səʊʃl]	*asozial*	<>	socially acceptable
▸ **behaviour**	*Verhalten*	vi	to behave
▸ **randomly**	*nach dem Zufallsprinzip*	≈	at random
▸ **low-level**	*geringfügig*	≈	a low level of
▸ **high-level**	*hochrangig*	≈	a high level of
▸ **attitude towards**	*Einstellung gegenüber*	≈	standpoint on
▸ **risky**	*riskant*	n	risk
▸ **pastime**	*Zeitvertreib*	≈	leisure activity
▸ **to measure** ['meʒə]	*messen*	n	measurement
▸ **mood**	*Stimmung, Laune*	adj	moody – *launisch*
▸ **uncooperative**	*unkooperativ*	v prep	to cooperate with
▸ **conflict**	*Konflikt*	v prep	to conflict with
▸ **social interaction**	*soziale Beziehungen*	v prep	to interact with
▸ **permissive**	*freizügig*	n	permissiveness
▸ **socioeconomic background**	*sozioökonomische Herkunft*	cf	socioeconomic status
▸ **to experience**	*erleben*	n	experience
▸ **to make no difference**	*keine Rolle spielen*		
▸ **transitory**	*vorübergehend*	≈	passing
▸ **lasting**	*andauernd*	≈	permanent
▸ **long-term**	*langfristig*	<>	short-term
▸ **phenomenon**	*Phänomen*	pl	phenomena
▸ **evidence**	*Beweis(e)*	adj	evident – *offensichtlich*
▸ **exposure to**	*Aussetzung (einer Sache)*	vt	to expose sb to sth
▸ **childhood**	*Kindheit*	phr	to have a difficult ~
▸ **aggressive**	*aggressiv*	n	aggression
▸ **criminality**	*Kriminalität*	adj	criminal
▸ **adulthood**	*Erwachsenenalter*	phr	to reach ~
▸ **to take into account**	*berücksichtigen*	≈	to consider
▸ **parenting**	*Elternschafts-*	phr	~ skills
▸ **to desensitize**	*abstumpfen*	phr	to become ~d to sth
▸ **aversion to**	*Abneigung gegen*	adj	averse to
▸ **to reward**	*belohnen*	<>	to punish
▸ **non-violent**	*gewaltlos*	n	non-violence
▸ **acceptable**	*akzeptabel*	n	acceptability
▸ **desirable**	*wünschenswert*	n	desirability
▸ **ingrained**	*tief verwurzelt*	phr	~ attitudes, beliefs
▸ **widespread**	*weit verbreitet*	<>	uncommon
▸ **belief**	*Glaube*	vt	to believe
▸ **to vent**	*abreagieren*	≈	to find an outlet for

http://technology.timesonline.co.uk

Internet users could be banned over illegal downloads

People who illegally download films and music will be disconnected from the internet under a proposed new law. Internet service providers (ISPs) will be legally required to take action against users who access pirated material. Users who are detected downloading films or music will receive a warning e-mail for the first offence, a suspension for the second and the termination of their internet contract if caught a third time. Broadband companies who fail to enforce the law would be prosecuted and customers' details could be made available to police. The Government has yet to decide if information on offenders should be shared between ISPs.
Six million broadband users download files illegally every year in this country. Music and film companies claim this is costing them billions of pounds in lost income annually.
Britain's four biggest ISPs have been in talks with Hollywood's biggest studio and distribution companies for six months over a voluntary scheme. However, negotiations between Britain's music industry and ISPs have been going on for two years without reaching agreement.

Have your say

How will they implement this law? Will the ISP monitor and check every URL I look at, every transaction I make, every bit of information I upload or download? That would be an invasion of privacy. Besides, new ways will be found to get around tracking. *James, London, UK*

It's not theft, since you're not taking a product from the musicians. They have not *lost* anything. Besides, I've often bought the CD after downloading a track 'illegally'. *Aaron, TN, USA*

Whether you like to admit it or not, if you download copyright material illegally then you are a thief. *Pam, Adelaide, Australia*

You have to be stupid to think piracy is OK because 'We're only stealing from the big greedy film companies!' What about the local independent DVD stores that are being put out of business? What about the jobs that are being lost? *John, Deal, UK*

And how does the ISP know it is really me downloading those files and not some kid who has hacked into my wifi connection? *Mohammed, London, UK*

[Shortened and adapted: http://technology.timesonline.co.uk]

4 Censorship and control

▸ **internet user**	*Internetnutzer/in*	≈	web user
▸ **to ban**	*ausschließen, (den Zugang) sperren*	n	ban
▸ **to disconnect**	*(jmd den Anschluss) abstellen*	n	disconnection
▸ **to propose**	*vorschlagen*	n	proposal
▸ **internet service provider**	*Internetanbieter*	vt	to provide
▸ **to require**	*auffordern*	n	requirement
▸ **to take action against**	*Schritte unternehmen gegen*		
▸ **to access**	*zugreifen auf*	adj	accessible
▸ **to pirate**	*raubkopieren*	adj	pirated (software, music)
▸ **to detect**	*entdecken*	n	detection
▸ **offence**	*Vergehen*	vti	to offend
▸ **suspension**	*(zeitweiliger) Ausschluss*	vt	to suspend
▸ **termination**	*Beendigung, Auflösung*	vt	to terminate
▸ **contract** ['kɒntrækt]	*Vertrag*	phr	to sign a ~
▸ **to enforce**	*durchsetzen*	n	enforcement
▸ **to prosecute**	*strafrechtlich belangen*	n	prosecution
▸ **offender**	*Straftäter/in*	≈	wrongdoer
▸ **to claim**	*erklären*	n	claim
▸ **income**	*Einkommen*	<>	expenditure
▸ **distribution** [ˌdɪstrɪ'bjuːʃn] **company**	*Vertriebsgesellschaft*	vt	to distribute
▸ **voluntary**	*freiwillig*	<>	compulsory
▸ **to reach agreement**	*sich einigen*	vt, v prep	to agree (to) sth
▸ **to implement**	*durchführen*	n	implementation
▸ **to monitor**	*überwachen*	⚠	≠ to control – *steuern*
▸ **to check**	*überprüfen*	⚠	≠ to prove – *beweisen*
▸ **transaction**	*Vorgang*	phr	financial, business ~
▸ **invasion of privacy**	*Eindringen in die Privatsphäre*	vt	to invade
▸ **to get around**	*umgehen*	≈	to circumvent
▸ **to track**	*(zurück)verfolgen*	≈	to trace, to follow
▸ **theft**	*Diebstahl*	vt	to steal
▸ **musician** [mjuː'zɪʃn]	*Musiker/in*	adj	musical
▸ **track**	*Spur, Stück, Lied*	≈	song
▸ **to admit**	*zugeben*	<>	to deny
▸ **copyright**	*Urheberrecht*	phr	breach of ~ – *Urheberrechtsverletzung*
▸ **thief**	*Dieb/in*		
▸ **piracy**	*Raubkopieren*	n	pirate
▸ **to steal**	*stehlen*	n	stealing, theft
▸ **greedy**	*(hab)gierig*	n	greed
▸ **to put out of business**	*aus dem Geschäft verdrängen*	≈	to ruin
▸ **file**	*Datei*	phr	music, video, data ~
▸ **to hack into**	*unrechtmäßig eindringen*	n	hacker
▸ **wifi** ['waɪfaɪ] **connection**	*drahtlose Verbindung*	≈	wireless connection

Regulating the internet

Interviewer In the studio with me today are Harriette Duncan from internet watchdog InterWatch, and Alex Salter, a civil liberties campaigner. Ms Duncan, do we need to regulate the internet?

Duncan Clearly we do. Paedophile rings are using the internet to distribute child pornography. Then there are websites which incite racial hatred and which promote terrorism. We need to shut down these illegal activities.

Interviewer But most of the illegal material is hosted on servers overseas, and international law has been ineffective in shutting them down.

Duncan True. That's why we want to protect ordinary British internet users from illegal material by monitoring internet traffic and blocking illegal content.

Interviewer Mr Salter, where do you stand on this issue?

Salter I think we have to be wary of media hysteria and knee-jerk reactions by governments. We could end up with censorship of anything which the government considers offensive or undesirable. That would be the end of the right to free speech.

Interviewer So you don't agree that child porn websites need to be banned and their owners prosecuted?

Salter Oh, yes. I agree with Ms Duncan there. The same applies to websites that recruit people for terrorism. But she wants to give the police powers to spy on ordinary citizens online. That is an infringement of civil liberties.

Interviewer What kind of approach would you like to see?

Salter I would like to see international law improved to make it easier to combat paedophile and terrorist material online. Other than that, to be honest, I think we need less regulation, not more. At present, we have a system of self-regulation by internet service providers. The problem is, these are private organizations. They are not democratically accountable, and their decisions are not transparent. There have been many cases of innocent websites being blacklisted by an ISP …

4 Censorship and control

▸ **to regulate**	*kontrollieren, regeln*	n	regulation
▸ **watchdog**	*Aufsichtsbehörde*	≈	guardian ['gɑːdiən]
▸ **civil liberties**	*Bürgerrechte*	≈	civil rights
▸ **campaigner**	*Aktivist/in*	vi	to campaign (for/against)
▸ **paedophile ring**	*Pädophilenring*	≈	child porn(ography) ring
▸ **to distribute**	*vertreiben*	n	distribution
▸ **child pornography** [pɔː'nɒgrəfi]	*Kinderpornografie*	adj	pornographic [ˌpɔːnə'græfɪk]
▸ **to incite**	*schüren*	n	incitement
▸ **racial hatred**	*Rassenhass*	vt	to hate
▸ **to promote**	*fördern*	n	promotion
▸ **terrorism**	*Terrorismus*	cf	terrorist
▸ **to shut down**	*schließen*	≈	to close
▸ **to host**	*(auf Zentralrechner) verwalten*	n	host
▸ **overseas**	*im Ausland*	≈	abroad
▸ **law**	*Recht*	adj	legal
▸ **ineffective**	*wirkungslos*	<>	effective
▸ **to protect from**	*schützen vor*	<>	to endanger
▸ **internet user**	*Internetnutzer/in*	≈	surfer
▸ **to monitor**	*überwachen*	n	monitoring
▸ **internet traffic**	*Internetverkehr*		
▸ **to block**	*sperren*	<>	to let through
▸ **content** ['kɒntent]	*Inhalt(e)*		
▸ **issue**	*Frage, Thema*	≈	matter, question
▸ **to be wary of**	*sich hüten vor*	n	wariness
▸ **hysteria**	*Hysterie*	adj	hysterical
▸ **knee-jerk reaction**	*Kurzschlussreaktion*	≈	hasty reaction
▸ **government**	*Regierung*	vt	to govern
▸ **censorship**	*Zensur*	vt	to censor
▸ **to consider sth sth**	*etw als etw betrachten*	≈	to regard sth as sth
▸ **offensive**	*anstößig*	vt	to offend
▸ **undesirable**	*unerwünscht*	≈	unwelcome
▸ **right to**	*Recht auf*	adj	rightful
▸ **free speech**	*Meinungsfreiheit*	≈	freedom of speech
▸ **to ban**	*verbieten*	n	ban
▸ **to prosecute**	*strafrechtlich verfolgen*	n	prosecution
▸ **to recruit**	*anwerben*	n	recruitment
▸ **power**	*Befugnis*	n	authority
▸ **to spy on**	*ausspähen*	n	spy
▸ **infringement**	*Verletzung*	vt	to infringe
▸ **to combat**	*bekämpfen*	≈	to fight against
▸ **regulation**	*Regulierung, Kontrolle*	≈	control, supervision
▸ **internet service provider**	*Internetanbieter*	abbr	ISP
▸ **democratically accountable**	*demokratisch verantwortlich*	n	accountability
▸ **innocent**	*harmlos, unschuldig*	<>	guilty
▸ **to blacklist**	*auf die schwarze Liste setzen*		

F

Politics

1 Systems and institutions

2 Issues and policies

3 Campaigning and protest

Elections in the United States

Tina I don't really understand the electoral system here in the US. For example, what exactly are 'primaries'?

Dave Elections in which a party's candidates for public office are nominated. The winners of the primary run in the general election.

Tina Nominated by whom? By the electorate as a whole?

Dave That depends. Because we have a federal system, regulations vary from state to state. Most states have a 'closed primary' system – only party members can vote in that party's primary. But some states have 'open primaries': anyone who is on the electoral register may vote in any primary. Others again have a caucus system, in which party leaders and activists nominate the candidates.

Tina So, a Republican supporter in an open primary could cast a vote for the weakest Democratic candidate, because he or she would be easier to defeat in the general election?

Dave That's right. But in most states, you are only eligible to vote in one primary. So your Republican would forfeit the right to vote in his own party's primary.

Tina I see … Are presidential candidates nominated in the same way?

Dave Not exactly. They're nominated by a national convention of their party. But the delegates to these conventions are picked in primaries – presidential primaries.

Tina So the presidential hopefuls just sit around in Washington waiting to be nominated?

Dave You've got to be joking! The candidates travel from state to state campaigning. A large proportion of the campaign funds are contributed by special-interest groups.

Tina Surely that must give them unfair political influence?

Dave That's one of the criticisms levelled at the system. Another is that presidential primaries become huge media circuses, focusing on personalities instead of serious issues. A third is that the candidates aren't really accountable to their parties. But no system is perfect!

Tina Do most people vote in the primaries?

Dave No, they usually attract a low turnout. That means that an active minority can distort the result. Also, the early primaries are disproportionately important, as they can establish – or destroy – a candidate's reputation and sway voters in later primaries.

▸ **election**	*Wahl*	vt	to elect
▸ **electoral system**	*Wahlsystem*		
▸ **primary**	*Vorwahl*		
▸ **candidate** ['kændɪdət]	*Kandidat/in*	cf	candidacy – *Kandidatur*
▸ **public office**	*öffentliches Amt*		
▸ **to nominate**	*nominieren*	n	nomination
▸ **to run**	*kandidieren*	≈	to stand
▸ **general election**	*Parlamentswahlen*		
▸ **electorate** [ɪ'lektərət]	*Wählerschaft*		
▸ **federal**	*föderalistisch*	n	federalism
▸ **regulation**	*Vorschrift, Bestimmung*	≈	rule
▸ **party member**	*Parteimitglied*	cf	membership – *Mitgliedschaft*
▸ **to vote**	*wählen, die Stimme abgeben*	n	vote – *Stimme; Abstimmung*
▸ **electoral** [ɪ'lektərəl] **register**	*Wählerverzeichnis*	vti	to register
▸ **caucus**	*Ausschuss-*		
▸ **supporter**	*Anhänger/in*	vt	to support
▸ **to cast a vote**	*eine Stimme abgeben*	≈	to vote
▸ **to defeat**	*besiegen*	n	defeat
▸ **eligible** ['elɪdʒəbl]	*berechtigt*	<>	ineligible
▸ **to forfeit** ['fɔːfɪt]	*verwirken*	adj	forfeit
▸ **presidential candidate**	*Präsidentschaftskandidat/in*		
▸ **national convention**	*Nationalversammlung*	vti	to convene
▸ **delegate to** ['delɪgət]	*Delegierte/r für*	vt	to delegate
▸ **presidential primary**	*Vorwahl für die Präsidentschaft*	cf	president
▸ **presidential hopeful**	*Präsidentschaftsanwärter/in*	cf	hopeful – *hoffnungsvoll*
▸ **to campaign** [kæm'peɪn]	*den Wahlkampf führen*	n	campaign
▸ **funds**	*Mittel, Gelder*	vt	to fund
▸ **to contribute**	*spenden, beisteuern*	n	contribution
▸ **special-interest group**	*Interessengruppe*	≈	lobby
▸ **to level a criticism at**	*eine Kritik erheben gegen*	≈	to criticize
▸ **media circus**	*Medienzirkus*		
▸ **to focus on**	*sich konzentrieren auf*	≈	to concentrate on
▸ **issue**	*Frage, Thema*	≈	question, topic
▸ **to be accountable to sb**	*jdm verantwortlich sein*	n	accountability
▸ **turnout**	*Wahlbeteiligung*	vi	to turn out
▸ **minority**	*Minderheit*	<>	majority
▸ **to distort**	*verzerren*	n	distortion
▸ **disproportionately**	*unverhältnismäßig*	<>	proportionately
▸ **reputation**	*Ruf*		
▸ **to sway**	*beeinflussen*	≈	to influence

General elections in the UK

Dear Alex,

Watching the run-up to the general election here in the UK has been really interesting. The British like to think that they invented parliamentary democracy, but their political system doesn't seem all that democratic to me: they have 'first-past-the-post' elections here, so in theory one party can win, even though another party got more votes! The system of proportional representation that we have back home seems much fairer.

When I ask my British friends about that, they point out that under the British system, coalition governments are less likely, and they see that as a positive aspect of their electoral system. They prefer a more confrontational, decisive style of government here, rather than compromise and negotiation.

The second-largest party forms the Official Opposition and is expected to oppose almost everything the government does! Debates in the House of Commons (the Lower House) are often very heated as a result.

Anyway, this is how their system works: in each constituency there is one candidate for each party, and the candidate who gets the largest number of votes becomes the member of parliament for that constituency: then the party which has a majority of MPs wins the election and forms the new government. The leader of that party becomes the prime minister.

The election campaign is in full swing. I have just seen a party political broadcast on TV by the Liberal Democrats. Their manifesto is much more radical and imaginative than those of the two major parties (Labour and Conservative), but they have no chance of getting a majority. Opinion polls show that Labour and the Conservatives are neck-and-neck.

The local Conservative candidate came round our area canvassing a few days ago, and knocked on my door. I was very interested to hear about his policies – but he soon lost interest in me when he realized that I'm not eligible to vote in this country!

▸ **general election**	*Parlamentswahl*	cf	by-election – *Nachwahl*
▸ **run-up to**	*Vorbereitungszeit für*		
▸ **to invent**	*erfinden*	n	inventor
▸ **parliamentary democracy** [dɪ'mɒkrɪsi]	*parlamentarische Demokratie*	cf	dictatorship – *Diktatur*
▸ **political**	*politisch*	n	politics (pl)
▸ **democratic**	*demokratisch*	n	democrat – *Demokrat/in*
▸ **first-past-the-post election**	*Mehrheitswahl*	cf	to elect – *wählen*
▸ **party**	*Partei*		
▸ **vote**	*Stimme*	vi, v prep	to vote (for)
▸ **proportional representation**	*Verhältniswahlsystem*	vt	to represent
▸ **coalition government**	*Koalitionsregierung*	vti	to govern
▸ **electoral system**	*Wahlsystem*	vt	to elect
▸ **confrontational**	*konfrontativ*	vt	to confront
▸ **decisive**	*entscheidend*	<>	indecisive
▸ **compromise**	*Kompromiss*	phr	to reach a ~
▸ **negotiation**	*Verhandlung*	vt, v prep	to negotiate (with)
▸ **to form**	*bilden*	n	formation
▸ **to oppose**	*sich widersetzen*	<>	to support
▸ **debate**	*Debatte*	vt	to debate
▸ **House of Commons**	*(britisches) Unterhaus*	cf	House of Lords – *(britisches) Oberhaus*
▸ **Lower House**	*Unterhaus*	cf	Upper House – *Oberhaus*
▸ **constituency** [kən'stɪtjuənsi]	*Wahlkreis*	cf	constituent – *Wähler/in*
▸ **candidate**	*Kandidat/in*	⚠	to stand for election – *kandidieren*
▸ **member of parliament**	*Abgeordnete/r (des Unterhauses)*	abbr	MP
▸ **majority**	*Mehrheit*	<>	minority
▸ **leader**	*Vorsitzende/r*	vt	to lead
▸ **prime minister**	*Premierminister/in*		
▸ **election campaign** [kæm'peɪn]	*Wahlkampf*	vi	to campaign
▸ **to be in full swing**	*in vollem Gange sein*		
▸ **party political broadcast**	*Wahlsendung*	cf	to broadcast – *senden*
▸ **manifesto**	*Parteiprogramm*		
▸ **radical**	*radikal*	<>	moderate
▸ **imaginative**	*einfallsreich, fantasievoll*	n	imagination
▸ **major**	*größer*	<>	minor
▸ **opinion poll**	*Meinungsumfrage*	≈	opinion survey
▸ **to be neck-and-neck**	*Kopf an Kopf liegen*		
▸ **local**	*örtlich, lokal*	phr	the ~ area
▸ **to canvass**	*um Stimmen werben*	n	canvasser – *Wahlhelfer/in*
▸ **policy**	*Politik, politische Linie*		
▸ **eligible to vote**	*wahlberechtigt*	n	eligibility

Book review
The European Dream by Jeremy Rifkin

The American Dream is becoming ever more difficult to achieve. Americans are increasingly overworked, underpaid, time-poor and unsure about their prospects for a better life. One third of all Americans say that they no longer even believe in the American Dream.

While the American Dream is declining, says bestselling author Jeremy Rifkin, a new European Dream is capturing the attention and imagination of the world.

The European Union's GDP now rivals the United States', making it the largest economy in the world. The EU is already the world's leading exporter and largest internal market. Moreover, much of Europe enjoys a longer lifespan and greater literacy, and has less poverty and crime, less urban sprawl, longer vacations, and shorter commutes to work than we do in the United States. When one considers what makes a people great and what constitutes a better way of life, observes Rifkin, Europe is beginning to surpass America.

More important, Europe has become a giant laboratory for rethinking humanity's future. In many respects, the European Dream is the mirror opposite of the American Dream. While the American Dream emphasizes economic growth, personal wealth and individual self-interest, the European Dream focuses more on sustainable development, quality of life and community.

We Americans live (and die) by the work ethic. Europeans place more importance on leisure and even idleness. America has always seen itself as a great melting pot. Europeans, instead, prefer to preserve their rich multicultural diversity. We believe in maintaining an unrivalled military presence in the world. Europeans, by contrast, emphasize cooperation and consensus over go-it-alone approaches to foreign policy.

All of this does not suggest that Europe has suddenly become a utopia. Its problems, Rifkin cautions, are complex and its weaknesses glaringly obvious. What's crucial is that Europe has a bold new vision for the future of humanity that differs in many of its most fundamental aspects to America's.

Two hundred years ago, America's founders created a new dream for humanity that transformed the world. Today, suggests Rifkin, a new generation of Europeans is creating a radical new dream – one better suited to meet the challenges of a globalized world in the 21st century.

[Shortened and slightly adapted: http://www.foet.org]

1 Systems and institutions

▸ **overworked**	*überarbeitet*	vt	to overwork sb
▸ **underpaid**	*unterbezahlt*	<>	overpaid
▸ **time-poor**	*unter Zeitmangel leidend*	<>	time-rich
▸ **unsure**	*unsicher, ungewiss*	≈	uncertain
▸ **to decline**	*verfallen*	n	decline
▸ **GDP**	*Bruttoinlandsprodukt*	abbr	gross domestic product
▸ **to rival** ['raɪvl]	*sich messen lassen können mit*	n	rival *(person)*, rivalry
▸ **economy**	*Wirtschaft*	adj	economic
▸ **exporter**	*Exporteur*	vti	to export
▸ **internal market**	*Binnenmarkt*	≈	domestic market
▸ **lifespan**	*Lebensdauer, -erwartung*		
▸ **literacy** ['lɪtərəsi]	*Lese- und Schreibfähigkeit*	adj	literate
▸ **poverty**	*Armut*	adj	poor
▸ **crime**	*Kriminalität*	adj	criminal
▸ **urban sprawl**	*städtische Ausdehnung*	vi	to sprawl
▸ **commute**	*Fahrt zur Arbeit*	vi	to commute
▸ **way of life**	*Lebensstil*	≈	lifestyle
▸ **to surpass**	*übertreffen*	≈	to outdo
▸ **to rethink**	*überdenken*	≈	to reconsider
▸ **humanity**	*Menschheit*	adj	human
▸ **growth**	*Wachstum*		
▸ **wealth**	*Reichtum*	adj	wealthy
▸ **self-interest**	*Eigeninteresse*	<>	altruism
▸ **to focus on**	*sich konzentrieren auf*	n	focus on
▸ **sustainable development**	*nachhaltige Entwicklung*	n	sustainability
▸ **quality of life**	*Lebensqualität*		
▸ **community**	*Gemeinschaft(sgeist)*	adj	communal
▸ **work ethic**	*Arbeitsmoral*	adj	ethical
▸ **leisure**	*Freizeit*	≈	free time
▸ **idleness** ['aɪdlnəs]	*Faulheit, Nichtstun*	adj	idle
▸ **melting pot**	*Schmelztiegel*	phr	cultural ~
▸ **to preserve**	*erhalten*	n	preservation
▸ **diversity**	*Vielfalt*	adj	diverse
▸ **unrivalled**	*unübertroffen*	≈	unparalleled
▸ **military presence**	*Militärpräsenz*	phr	to maintain a ~
▸ **cooperation**	*Zusammenarbeit*	vi, v prep	to cooperate (with)
▸ **go-it-alone approach**	*Alleingang*	vt	to approach
▸ **foreign policy**	*Außenpolitik*	<>	domestic policy
▸ **weakness**	*Schwäche*	<>	strength
▸ **glaringly obvious**	*ins Auge springend*	≈	apparent
▸ **vision**	*Vision*	vt	to envisage (BE), to envision (AE)
▸ **founder**	*Gründer(väter)*	vt	to found
▸ **to transform**	*verwandeln*	n	transformation
▸ **challenge**	*Herausforderung*	vt	to challenge
▸ **globalized**	*globalisiert*	n	globalization

www.unac.org

THE UN IN BRIEF

Most of us have heard about United Nations peacekeeping and humanitarian assistance. But the many other ways the UN affects all our lives are not always so well known. The United Nations is central to global efforts to solve problems which challenge humanity. Cooperating in this effort are more than 30 affiliated organizations known together as the UN system. Day in and day out, the UN and its family of organizations work to promote respect for human rights, protect the environment, fight disease, promote development and reduce poverty. The United Nations leads the international campaigns against illicit drug trafficking and terrorism. Throughout the world, the UN and its agencies assist refugees and set up programmes to clear landmines, help improve the quality of drinking water and expand food production, make loans to developing countries and help stabilize financial markets.

HOW THE UN WORKS

The United Nations was established on 24 October 1945 by 51 countries committed to preserving peace through international cooperation and collective security. Today, nearly every nation in the world belongs to the UN – 192 countries in all. When states become Members of the United Nations, they agree to accept the obligations of the UN Charter, an international treaty which sets out basic principles of international relations. According to the Charter, the UN has four purposes: to maintain international peace and security, to develop friendly relations among nations, to cooperate in solving international problems and in promoting respect for human rights, and to be a centre for harmonizing the actions of nations. UN Members are sovereign countries. The United Nations is not a world government, and it does not make laws. It does, however, provide the means to help resolve international conflict and formulate policies on matters affecting all of us. The United Nations has six main organs. Five of them – the General Assembly, the Security Council, the Economic and Social Council, the Trusteeship Council and the Secretariat – are based at UN Headquarters in New York. The sixth, the International Court of Justice, is located in The Hague, Netherlands.

[Adapted extracts: http://un.by/en/about/; http://www.unac.org]

1 Systems and institutions

peacekeeping	*Friedenssicherung*	vt	to keep the peace
humanitarian assistance	*humanitäre Hilfe*	≈	humanitarian aid
effort	*Bemühung*	phr	to make an ~ to do sth
to challenge	*herausfordern*	n	challenge
to cooperate	*kooperieren*	≈	to collaborate
affiliated [ə'fɪlieɪtɪd]	*angeschlossen*	n	affiliation
to promote	*fördern*	<>	to discourage
human rights	*Menschenrechte*		
poverty	*Armut*	adj	poor
campaign [kæm'peɪn]	*Kampagne*	vi	to campaign
illicit	*illegal*	≈	illegal
drug trafficking	*Drogenhandel*	≈	drug dealing
terrorism	*Terrorismus*	cf	terrorist
to assist	*helfen*	cf	aid – *Hilfe*
refugee	*Flüchtling*	cf	asylum – *Asyl*
to set up	*einrichten*	≈	to establish
to clear landmines	*Landminen räumen*	<>	to lay landmines
to expand	*erweitern*	n	expansion
loan	*Darlehen*	cf	grant – *Subvention*
developing country	*Entwicklungsland*	<>	developed country
to stabilize	*stabilisieren*	adj	stable
financial market	*Finanzmarkt*		
to establish	*gründen*	≈	to found
to be committed to	*sich einsetzen für*	n	commitment – *Engagement*
to preserve	*erhalten*	n	preservation
security	*Sicherheit*	<>	insecurity
obligation	*Verpflichtung*	adj	obliged
charter	*Charta*		
to set out	*darlegen*	≈	to state
basic principle	*Grundsatz*	≈	fundamental principle
international relations	*internationale Beziehungen*		
to maintain	*bewahren*	≈	to preserve
to develop	*entwickeln*	n	development
to harmonize	*aufeinander abstimmen*	n	harmonization
sovereign country	*souveräner Staat*	n	sovereignty
to resolve	*lösen*	n	resolution
to formulate	*formulieren*	n	formula
General Assembly	*Vollversammlung*	cf	Secretary General – *Generalsekretär/in*
Security Council	*Sicherheitsrat*		
to be based	*seinen Sitz haben*		
headquarters	*Zentrale*	⚠	Plural
to be located	*sich befinden*	n	location

http://forum.newsonline.info/readerpoll.asp

The News – Online Forum

Talkback: Is Britain's immigration policy too lenient?

Last year around 25,000 people applied for asylum in the UK. Meanwhile there were an estimated 500,000 failed asylum seekers living in the country. These are people whose applications for asylum have been rejected, but who have not been deported to their home countries. Is it time to stem the tide of refugees?

Answers

Quite the opposite is true – Britain's immigration laws are far too tough. The policy is to make it as difficult as possible for people to apply for asylum. New arrivals in Britain have only a short period of time to collect evidence to substantiate an asylum application. Remember that these are people who are destitute, are traumatized by their experiences in their home countries, often have no local contacts and may not be able to speak English.
Clara, Newcastle-upon-Tyne

We should keep all asylum seekers in detention camps until their applications have been processed. Those who are found not to be eligible should be deported swiftly and without appeal. At the moment, bogus asylum seekers – economic migrants – are living here at the taxpayer's expense, receiving cash handouts and living in luxury. **Mike, Exeter**

You clearly have no experience of the life of an asylum seeker in Britain. Asylum seekers are sent to specific accommodation (maybe hundreds of miles from friends and family), are not given cash handouts but vouchers that they must use at specific supermarkets, and receive only enough assistance for basic subsistence. You call that luxury?

If their asylum application fails, they are often too scared to return to their home countries and so choose to stay in Britain illegally, depending on charities such as the Red Cross for their survival and often living on as little as £1 per day.
Sukhdev, Canterbury

Another result of the current bureaucratic system is that many asylum seekers join the 'black economy', working in sweatshops without paying taxes and without any protection from exploitation.

Ironically, if the decision procedure were more lenient, it would also be quicker and cheaper to run. Refugees could integrate into society, get proper jobs and contribute to the national economy instead of being a burden on it.
Lucy, Leicester

2 Issues and policies

immigration policy	*Einwanderungspolitik*	cf	immigrant
lenient ['li:niənt]	*milde, nachsichtig*	<>	strict
to apply for	*beantragen*	n	applicant – *Bewerber/in*
asylum [ə'saɪləm]	*Asyl*	phr	to seek ~
failed	*abgelehnt*	n	failure
asylum seeker	*Asylbewerber/in*		
application	*Antrag*	phr	~ procedure
to reject	*ablehnen*	n	rejection
to deport	*abschieben*	n	deportation
home country	*Heimatland*	≈	native country
to stem the tide	*den Zustrom eindämmen*		
refugee	*Flüchtling*		
tough	*streng*	≈	harsh
new arrival	*Neuankömmling*	vi	to arrive
evidence	*Beweis(e)*	cf	to prove – *beweisen*
to substantiate	*begründen*	≈	to justify
destitute	*mittellos*	n	destitution
traumatized	*traumatisiert*	n	trauma
contact	*Kontakt*	phr	to be in ~ with
detention camp	*Internierungslager*	vt	to detain
to process	*bearbeiten*	n	processing
eligible	*berechtigt*	n	eligibility
appeal	*Einspruch, Berufung*	vi, v prep	to appeal (against)
bogus	*Schein-*	<>	genuine
economic migrant	*Wirtschaftsflüchtling*	vi	to migrate
at sb's expense	*auf jds Kosten*		
taxpayer	*Steuerzahler/in*	cf	tax office – *Finanzamt*
handout	*Almosen*	v prep	to hand out
luxury	*Luxus*	adj	luxurious
accommodation	*Unterkunft*	≈	housing
voucher	*Gutschein*		
assistance	*Unterstützung*	vt	to assist
subsistence	*Lebensunterhalt*	vi	to subsist
scared	*verängstigt*	≈	frightened
illegally	*illegal*	<>	legally
to depend on	*angewiesen sein auf*	n	dependence on
charity	*Wohltätigkeitsorganisation*	adj	charitable
survival	*Überleben*	vti	to survive
to live on	*leben von*	≈	to survive on
bureaucratic	*bürokratisch*	n	bureaucracy
black economy	*Schattenwirtschaft*		
sweatshop ['swetʃɒp]	*Ausbeuterbetrieb*	vi	to sweat – *schwitzen*
to pay taxes	*Steuern zahlen*	n	taxation
protection	*Schutz*	vt	to protect
exploitation	*Ausbeutung*	vt	to exploit
to integrate into	*sich integrieren in*	n	integration
society	*Gesellschaft*	adj	social
burden on	*Belastung für*	vt	to burden sb with sth

Web poll:

Did the US 'War on Terror' achieve anything?

On September 11, 2001, hijacked passenger jets were used to destroy the World Trade Center in New York and damage the Pentagon. The attacks caused great loss of civilian life and were internationally condemned as an atrocity.

US president George W Bush declared the 'War on Terror', largely in response to the 9/11 attacks. This led to military interventions in Afghanistan and Iraq. With the benefit of hindsight, do we feel his actions were justified and did they achieve anything?

YES 0 0 1 5 9 **NO** 0 1 2 4 4

Comments

The War on Terror has been used to justify unilateral preemptive war (the invasion of Iraq), human rights abuses (Abu Ghraib; Guantanamo Bay) and other violations of international law. It has alienated many people from the aims and values of the US and has discredited Western democracy generally in developing countries.

In short, it has been an extremely effective means of increasing terrorist recruitment – far more effective than anything al-Qaeda and Osama bin Laden could have come up with.

Trudi van K, The Netherlands

The United States and its allies committed themselves to a war without clearly defined objectives. They never really understood how their enemies thought, so they had no idea how to defeat them. Instead, they just labelled them as 'evil' and 'enemies of freedom' and tried to destroy them with massive military superiority. The rest, as they say, is history.

The USA also used the war as a pretext to justify drastic restrictions to civil rights at home. The US Government in particular tried to subvert the Geneva Conventions in its inhumane and unlawful treatment of prisoners of war from the Afghan and Iraqi conflicts.

Brad, New Zealand

Like any other state, the USA has a right to defend itself against foreign aggressors. 9/11 was an act of war and the War on Terror was a legitimate response to it. It weakened al-Qaeda's power base in Afghanistan and removed a vicious dictator from power in Iraq.

It's easy to criticize that foreign policy now, but it's a significant fact that there were no further terrorist attacks on US soil during George W Bush's eight years as US president.

Stars&Stripes, USA

2 Issues and policies

▸ **to achieve**	*erreichen*	n	achievement
▸ **to hijack** ['haɪdʒæk]	*entführen*	n	hijacking
▸ **to destroy**	*zerstören*	n	destruction
▸ **to damage**	*beschädigen*	n	damage
▸ **loss of life**	*Todesopfer*	cf	fatalities – *Todesfälle*
▸ **civilian**	*zivil*	<>	military
▸ **to condemn**	*verurteilen*	n	condemnation
▸ **atrocity** [ə'trɒsəti]	*Gräueltat*	phr	to commit an ~
▸ **to declare war**	*den Krieg erklären*	n	declaration of war
▸ **in response to**	*als Reaktion auf*	vi, v prep	to respond (to)
▸ **military intervention**	*militärische Intervention*	vi	to intervene
▸ **with the benefit of hindsight**	*im Nachhinein*	v prep	to benefit from
▸ **justified**	*gerechtfertigt*	n	justification
▸ **unilateral**	*einseitig*	<>	multilateral
▸ **preemptive**	*Präventiv-*	phr	~ strike, ~attack
▸ **human rights abuse** [ə'bjuːs]	*Menschenrechtsverletzung(en)*	vt	to abuse [ə'bjuːz]
▸ **violation**	*Verletzung*	≈	contravention
▸ **law**	*Recht*	adj	lawful, legal
▸ **to alienate** ['eɪliəneɪt]	*entfremden*	n	alienation
▸ **to discredit**	*diskreditieren*	≈	to destroy confidence in
▸ **recruitment**	*Rekrutierung*	vt	to recruit
▸ **ally**	*Verbündete/r*	adj	allied
▸ **clearly defined**	*klar definiert*	<>	vague
▸ **objective**	*Ziel*	≈	aim, goal
▸ **to defeat**	*besiegen*	n	defeat
▸ **to label as**	*bezeichnen als*	≈	to dub
▸ **evil**	*böse*	n	evil
▸ **freedom**	*Freiheit*	≈	liberty
▸ **superiority**	*Überlegenheit*	<>	inferiority
▸ **pretext**	*Vorwand*	≈	excuse
▸ **restriction**	*Einschränkung*	vt	to restrict
▸ **civil rights**	*Bürgerrechte*	phr	~ movement, ~ lawyer
▸ **to subvert**	*untergraben*	adj	subversive
▸ **unlawful**	*widerrechtlich*	≈	illegal
▸ **prisoner of war**	*Kriegsgefangene/r*	abbr	POW
▸ **conflict**	*Konflikt*	≈	war
▸ **to defend**	*verteidigen*	n	defence
▸ **aggressor**	*Aggressor*	adj	aggressive
▸ **act of war**	*kriegerische Handlung*	vgl	act of aggression
▸ **legitimate**	*legitim*	<>	illegitimate
▸ **to weaken**	*schwächen*	<>	to strengthen
▸ **power base**	*Machtbasis*	adj	powerful
▸ **vicious** ['vɪʃəs]	*bösartig*	n	viciousness
▸ **foreign policy**	*Außenpolitik*	<>	domestic policy

Amnesty International

Mel I was pretty shocked by the news last night about the latest human rights violations in Burma. The UN has imposed sanctions, but when have sanctions ever had any effect on totalitarian governments?

James I think that sometimes diplomatic pressure and sanctions have more effect behind the scenes than we realize, although perhaps not in this case. Did you know that there were reliable reports of torture and ill-treatment by security forces in 130 countries last year? Or that people were executed without a fair trial in 40 countries?

Mel That's awful … But I guess there's not a lot we can do about it – as individuals, I mean.

James As individuals, no. On the other hand, I joined Amnesty International recently.

Mel Right. Well I don't get involved in politics …

James But Amnesty is completely non-political! It simply promotes human rights around the world. It campaigns to free prisoners of conscience, ensure fair trials, abolish the death penalty and torture – things like that.

Mel OK. So it 'promotes' and 'campaigns' … What does that mean exactly?

James Well, for example, Amnesty visits countries worldwide to observe trials, talk with victims of human rights abuses and interview local activists and officials. It gathers information, being careful not to just pass on unsubstantiated rumours and allegations. Then it raises public awareness and mobilizes public opinion through petitions and publicity campaigns. It also confronts the offending governments with its evidence directly in detailed reports, and it lobbies other governments and the UN to take action.

Mel Cool. But what's your contribution to all this?

James I'm going to write letters to prisoners of conscience – letting them know that they haven't been forgotten – and also to governments expressing my concerns about their human rights violations. And I'm going to get involved in fundraising events.

Mel And do you think it will make a difference, or will it just make you feel better?

James It's difficult to be sure how much difference it will make, but I'm sure that Amnesty raises public awareness. After all, I've just raised your awareness, haven't I?

3 Campaigning and protest

▸ **to shock**	*erschüttern, schockieren*	n	shock
▸ **human rights**	*Menschenrechte*	phr	~ activist
▸ **violation**	*Verletzung*	vt	to violate
▸ **to impose**	*auferlegen*	n	imposition
▸ **totalitarian**	*totalitär*	n	totalitarianism
▸ **diplomatic**	*diplomatisch*	n	diplomacy
▸ **pressure**	*Druck*	phr	to put ~ on sb
▸ **behind the scenes**	*hinter den Kulissen*		
▸ **torture** ['tɔːtʃə]	*Folter*	vt	to torture
▸ **ill-treatment**	*Misshandlung*	vt	to ill-treat
▸ **security forces**	*Sicherheitskräfte*	cf	armed forces – *Streitkräfte*
▸ **to execute**	*hinrichten*	n	execution
▸ **trial**	*Gerichtsverfahren*	phr	to put sb on ~
▸ **to get involved in politics**	*sich politisch engagieren*	n	involvement
▸ **to promote**	*fördern*	n	promotion
▸ **to campaign** [kæm'peɪn]	*sich einsetzen (für)*	n	campaign
▸ **prisoner of conscience** ['kɒnʃəns]	*Gefangene/r aus Gewissensgründen*		
▸ **to ensure**	*gewährleisten*	<>	to make sure
▸ **to abolish**	*abschaffen*	n	abolition
▸ **death penalty**	*Todesstrafe*	≈	capital punishment
▸ **worldwide**	*weltweit*	≈	globally
▸ **to observe**	*beobachten*	≈	to witness
▸ **victim**	*Opfer*	vt	to victimize
▸ **abuse** [ə'bjuːs]	*Missbrauch*	vt	to abuse [ə'bjuːz]
▸ **official**	*Amtsträger/in*	adj	official
▸ **unsubstantiated** [ˌʌnsəb'stænʃieɪtɪd]	*unbewiesen, haltlos*	vt	to substantiate
▸ **rumour** ['ruːmə]	*Gerücht*	phr	to spread a ~
▸ **allegation**	*Behauptung*	vt	to allege (that)
▸ **to raise awareness**	*das Bewusstsein stärken*	≈	to increase awareness
▸ **public**	*der Öffentlichkeit*	<>	private
▸ **to mobilize**	*mobilisieren*	≈	to rally
▸ **petition**	*Petition*	phr	to sign a ~
▸ **publicity campaign**	*Öffentlichkeits-kampagne*	vi, v prep	to campaign (for/against)
▸ **to confront**	*konfrontieren*	n	confrontation
▸ **offending**	*schuldig, zuwiderhandelnd*	n	offender, offence
▸ **evidence**	*Beweis(e)*		
▸ **to lobby**	*sich einsetzen (bei)*	cf	lobby group
▸ **to take action**	*aktiv werden*	adj	active
▸ **contribution**	*Beitrag*	vti	to contribute sth (to sth)
▸ **fundraising event**	*Spendenaktion*	cf	funds – *Gelder*
▸ **to make a difference**	*etwas bewirken*	≈	to achieve sth

Sea Shepherd – sea terrorists or Neptune's Navy?

Sea Shepherd Conservation Society sees its mission as enforcing international law under the UN World Charter for Nature. Specifically, it aims to protect marine wildlife worldwide, including seals, dolphins and whales.

Unlike Greenpeace, Sea Shepherd's activities are not confined to peaceful protest and publicity stunts. Its activists are prepared to sink ships and damage or destroy property, where this can be done without endangering human life. Since 1979 the organization has sunk 10 ships, but nobody has been killed or seriously injured during any of its actions.

Sea Shepherd's method of direct action attracts plenty of critics, including of course its targets, especially countries that are involved in hunting and killing whales. The organization's opponents have referred to Sea Shepherd as 'pirates' and 'terrorists' and claim that its activities are illegal. Japan has repeatedly asked the USA to declare Sea Shepherd a terrorist organization.

To others, Sea Shepherd's crews are heroes and 'eco-warriors'. Its crews are mostly young volunteers from many different countries. When in port its ships are frequently visited by enthusiastic members of the public who wish to show their approval of and support for Sea Shepherd's work.

Sea Shepherd's activities – including operating three ships and some smaller boats – are extremely expensive. The organization relies on donations from individuals and from companies to fund its activities. In the US and the Netherlands it is registered as a not-for-profit organization and Sea Shepherd UK is a registered charity.

Sea Shepherd argues that it is in fact upholding and enforcing laws that national governments are not prepared to enforce for fear of endangering trade agreements and diplomatic relations with the countries that violate international law in the world's oceans.

Sea Shepherd's methods are controversial and many environmentalists argue that, though well-meaning, Sea Shepherd does more harm than good, by giving the environmentalist movement a radical image and encouraging extremist animal rights activitists through its example.

▸ **navy** ['neɪvi]	*Marine*	adj	naval
▸ **conservation**	*(Natur-)Schutz*	vt	to conserve
▸ **mission** ['mɪʃn]	*Aufgabe*	phr	~ statement
▸ **to enforce**	*durchsetzen*	n	enforcement
▸ **law**	*Recht*	adj	lawful, legal
▸ **to protect**	*schützen*	n	protection
▸ **wildlife**	*Tierwelt*	≈	fauna
▸ **activity**	*Aktivität, Handlung*	adj	active
▸ **to be confined to**	*sich beschränken auf*	≈	to be limited to
▸ **peaceful**	*friedlich*	n	peace
▸ **publicity stunt**	*öffentlichkeitswirksamer Einsatz*	vt	to publicize
▸ **activist**	*Aktivist/in*	cf	activism
▸ **to damage**	*beschädigen*	n	damage
▸ **to destroy**	*zerstören*	n	destruction
▸ **property**	*Eigentum*	≈	possessions
▸ **to endanger**	*gefährden*	≈	to put in danger
▸ **to injure**	*verletzen*	n	injury
▸ **direct action**	*direkte Aktion*	phr	to take ~
▸ **critic**	*Kritiker/in*	vt	to criticize
▸ **target**	*Ziel*	vt	to target
▸ **opponent**	*Gegner/in*	vt	to oppose
▸ **to declare sb sth**	*jdn zu etw erklären*	n	declaration
▸ **terrorist organization**	*Terrororganisation*	cf	terrorism
▸ **hero**	*Held*	adj	heroic
▸ **eco-warrior**	*Ökokrieger*	cf	ecology – *Umweltschutz, Ökologie*
▸ **volunteer**	*Freiwillige/r*	vi, v prep	to volunteer (for)
▸ **member of the public**	*Angehörige/r der Öffentlichkeit*	≈	person in the street
▸ **approval**	*Zustimmung*	vti, v prep	to approve (of)
▸ **support**	*Unterstützung*	vt	to support
▸ **donation**	*Spende*	vt	to donate
▸ **to fund**	*finanzieren*	n	funding
▸ **to register**	*eintragen*	n	registration
▸ **not-for-profit organization**	*gemeinnützige Organisation*	≈	non-profit-making organization
▸ **charity**	*Wohltätigkeitsorganisation*	adj	charitable
▸ **to uphold**	*wahren, schützen*	≈	to maintain, defend
▸ **trade agreement**	*Handelsabkommen*	≈	trade treaty
▸ **diplomatic relations**	*diplomatische Beziehungen*	n	diplomacy
▸ **to violate**	*verletzen*	n	violation
▸ **controversial**	*umstritten*	n	controversy
▸ **environmentalist**	*Umweltschützer/in*	adj	environmental
▸ **well-meaning**	*mit guten Absichten*	≈	well-intentioned
▸ **harm**	*Schaden*	vt	to harm
▸ **animal rights**	*Tierrechte*	phr	~ group

http://newsserver.stayinformed.info/wto.aspx

WTO Conference:

Eyewitness reports from the demonstrations

"There are around 50,000 citizens protesting peacefully here. Sure, there are a few extremists and trouble-makers among them, but the police have been very heavy-handed. There was no need to use tear gas and rubber bullets to break up the demonstrations, or to arrest hundreds of people. After all, intolerance of dissent is a characteristic of dictatorship, not of democracy."

– Local student

"The police have done a great job in difficult circumstances, showing restraint under extreme provocation. We have seen rioting and destruction of property on a shocking scale. The authorities were right to declare a state of emergency and impose a curfew. The moderate protesters have a legitimate message, but there is no excuse for resorting to violence and rampaging through our city intimidating local residents and looting stores."

– Local resident

"The activists and ordinary citizens out on the streets are defending the common rights of all people, upholding the principles of justice and sustainability. Citizens from all walks of life and all parts of the world are united here in rejecting the economic dictatorship of the World Trade Organization. Petitions, marches and rallies around the globe show that we have a broad base of support."

– Environmental protester

"We respect that the protesters are standing up for their rights, but the talks must go on. We must be able to voice our legitimate concerns to the rich countries, and this is the best place for us to do so. The protesters are well-intentioned, but they're doing more harm than good."

– African delegate to the talks

▸ **citizen**	*Bürger/in*		
▸ **to protest** [prə'test]	*protestieren*	n	protest ['prəʊtest]
▸ **peacefully**	*friedlich*	n	peace
▸ **trouble-maker**	*Unruhestifter/in*	cf	to make trouble
▸ **heavy-handed**	*hart durchgreifend*	<>	restrained
▸ **tear gas** [tɪə]	*Tränengas*		
▸ **rubber bullet**	*Gummigeschoss*		
▸ **to break up**	*auflösen*		
▸ **to arrest**	*verhaften*	n	arrest
▸ **intolerance of**	*Intoleranz gegenüber*	adj	intolerant
▸ **dissent**	*abweichende Meinung*	vi	to dissent
▸ **dictatorship**	*Diktatur*	adj	dictatorial
▸ **democracy**	*Demokratie*	adj	democratic
▸ **restraint**	*Zurückhaltung*	vt	to restrain
▸ **provocation**	*Provokation*	vt	to provoke
▸ **rioting**	*Randale, Krawalle*	n	riot – *Aufstand*
▸ **destruction**	*Zerstörung*	vt	to destroy
▸ **property**	*Eigentum*		
▸ **authorities** [ɔː'θɒrətiz]	*Behörden*	cf	authority – *Autorität*
▸ **to declare a state of emergency**	*den Notstand ausrufen*		
▸ **to impose a curfew**	*eine Ausgangssperre verhängen*		
▸ **moderate** ['mɒdərət]	*gemäßigt*	<>	extreme, radical
▸ **legitimate** [lɪ'dʒɪtɪmət]	*berechtigt, begründet*	n	legitimacy
▸ **message**	*Botschaft*	cf	statement – *Aussage*
▸ **to resort to violence**	*gewalttätig werden*		
▸ **to rampage**	*randalieren*	≈	to go on the rampage
▸ **to intimidate**	*einschüchtern*	n	intimidation
▸ **resident**	*Einwohner/in*	adj	residential
▸ **to loot**	*plündern*	n	looting
▸ **to defend**	*verteidigen*	n	defence
▸ **common rights**	*allgemeine (Menschen-)Rechte*	cf	to have in common – *gemeinsam haben*
▸ **to uphold**	*(unter)stützen*		
▸ **justice**	*Gerechtigkeit*	adj	just
▸ **sustainability**	*nachhaltigkeit*	adj	sustainable
▸ **to unite**	*vereinen*	n	unity
▸ **to reject**	*ablehnen*	n	rejection
▸ **petition**	*Petition*	phr	to sign a ~
▸ **march**	*(Protest-)Marsch*	vi	to march
▸ **rally**	*(Protest-)Kundgebung*	phr	to hold a ~
▸ **broad base**	*breite Basis*		
▸ **support**	*Unterstützung*	vt	to support
▸ **to stand up for**	*sich einsetzen für*		
▸ **talks**	*Gespräche*	⚠	speech – *Rede*
▸ **to voice a concern**	*einer Sorge Ausdruck verleihen.*	vt	to concern
▸ **well-intentioned**	*mit guten Absichten*	n	good intentions
▸ **delegate** ['delɪgət]	*Delegierte/r*	vtl	to delegate ['delɪgeɪt]

G

Science and technology

1 Information technology

2 Energy technology

3 Transportation

4 Biotechnology and medicine

OPINION

State-of-the-art? Not for long!

Steve Nevell, video editor

As a freelance video editor, I need a reasonably powerful computer for my work, because encoding video is a processor-intensive task.

Three years ago, fresh out of college, I bought the latest, fastest, state-of-the-art computer – the best I could afford and at the cutting edge of PC technology. It ran all my applications at lightning speed and hardly ever crashed. Its processing power was impressive and its hard disk capacity enormous – far more, I thought, than I would ever need.

Six months later, my model was selling for half the price I had paid. A year later, my model was no longer being manufactured, so I was the owner of an officially obsolete computer, though it was still shiny and relatively new. I knew all this because I read computer magazines regularly, in order to keep up to date with technological advances.

After two years, I had upgraded my computer as far as possible: I had bought a faster processor and as much extra memory as I could fit in the case. An external hard drive was added to back up my files. I had installed a new graphics card. Despite these improvements, my computer seems to be getting slower. With little processing power and a tiny hard disk, it struggles even to run the latest version of the operating system. The powerful machine that I used to create amazing graphics three years ago is now so slow that it hardly seems adequate for typing a letter or sending an email.

I would like to buy a new monitor, printer and scanner, but the latest peripherals are not compatible with my old computer – their system requirements are just too high. So now I'm thinking of buying the latest, fastest, state-of-the-art model, with more processing power and hard disk capacity than I will ever need. Again.

1 Information technology

▸ **state-of-the-art**	*auf dem neuesten Stand*	≈	cutting-edge
▸ **video editor**	*Videoredakteur/in*	vt	to edit
▸ **freelance**	*freiberuflich*	n	freelancer
▸ **powerful**	*leistungsstark*	n	power
▸ **to encode**	*kodieren*	<>	to decode
▸ **processor-intensive**	*viel Rechnerleistung erfordernd*		
▸ **task**	*Aufgabe*		
▸ **latest**	*neuest*	<>	earliest
▸ **at the cutting edge**	*an der Spitze*		
▸ **technology**	*Technologie*	adj	technological
▸ **to run**	*laufen lassen*		
▸ **application**	*Anwendung, Computerprogramm*	≈	program
▸ **at lightning speed**	*mit Lichtgeschwindigkeit*		
▸ **to crash**	*abstürzen*	n	crash
▸ **processing power**	*Rechenleistung*	vt	to process
▸ **impressive**	*eindrucksvoll*	vt	to impress
▸ **hard disk**	*Festplatte*	≈	hard drive
▸ **capacity**	*(Speicher-)Kapazität*	≈	space
▸ **model**	*Modell*		
▸ **to manufacture**	*herstellen, produzieren*	≈	to produce
▸ **obsolete**	*veraltet, überholt*	≈	out of date
▸ **to keep up to date**	*auf dem Laufenden bleiben*		
▸ **technological advance**	*technischer Fortschritt*	vti	to advance
▸ **to upgrade** [ˌʌp'greɪd]	*nach-, aufrüsten*	n	upgrade ['ʌpgreɪd]
▸ **processor**	*Prozessor, Rechner*	cf	central processing unit (CPU)
▸ **memory**	*Speicher*	cf	random access memory (RAM)
▸ **case**	*Gehäuse*	≈	housing
▸ **external hard drive**	*externe Festplatte*	<>	internal hard drive
▸ **to back up**	*(als Sicherungskopie) speichern*	n	backup
▸ **file**	*Datei*		
▸ **graphics card**	*Grafikkarte*		
▸ **improvement**	*Verbesserung*	vti	to improve
▸ **to struggle to do sth**	*Mühe haben, etwas zu tun*	≈	to have difficulty doing sth
▸ **operating system**	*Betriebssystem*	vt	to operate
▸ **to create**	*erstellen*		
▸ **graphics**	*Grafiken*	adj	graphical
▸ **adequate** ['ædɪkwət]	*ausreichend*	<>	inadequate
▸ **monitor**	*Monitor*	≈	display, screen
▸ **printer**	*Drucker*	vt	to print (out)
▸ **scanner**	*Scanner*	vt	to scan (in)
▸ **peripheral** [pəˈrɪfərəl]	*Zusatz-, Peripheriegerät*	adj	peripheral
▸ **compatible**	*kompatibel*	n	compatibility
▸ **system requirements**	*Systemanforderungen*	vt	to require

Smart future for swarming robots

Swarms of robots could one day explore space or do hazardous jobs on Earth, say researchers. Prototypes of cooperating robots were on show at the Artificial Life conference this week.

Advances in technology mean that it is now possible to create tiny robots for as little as £24. Roboticists say the swarms of robots could prove more adaptable and smarter than individual, self-contained ones.

"For a long time in robotics there was this focus on a 'smart machine', an android that would make you breakfast and go out and buy your shopping," said Dr Seth Bullock from the University of Southampton.

"But that's extremely challenging; it's far easier for us to engineer little simple things and rely on them to organize themselves."

To that end, a group of undergraduate students at the University of Southampton has developed a swarm of identical, matchbox-sized robots, each of which costs just £24 to produce.

Demonstrated at the conference, the prototypes showed how swarm robots can independently divide up tasks, with no central program controlling them. They communicate with each other via infrared technology like that used in mobile phones.

"You might have a complex robot that is sent to Mars develop a technical fault, and then the mission is basically over," said Klaus-Peter Zauner, the leader of the Southampton project.

"With swarm robots, even if some of them fail, they'll still be able to achieve their goal."

The robots can also cope with events their designers never predicted. They have been equipped with software that learns and adapts as it encounters new situations.

Planetary exploration and assembly of satellites and space stations are two applications for swarm robots, but they could also be of great use on Earth.

Swarms of tiny robots could be deployed in a collapsed building, for instance, dividing their tasks among looking for survivors and checking for further dangers such as gas leaks.

[http://news.bbc.co.uk/go/pr/fr/-/2/hi/technology/7549059.stm]

1 Information technology

▸ **to swarm**	*ausschwärmen*		
▸ **swarm**	*Schwarm*	phr	~ of bees, wasps, insects
▸ **to explore**	*erforschen*	adj	exploratory
▸ **space**	*Weltall, -raum*	phr	to go into ~
▸ **hazardous**	*gefährlich*	≈	dangerous
▸ **researcher** [rɪ'sɜːtʃə]	*Forscher/in*	vt	to research
▸ **prototype**	*Prototyp*	vt	to prototype
▸ **to cooperate** [kəʊ'ɒpəreɪt]	*zusammenarbeiten*	n	cooperation
▸ **artificial**	*künstlich*	<>	natural
▸ **advance**	*Fortschritt*	vti	to advance
▸ **technology**	*Technologie, Technik*	⚠	≠ technique – *Methode*
▸ **adaptable**	*anpassungsfähig*	vti	to adapt
▸ **smart**	*intelligent*	≈	intelligent
▸ **self-contained**	*unabhängig, autark*	≈	stand-alone
▸ **robotics** [rəʊ'bɒtɪks]	*Robotik, Robotertechnik*	cf	roboticist [rəʊ'bɒtəsɪst]
▸ **focus on**	*Konzentration auf*	v prep	to focus on
▸ **challenging**	*herausfordernd*	vt	to challenge
▸ **to engineer**	*entwickeln*	n	engineering
▸ **simple**	*einfach*	<>	complex
▸ **to rely on sb/sth**	*es jdm/etwas überlassen*	adj	reliable
▸ **to develop**	*entwickeln*	n	development
▸ **to produce**	*herstellen, produzieren*	n	production
▸ **independently**	*unabhängig*	≈	autonomously
▸ **task**	*Aufgabe*	≈	assignment
▸ **to communicate**	*kommunizieren*	n	communication
▸ **infrared**	*infrarot*	<>	ultraviolet
▸ **complex**	*kompliziert*	n	complexity
▸ **fault**	*Defekt, Fehler*	≈	error, glitch (coll)
▸ **mission**	*Mission*	phr	~ accomplished
▸ **to be over**	*vorbei sein*	≈	to be at an end
▸ **to fail**	*versagen*	n	failure
▸ **to achieve**	*erreichen*	n	achievement
▸ **goal**	*Ziel*	≈	objective
▸ **to cope with**	*fertig werden mit*	≈	to deal with, to handle
▸ **event**	*Ereignis*	≈	occurrence
▸ **to predict**	*vorhersehen*	≈	to anticipate
▸ **to equip with**	*ausstatten mit*	n	equipment
▸ **to adapt**	*(sich) anpassen*	n	adaptation
▸ **to encounter**	*stoßen auf*	n	encounter
▸ **planetary** ['plænətri]	*Planeten-*	phr	inter~ space flight
▸ **exploration**	*Erkundung*	cf	explorer
▸ **assembly**	*Montage*	vt	to assemble
▸ **space station**	*Raumstation*	cf	space craft
▸ **application**	*Anwendung*	vt	to apply sth to sth
▸ **to deploy**	*einsetzen*	n	deployment
▸ **survivor**	*Überlebende/r*	vti	to survive
▸ **danger**	*Gefahr*	≈	hazard

Artificial intelligence

Interviewer … Dr Franklin, what exactly is artificial intelligence?

Franklin A branch of science concerned with creating computers which "think". Finding solutions to that problem involves computer science and robotics – but also psychology, linguistics and so on. Different research teams around the world have adopted different approaches – and different definitions of the goal.

Interviewer Why is that?

Franklin Well, we frankly can't agree on a universal definition of intelligence. The British scientist Alan Turing considered that a computer is intelligent if its behaviour is indistinguishable from that of a human. But is that just the simulation of intelligence?

Interviewer What's your definition?

Franklin Personally, I don't think it matters in the short term. What we are aiming for is a computer which is able to learn – that is, which is able to experiment with ways of achieving a goal, and come up with more and more efficient solutions. That requires making decisions, gathering, analysing and comparing data and making deductions – which lead to improved decisions. At first, its decisions will be made randomly and it will proceed by pure trial and error; as it acquires more knowledge, it will be able to reason.

Interviewer And in the longer term?

Franklin We may have to address more difficult issues. Does true intelligence require personality? Do we need to create a synthetic life form which has emotions and opinions? Which has self-awareness?

Interviewer Why do you say you may have to address these issues?

Franklin It depends on what we want. Will we be satisfied with practical applications of artificial intelligence – such as computers which can interact with us in natural language and robots which can perform intricate tasks like surgery without supervision? Or must we push back the boundaries until we create computers with superhuman intelligence – which could evolve into god-like beings?

Interviewer That sounds a terrifying prospect!

Franklin Yes, but an interesting challenge, don't you think?

artificial intelligence	*künstliche Intelligenz*		
branch	*Zweig*		
science ['saɪəns]	*Wissenschaft*	adj	scientific [ˌsaɪən'tɪfɪk]
computer science	*Informatik*	cf	computer scientist
robotics [rəʊ'bɒtɪks]	*Robotik, Robotertechnik*	cf	robot ['rəʊbɒt] – *Roboter*
linguistics	*Linguistik*	adj	linguistic
research team	*Forscherteam*	vt	to research
to adopt an approach	*einen Ansatz wählen*	vt	to approach
goal	*Ziel*	≈	objective
universal	*universell, allgemein*	n	universality
scientist ['saɪəntɪst]	*Wissenschaftler/in*		
indistinguishable [ˌɪndɪ'stɪŋgwɪʃəbl]	*nicht zu unterscheiden*	vt	to distinguish – *unterscheiden*
in the short term	*vorläufig, kurzfristig*	adj	short-term
to experiment	*experimentieren*	n	experiment
to achieve	*erreichen*	n	achievement
to gather	*sammeln*	≈	to collect
to analyse ['ænəlaɪz]	*analysieren*	n	analysis [ə'næləsɪs]
data	*Daten*		
to make a deduction	*eine Schlussfolgerung ziehen*	adj	deductive
randomly	*zufällig*	≈	at random
to proceed	*vorgehen*	n	procedure
trial and error	*Ausprobieren, Versuch und Irrtum*		
to acquire	*sich aneignen*	n	acquisition
knowledge	*Wissen*	adj	knowledgeable
to reason	*logisch denken*	n	reasoning
personality	*Persönlichkeit*		
synthetic [sɪn'θetɪk]	*synthetisch, künstlich*	≈	artificial
life form	*Lebensform*	≈	form of life
self-awareness	*Selbstbewusstsein*	adj	self-aware
practical	*praktisch*	n	practice
application	*Anwendung*	vt	to apply
to interact with	*interagieren mit*	n	interaction
to perform a task	*eine Aufgabe ausführen*	≈	to carry out a task
intricate ['ɪntrɪkət]	*kompliziert*	n	intricacy
surgery	*Chirurgie*	cf	surgeon – *Chirurg/in*
supervision	*Aufsicht*	vt	to supervise
to push back the boundaries	*die Grenzen weiter hinausschieben*	≈	to push back the frontiers
superhuman	*übermenschlich*	<>	subhuman
to evolve into	*sich entwickeln zu*	n	evolution
prospect	*Aussicht*		
challenge	*Herausforderung*	vt	to challenge

www.blogspot.info/techblogIO.php

Joe's Blog

Tech-Blog: random thoughts of an IT geek:

The future of mobile phones

It's difficult to predict what mobile phones will be like in 10 years' time, but here are some trends which are already changing the design of phones.

Convergence

This is the idea of having one device that will perform a variety of functions. Mobile phones already incorporate a camera capable of taking photos and videos with sound, and a music player. They also run software applications such as a web browser, a photo library and a calendar. After all, a phone has a microprocessor and a solid-state memory, so in theory it can do anything a computer can do.

Miniaturization

There are practical limits to how far you can miniaturize screens, keys, etc. because if a phone is too small for human hands and human eyes it is useless. So the actual physical size of phones will stay constant (but see bionics below). What we will certainly see is further miniaturization of printed circuits, leading to smaller, more powerful processors, and the development of smaller, longer-lasting power sources. The phone of 10 years' time will probably have more computing power than the average PC today.

New user interfaces

Up until recently, mobile phone users required a keypad to control their phones. PDAs and other phone-like devices have experimented with the use of a stylus to write text, but that isn't a useful option for phones. The iPhone was the first commercially successful phone to use a touch-sensitive screen and orientation sensor instead of a keypad. Voice control for a phone seems a bit problematic – how does the phone recognize that you are talking to it and not to the person you are phoning?

Bionics

We may see communication devices actually embedded in people's bodies. This would enable them to monitor the user's health as well as function as a phone. The human body could also provide a convenient, ever-lasting power source for the device. A telepathic interface would be used to control the device: the user would think of calling someone and a communication link would be established. Hmm, maybe that idea's a bit too freaky to catch on ...

1 Information technology

▸ **random**	*zufällig*		
▸ **geek**	*Computerfreak*		
▸ **mobile phone** (BE)	*Handy, Mobiltelefon*	AE	cell(ular) phone
▸ **to predict**	*vorhersagen*	n	prediction
▸ **design**	*Design*	vt	to design
▸ **convergence** [kən'vɜːdʒəns]	*Zusammenpassen*	vi, v prep	to converge (with)
▸ **device**	*Gerät*	≈	piece of equipment
▸ **to perform**	*erledigen*	≈	to carry out
▸ **variety**	*Vielfalt*	adj	varied
▸ **function**	*Funktion*	adj	functional
▸ **to incorporate**	*enthalten*	≈	to include
▸ **application**	*Anwendung, Programm*	≈	program
▸ **photo library**	*Fotoarchiv*	cf	photo album
▸ **calendar**	*Kalender*	cf	diary – *Tagebuch, Terminkalender*
▸ **solid-state memory**	*Halbleiterspeicher*	cf	solid-state drive (SSD)
▸ **in theory**	*theoretisch*	<>	in practice
▸ **miniaturization**	*Miniaturisierung*	vt	to miniaturize
▸ **limit**	*Grenze*	adj	limited
▸ **screen**	*Bildschirm*	≈	display
▸ **key**	*Taste*	cf	keyboard – *Tastatur*
▸ **useless**	*nutzlos*	<>	useful
▸ **to stay constant**	*konstant bleiben*	≈	to stay the same
▸ **printed circuit**	*gedruckter Schaltkreis*	vt	to print
▸ **powerful**	*stark*	n	power
▸ **development**	*Entwicklung*	vti	to develop
▸ **long-lasting**	*lange reichend*	≈	long-lived
▸ **power source**	*Akku, Stromquelle*	≈	power supply
▸ **computing power**	*Rechenleistung*	vt	to compute
▸ **user interface**	*Benutzeroberfläche*	phr	graphical ~ (GUI)
▸ **keypad**	*Tastatur*	v prep	to key in
▸ **commercially**	*kommerziell*	adj	commercial
▸ **successful**	*erfolgreich*	vi	to succeed
▸ **touch-sensitive**	*berührungsempfindlich*	cf	to be sensitive to sth
▸ **orientation sensor**	*Orientierungssensor*	vt	to sense – *wahrnehmen*
▸ **voice control**	*Sprachsteuerung*	cf	speech recognition – *Spracherkennung*
▸ **to recognize**	*erkennen*	n	recognition
▸ **to embed**	*einsetzen, implantieren*	≈	to implant
▸ **to monitor**	*überwachen*	n	monitor
▸ **to function as**	*funktionieren als*	≈	to serve as
▸ **convenient**	*bequem*	n	convenience
▸ **ever-lasting**	*immerwährend*	<>	temporary
▸ **communication link**	*Sprechverbindung*	vt	to link sth with sth
▸ **to establish**	*herstellen*	≈	to set up
▸ **freaky** (coll)	*verrückt*	≈	weird, bizarre
▸ **to catch on**	*sich durchsetzen*	≈	to become popular

www.lifeaftertheoilcrash.net

End of the oil age

Known reserves of oil are going to run out some time in the next few decades, but a long time before they run out, they will become prohibitively expensive to extract from the ground. We need to plan for the end of cheap oil.

On the face of it, the solution seems relatively easy: switch to electric cars and other alternative forms of transport. However, oil is needed for many other purposes than fuelling cars. Nearly every economic activity – including manufacturing, construction and transport – depends on energy which is derived from fossil fuels, and on materials which are made from petrochemicals.

Let's look at a basic necessity, food:

In industrialized countries, approximately 10 kilojoules of fossil fuels are required to produce every 1 kilojoule of food. This is because every step of modern food production is powered by fossil fuels and petrochemicals:

- Pesticides and other agricultural chemicals are made from oil.
- Commercial fertilizers are made from ammonia, which is made from natural gas.
- Farm machinery such as tractors is constructed and powered using fuels derived from oil.
- Refrigerators are manufactured in oil-powered plants, distributed using oil-powered transport and run on electricity.

All electrical devices make use of silver, copper, aluminium and platinum, each of which is discovered, extracted and processed using oil or natural gas powered machinery. So no oil might mean no computers, no internet, no mobile phones.

Some people see the solution to the looming oil shortage in biofuels. However, it's important to bear in mind that the crops used for biofuels such as biodiesel and ethanol are grown using the high-tech, oil-powered industrial methods of farming described above. In other words, the so-called 'alternatives' to oil are actually derivatives of oil.

It's a similar story when it comes to other 'alternative' sources of energy. Solar arrays, wind farms, hydrogen fuel cells and nuclear power plants all rely on sophisticated technology and energy-intensive forms of metallurgy. In fact, it's difficult to think of an aspect of modern technology that isn't directly or indirectly a petroleum product.

[Adapted extracts: www.lifeaftertheoilcrash.net]

▸ **oil**	*(Erd-)Öl*	phr	crude ~, ~ refinery
▸ **reserve**	*Reserve*	phr	to have sth in ~
▸ **to run out**	*zu Ende gehen*	≈	to be exhausted, used up
▸ **prohibitively**	*unerschwinglich, untragbar*	≈	excessively
▸ **to extract**	*herausholen*	n	extraction
▸ **solution (to)**	*Lösung (für)*	vt	to solve
▸ **to switch to**	*umstellen auf*	≈	to change (over) to
▸ **to fuel**	*antreiben*	n	fuel
▸ **manufacturing**	*Produktion*	vt	to manufacture
▸ **construction**	*Bau*	vt	to construct
▸ **to depend on**	*abhängen von*	n	dependence on
▸ **to be derived from**	*stammen aus*	n	derivation
▸ **fossil fuel**	*fossiler Brennstoff*		
▸ **petrochemical**	*Petrochemikalie*		
▸ **basic necessity**	*Grundbedürfnis*	≈	fundamental need
▸ **to power**	*antreiben*	n	power
▸ **agricultural**	*landwirtschaftlich*	n	agriculture
▸ **chemical**	*Chemikalie*	adj	chemical
▸ **fertilizer**	*Dünger*	adj	fertile
▸ **natural gas**	*Erdgas*	cf	town gas – *Leuchtgas*
▸ **machinery**	*Maschinen(park)*	≈	machines
▸ **to construct**	*bauen*	≈	to build
▸ **refrigerator**	*Kühlschrank*	≈	fridge
▸ **to manufacture**	*herstellen*	≈	to make
▸ **oil-powered**	*durch Öl angetrieben*	vt	to power
▸ **plant**	*Fabrik, Betrieb*	≈	power station
▸ **to distribute**	*ausliefern*	n	distribution
▸ **to run on**	*betreiben mit*		
▸ **electrical**	*elektrisch, Elektro-*	n	electricity
▸ **device**	*Gerät*	≈	(piece of) equipment
▸ **copper**	*Kupfer*		
▸ **to discover**	*entdecken*	n	discovery
▸ **to process**	*verarbeiten*	phr	processing plant
▸ **to loom**	*sich abzeichnen*	≈	to be impending
▸ **shortage**	*Knappheit, Mangel*	cf	to be short of
▸ **biofuel**	*Biotreibstoff*	cf	biodiesel
▸ **crop**	*Ernte*	phr	to harvest a ~
▸ **industrial**	*industriell*	n	industry
▸ **derivative of oil**	*Ölderivat*	≈	product of oil
▸ **source**	*Quelle*	vt	to source sth
▸ **solar array**	*Solaranlage*	cf	solar power
▸ **wind farm**	*Windpark, -kraftanlage*	cf	wind power
▸ **hydrogen**	*Wasserstoff*	phr	~ bomb
▸ **fuel cell**	*Brennstoffzelle*		
▸ **nuclear power plant**	*Kernkraftwerk*	≈	nuclear power station
▸ **to rely on**	*angewiesen sein auf*	n	reliable
▸ **sophisticated**	*kompliziert*	n	sophistication
▸ **energy-intensive**	*energieintensiv*	cf	energy-efficient
▸ **(in)directly**	*(in)direkt*	adj	(in)direct

World of Science

Solar power

Solar power is perhaps the ultimate 'clean, green' energy: it has an inexhaustible fuel source, produces no pollution and is extremely versatile – it can be used to run items as diverse as domestic appliances, solar cars and satellites.

Broadly speaking, there are three methods of harnessing energy from the sun's rays: photovoltaic, passive and active.

Photovoltaic systems use solar cells, combined in solar panels, which in turn are connected together to form solar arrays. The cells are made of a semiconductor material such as silicon, and convert light directly into electricity. They are used in many everyday devices.

Passive systems have no moving parts. The sun's rays are simply absorbed by the structure. They are a cheap, low-tech method of using solar energy. For example, one type of solar oven is simply an insulated black box. It is extremely efficient in constant sunlight, and in developing countries offers a simple means of cooking food without burning wood. Solar ovens can be constructed from cheap, locally available materials.

Active systems use a fluid, often water. They are commonly used to provide hot water to residential and commercial buildings. One type uses an array of glass tubes with a vacuum inside them and copper pipes running through the centre, carrying water. The copper pipes are connected to a circulation pump which transfers the hot water to an insulated storage tank. Because it operates on a heat exchange principle, it does not require direct sunlight.

2 Energy technology

▸ **solar power**	*Sonnenenergie*	≈	solar energy
▸ **inexhaustible** [ˌɪnɪg'zɔːstəbl]	*unerschöpflich*	vt	to exhaust
▸ **fuel source** ['fjuːəl sɔːs]	*Kraftstoffquelle*	vt	to fuel
▸ **pollution**	*Umweltverschmutzung*	vt	to pollute
▸ **versatile**	*vielseitig*	n	versatility
▸ **domestic appliance**	*Haushaltgerät*	≈	household appliance
▸ **satellite**	*Satellit*		
▸ **to harness**	*nutzbar machen*	≈	to exploit, to employ
▸ **ray**	*Strahl*	cf	radiation – *(Aus-) Strahlung*
▸ **photovoltaic** [ˌfəʊtəʊvɒl'teɪɪk]	*photoelektrisch, -voltaisch*	n	photovoltaics (plural)
▸ **passive**	*passiv*	cf	inert – *träge, inert*
▸ **active**	*aktiv*	cf	dynamic
▸ **solar cell**	*Solarzelle*	adj	cellular
▸ **to combine**	*verknüpfen*	n	combination
▸ **solar panel**	*Sonnenkollektor*		
▸ **to connect**	*verbinden*	n	connection
▸ **solar array**	*Solaranlage*		
▸ **semiconductor**	*Halbleiter*	vt	to conduct
▸ **material**	*Material*	≈	substance
▸ **silicon**	*Silizium*	phr	~ chip, S~ Valley
▸ **to convert into**	*umwandeln in*	n	conversion into
▸ **directly**	*direkt*	<>	indirectly
▸ **electricity**	*Elektrizität, Strom*	adj	electric(al)
▸ **device**	*Gerät*	≈	piece of equipment
▸ **moving part**	*bewegliches Teil*	vti	to move
▸ **to absorb**	*absorbieren, aufnehmen*	adj	absorbent
▸ **structure**	*Konstruktion*	cf	construction – *Bau(weise)*
▸ **low-tech**	*technisch einfach*	<>	high-tech
▸ **oven**	*Ofen, Herd*	cf	cooker – *(Koch-)Herd*
▸ **to insulate**	*isolieren*	⚠	≠ isolate – *absondern*
▸ **efficient**	*leistungsfähig*	n	efficiency
▸ **sunlight**	*Sonnenlicht*		
▸ **to construct**	*bauen*	≈	to build
▸ **fluid**	*Flüssigkeit*	≈	liquid
▸ **residential**	*Wohn-*	≈	domestic
▸ **commercial**	*Büro-, gewerblich*	≈	business
▸ **tube**	*Röhre*		
▸ **vacuum**	*Vakuum*	phr	partial ~
▸ **copper**	*Kupfer*		
▸ **pipe**	*Rohr*	cf	pipework – *Rohrnetz*
▸ **to transfer**	*befördern*	n	transfer
▸ **storage tank**	*Wasserspeicher*	vt	to store
▸ **to operate**	*arbeiten*	n	operation
▸ **heat exchange**	*Wärmetausch-*	vt	to exchange
▸ **principle**	*Prinzip*		
▸ **to require**	*benötigen*	n	requirement

http://reference.greenwiki.org.au/windfarms.html

Wind farms – clean and green

Wind farms offer the promise of pollution-free electricity which does not deplete reserves of fossil fuels and does not have the inherent risk and waste-disposal problems of nuclear reactors.

The process of using wind power to generate electricity can be described in simple terms. The wind turns the blades of the wind turbine; this turns a generator which produces electricity. The electricity is fed into the power grid and becomes available to consumers.

One limitation of wind farms is that the wind is an intermittent power source. When the wind doesn't blow, the turbines produce no electricity. When it's too windy, the turbines may have to be turned off to prevent damage occurring. For this reason, wind power is currently seen as only a partial solution to meeting a country's energy needs. (In Denmark it accounts for around 20% of electricity generation.) Other forms of energy, such as conventional power stations, are still required to provide reliable baseload power.

However, as power grids are increasingly interlinked over whole continents, local variations in wind speed can be compensated for. It may eventually become practical to rely on wind power and other renewable power sources to provide all our electricity.

Another limitation is that wind turbines are not very intensive energy producers. You would need a lot of them to provide enough electricity to supply a medium-sized town or a large industrial plant, for example. If you want to generate large amounts of electricity from wind, you need a lot of space. In densely populated countries, this means that purchasing the land for a wind farm may simply be too expensive. To some extent, this problem can be solved by locating wind farms offshore.

Of course, resources are consumed in manufacturing and assembling wind turbines. Steel, concrete, aluminum and other materials have to be made and transported using energy-intensive processes, generally involving fossil fuels and hence carbon emissions. The good news is the 'payback time' on these initial carbon emissions is only around nine months of operation for offshore wind farms.

▸ **wind farm**	*Windpark, -kraftanlage*	cf	wind turbine
▸ **promise**	*Versprechen*	adj	promising
▸ **pollution-free**	*ohne Umweltverschmutzung*	<>	polluting
▸ **electricity**	*Elektrizität, Strom*	adj	electrical
▸ **to deplete**	*aufbrauchen*	n	depletion
▸ **reserve**	*Reserve*	≈	supply
▸ **fossil fuel**	*fossiler Brennstoff*	cf	coal – *Kohle*, oil – *Öl*
▸ **waste-disposal**	*Abfallentsorgung*	v prep	to dispose of
▸ **nuclear reactor**	*Kernkraftwerk*	v prep	to react to/with
▸ **wind power**	*Windkraft*	cf	solar power
▸ **to generate**	*erzeugen*	n	generation
▸ **blade**	*Schaufel*	≈	rotor ~
▸ **generator** ['dʒenəreɪtə]	*Generator, Stromerzeuger*	cf	wind ~
▸ **to feed sth into sth**	*etw in etw einspeisen*	<>	to draw sth from sth
▸ **power grid**	*Stromnetz*	≈	national grid
▸ **available**	*verfügbar*	n	availability
▸ **consumer**	*Verbraucher/in*	vt	to consume
▸ **limitation**	*Einschränkung*	adj	limited
▸ **intermittent**	*sporadisch*	<>	constant
▸ **power source**	*Stromquelle*		
▸ **damage**	*Beschädigung*	vt	to damage
▸ **partial**	*Teil-*	<>	complete
▸ **solution to**	*Lösung für*	vt	to solve
▸ **to meet one's needs**	*den Bedarf decken*		
▸ **to account for**	*ausmachen*	≈	to constitute
▸ **power station**	*Kraftwerk*	≈	power plant
▸ **reliable**	*zuverlässig*	v prep	to rely on
▸ **baseload power**	*Grundlaststrom*	<>	peak load power
▸ **to interlink**	*verbinden*	≈	to link together
▸ **local**	*lokal, örtlich*	<>	widespread
▸ **variation**	*Schwankung*	vti	to vary
▸ **to compensate for**	*ausgleichen*	n	compensation
▸ **renewable**	*erneuerbar*	vt	to renew
▸ **to supply**	*versorgen*	n	supply
▸ **industrial plant**	*Industriebetrieb*	≈	factory
▸ **densely populated**	*dicht besiedelt*	<>	sparsely populated
▸ **to locate**	*aufstellen*	n	location
▸ **offshore**	*vor der Küste*	<>	onshore
▸ **resource**	*Ressource*	phr	natural ~
▸ **to consume**	*verbrauchen*	n	consumption
▸ **to manufacture**	*herstellen*	≈	to construct, to produce
▸ **to assemble**	*montieren*	≈	to put together
▸ **steel**	*Stahl*	cf	iron – *Eisen*
▸ **concrete**	*Beton*	cf	cement – *Zement*
▸ **to transport**	*transportieren*	n	transport(ation)
▸ **energy-intensive**	*energieintensiv*	<>	energy-efficient
▸ **carbon emissions**	*Kohlendioxidausstoß*	vt	to emit
▸ **payback time**	*Amortisationszeit*	vt	to pay back

World of Science

Nuclear power

Nuclear power plants function in a similar way to oil and gas-fired plants. Heat energy is used to pressurize a gas, which drives a turbine linked to a generator. In a nuclear power plant, however, the heat comes from the fission of unstable isotopes of heavy metals.

There are currently approximately 440 nuclear power reactors in operation in over 25 countries around the world. Only a few years ago it seemed unlikely that new ones would be built, mainly because of the following problems:

- Radioactive waste is produced at almost every stage of the production and use of nuclear fuel. Although low-level waste can be disposed of relatively safely, there is still no accepted long-term solution to the problem of high-level waste.
- The consequences of accidents at nuclear power plants can be catastrophic. The melt-down of the reactor at Chernobyl is the worst example to date.

However, in recent years there has been a resurgence in popularity of nuclear power because of a growing awareness of the environmental impact of conventional power plants which burn fossil fuels.

New reactor designs could make nuclear fission far safer in the future, but perhaps a better long-term solution lies in nuclear fusion. If fusion reactors prove to be both technologically possible and commercially viable, they will provide inexhaustible energy from the hydrogen isotopes deuterium (found in water) and tritium (made in the reactor).

2 Energy technology

▸ **nuclear power**	*Kernenergie*	≈	atomic power
▸ **power plant**	*Kraftwerk*	≈	power station
▸ **to function**	*funktionieren, arbeiten*	≈	to operate
▸ **oil-fired**	*ölbetrieben*	≈	oil-powered
▸ **gas-fired**	*gasbetrieben*	≈	gas-powered
▸ **heat energy**	*Wärmeenergie*	cf	heat – *Hitze*
▸ **to pressurize**	*unter Druck setzen*	n	pressure – *Druck*
▸ **to drive**	*(an)treiben*	≈	to power
▸ **turbine** ['tɜːbaɪn]	*Turbine*		
▸ **to link to**	*verbinden mit*	≈	to connect to
▸ **generator** ['dʒenəreɪtə]	*Generator, Stromerzeuger*	vt	to generate
▸ **fission**	*Spaltung*	cf	to split – *spalten*
▸ **unstable**	*instabil*	n	instability
▸ **isotope** ['aɪsətəʊp]	*Isotop*		
▸ **heavy metal**	*Schwermetall*		
▸ **reactor** [ri'æktə]	*Reaktor*	v prep	to react to/with
▸ **in operation**	*in Betrieb*	vti	to operate
▸ **radioactive waste**	*Atommüll*	n	radioactivity
▸ **to produce**	*erzeugen*	≈	to create
▸ **stage**	*Stadium*	≈	step
▸ **production**	*Produktion*	vt	to produce
▸ **fuel**	*Brennstoff*	vt	to fuel
▸ **low-level**	*gering (strahlend)*	cf	a low level of
▸ **to dispose of**	*entsorgen*	n	disposal
▸ **long-term**	*langfristig*	phr	in the long term
▸ **solution to**	*Lösung für*	vt	to solve
▸ **high-level**	*stark (strahlend)*	cf	a high level of
▸ **consequence**	*Folge*	adv	consequently
▸ **accident**	*Unfall*	adj	accidental
▸ **catastrophic** [ˌkætə'strɒfɪk]	*katastrophal*	n	catastrophe [kə'tæstrəfi]
▸ **melt-down**	*Kernschmelze*	vi	to melt down
▸ **to date**	*bis dato*	≈	so far
▸ **resurgence in** [rɪ'sɜːdʒəns]	*Wiederaufleben der*	≈	renewal of
▸ **popularity**	*Popularität*	adj	popular
▸ **awareness**	*Bewusstsein*	adj	aware
▸ **environmental impact**	*Umweltbelastung*	v prep	to impact on
▸ **to burn**	*verbrennen*		
▸ **fossil fuel**	*fossiler Brennstoff*	adj	fossilized
▸ **design**	*Konstruktion*	vt	to design
▸ **nuclear fusion**	*Kernfusion*		
▸ **technologically**	*technisch*	n	technology
▸ **commercially**	*kommerziell*	adj	commercial
▸ **viable** ['vaɪəbl]	*realisierbar*	n	viability
▸ **to provide**	*liefern*	n	provision
▸ **inexhaustible** [ˌɪnɪg'zɔːstəbl]	*unerschöpflich*	vt	to exhaust
▸ **hydrogen** ['haɪdrədʒən]	*Wasserstoff*		

City council unveils plans for energy-efficient office block

Camford city council today revealed plans for a bizarre new office building on Rivermead Square in the city centre.

The block, which will be called Rivermead House, is designed for maximum energy efficiency and will employ the latest passive heating technology. It will be ventilated entirely by natural air currents created by its futuristic egg shape. Fresh air will enter the building through underground ducts. As the heat emitted by the building's human occupants and by office equipment warms the air, convection will cause it to rise, circulating through each floor before leaving the building through vents on the roof. This means artificial air conditioning will be unnecessary.

The triple-glazed windows in the block will provide highly effective thermal and acoustic insulation. In addition, 'smart' blinds will respond automatically to weather conditions in order to regulate temperature and light within the building. On cold, dull days, the blinds will open fully to admit direct sunlight, closing at night to conserve heat inside the building. On warmer, brighter days, the blinds will open partially, letting in light but not direct sunlight. The blinds are also designed to reflect light deep into the building, while fibre-optic cables will also channel daylight inside. This means that the need for artificial lighting during daylight hours will be reduced to a minimum.

Rivermead House: an artist's impression

The electricity consumption is projected to be only 15% of that of a conventional building of the same size.

▸ **energy-efficient**	*energiesparend*	<>	inefficient
▸ **office block**	*Bürogebäude*	≈	office building
▸ **to reveal**	*vorstellen*	<>	to hide, conceal
▸ **to design**	*konstruieren*	n	design
▸ **energy efficiency**	*Energieeinsparung*	<>	inefficiency
▸ **to employ**	*einsetzen*	n	employment
▸ **to ventilate**	*(be)lüften*	n	ventilation
▸ **air current**	*Luftstrom, -strömung*	cf	draught – *Luftzug*
▸ **futuristic**	*futuristisch*	≈	ultramodern
▸ **shape**	*Form*	≈	form
▸ **fresh air**	*Frischluft*	<>	stale air
▸ **underground**	*unterirdisch*	<>	above-ground
▸ **duct**	*Rohr(leitung)*		
▸ **heat**	*Wärme*	vt	to heat
▸ **to emit** [ɪ'mɪt]	*ausstrahlen*	n	emission
▸ **occupant**	*Bewohner/in*	vt	to occupy
▸ **office equipment**	*Büromaschinen*	≈	office machines
▸ **to warm**	*erwärmen*	n	warmth
▸ **convection**	*Wärmeströmung*		
▸ **to rise**	*ansteigen*	<>	to sink
▸ **to circulate**	*zirkulieren*	n	circulation
▸ **floor**	*Stockwerk*	≈	storey
▸ **vent**	*Öffnung, Lüftungsschlitz*	≈	opening
▸ **artificial** [ˌɑːtɪ'fɪʃl]	*künstlich*	<>	natural
▸ **air conditioning**	*Klimatisierung*	adj	air-conditioned
▸ **triple-glazed**	*dreifach verglast*		
▸ **highly effective**	*hochwirksam*	<>	ineffective
▸ **thermal**	*Wärme-*	≈	heat
▸ **acoustic** [ə'kuːstɪk]	*Geräusch-*	≈	sound
▸ **insulation**	*Isolierung, Dämmung*	⚠	isolation – *Abgeschiedenheit*
▸ **smart**	*intelligent*	≈	intelligent
▸ **blind**	*Jalousie*	cf	shutter – *Fensterladen*
▸ **to respond to**	*reagieren auf*	≈	to react to
▸ **weather conditions**	*Wetterbedingungen*		
▸ **to regulate**	*regulieren*	n	regulation
▸ **to admit**	*(her)einlassen*	<>	to block out
▸ **sunlight**	*Sonnenlicht*	adj	sunny
▸ **to conserve**	*erhalten, bewahren*	n	conservation
▸ **partially**	*teilweise*	adj	partial
▸ **to reflect**	*reflektieren*	n	reflection
▸ **fibre-optic cable**	*Glasfaserkabel*	cf	fibre optics – *Faseroptik*
▸ **to channel**	*leiten*	≈	to direct
▸ **daylight**	*Tageslicht*		
▸ **to reduce**	*reduzieren*	n	reduction
▸ **electricity consumption**	*Stromverbrauch*	vt	to consume
▸ **to project**	*prognostizieren*	n	projection – *Prognose*
▸ **conventional**	*herkömmlich*	≈	traditional

Web poll:

Vox pop: Solving traffic congestion

On our motorways and in our cities, traffic is increasing and congestion is growing. Everyone has his or her 'pet solution' to the problem, whether it is building more bypasses and adding more lanes to motorways, futuristic public transport schemes with monorails and driverless trams, or using congestion charges to make car use in city centres too expensive.

Yet the traffic jams get worse and road rage increases. What's your solution?

Comments

Congestion charges are definitely a good way of keeping cars out of city centres and they reduce pollution from exhaust fumes as well. Of course, they're not popular with car owners ...

Ken L, London, UK

A lot of city people don't really want to own a car, but sometimes you just need one for a short time. Here in Pittsburgh we have the Zipcar car-sharing service. You just pay an hourly or a daily fee to use one of the cars. You can reserve the car online or by phone; insurance and gas are included in the fee.

It reduces the number of car trips per person because you have to plan ahead – you can't just jump in a car and drive. It also helps to alleviate the shortage of parking spaces.

CJ, Pittsburgh, USA

I found this website about the City Car. It's a two-seater electric vehicle, designed to make the best use of limited public space. It has robotic wheels that contain all the moving parts, while the driver's controls operate electronically. That makes the car very light and flexible – you can actually fold up a City Car! The compact design means that eight City Cars take up the same space as one conventional car.

The idea is that commuters will be able to rent the vehicles from kiosks near train stations, airports and bus depots. I think that's a really clever idea to use in combination with public transport.

Kim, Amsterdam, The Netherlands

Replace traffic lights with roundabouts. The amount of petrol saved is huge because cars don't have to wait in queues with their engines running. Accidents are far fewer in those countries (France is by far the world leader) with roundabouts because drivers are more alert, slow down before reaching them and concentrate more on what they are doing. Also, you save on the electricity and servicing of traffic lights.

Jim, Berlin, Germany

▸ **traffic**	*Verkehr*	phr	heavy ~, light ~
▸ **congestion** [kən'dʒestʃən]	*Verstopfung, Stau*	adj	congested
▸ **motorway**	*Autobahn*	AE	freeway, Interstate, highway
▸ **bypass**	*Umgehungsstraße*	cf	ring road, (AE) beltway
▸ **lane**	*Fahrspur*	phr	slow ~, fast ~, overtaking ~
▸ **public transport**	*öffentlicher Nahverkehr*	AE	mass transit
▸ **monorail**	*Einschienenbahn*	cf	rail – *Bahn(schiene)*
▸ **driverless**	*ohne Fahrer*	vti	to drive
▸ **tram**	*Straßenbahn*	AE	trolley, streetcar
▸ **charge**	*Gebühr*	vt	to charge sb for sth
▸ **traffic jam**	*Verkehrsstau*	cf	gridlock – *Verkehrsinfarkt*
▸ **road rage**	*Verkehrsrowdytum*	phr	an attack of ~
▸ **pollution**	*Umweltverschmutzung*	vt	to pollute
▸ **exhaust fumes**	*Abgase*	cf	exhaust pipe – *Auspuff*
▸ **popular**	*beliebt*	n	popularity
▸ **car-sharing service**	*gemeinsame Pkw-Nutzung*	≈	car pool
▸ **fee**	*Gebühr*	phr	to pay a ~
▸ **insurance**	*Versicherung*	vt	to insure
▸ **gas(oline)** (AE)	*Treibstoff*	BE	petrol
▸ **car trip**	*Autofahrt*	≈	car journey
▸ **to plan ahead**	*vorausplanen*	n	forward planning
▸ **to alleviate** [ə'li:vieɪt]	*verringern*	≈	to ease
▸ **shortage of**	*Mangel an*	adj	short of
▸ **parking space**	*Parklücke, -platz*	cf	car park – *Parkplatz, -haus*
▸ **vehicle**	*Fahrzeug*	phr	passenger~, heavy goods ~
▸ **limited**	*begrenzt*	≈	restricted
▸ **robotic**	*Roboter-*	n	robot
▸ **moving part**	*bewegliches Teil*		
▸ **controls**	*Steuerung*	vt	to control
▸ **to operate**	*arbeiten*	≈	to work
▸ **electronically**	*elektronisch*	adj	electronic
▸ **flexible**	*flexibel*	n	flexibility
▸ **to fold up**	*zusammenlegen*	<>	to unfold, open out
▸ **compact**	*kompakt*	n	compactness
▸ **commuter**	*Pendler/in*	vi	to commute
▸ **in combination with**	*in Verbindung mit*	≈	together with
▸ **traffic lights**	*Ampel(n)*	phr	set of ~
▸ **roundabout** ['raʊndəbaʊt]	*Kreisverkehr*	AE	traffic circle, rotary
▸ **alert**	*aufmerksam*	vt	to alert sb (to sth)
▸ **to slow down**	*abbremsen*	<>	to speed up
▸ **to concentrate on**	*sich konzentrieren auf*	n	concentration
▸ **servicing**	*Wartung*	≈	maintenance

Designing the car of the future

At the moment, car travel is a hazardous, environmentally damaging activity. That will change in the near future, thanks to 'smart' cars – ones that use some form of artificial intelligence.

To some extent, cars today are already 'smart', in that they use on-board computers to improve engine performance and fuel economy, anti-lock braking systems (ABS) to shorten braking distances, cruise control to maintain a constant speed on long motorway journeys and satellite navigation systems to monitor the vehicle's own position and provide the driver with directions and traffic information.

We may soon see a whole range of new intelligent safety features become standard features of cars. These will probably include radar hazard avoidance to prevent collisions with other vehicles and pedestrians. Our cars will warn us when we change lanes on the motorway, when we exceed the speed limit and when we are about to fall asleep at the wheel.

Smart vehicles will also ease traffic congestion: satellite-based position monitoring will help them to choose the fastest, least congested route to the destination. Position monitoring will also make car theft a thing of the past.

In fact, cars of the future will be linked to a whole network of information sources: wireless connections will allow them to exchange information constantly with other vehicles.

Increasingly, driving will become automated. Cars will park themselves, steer themselves and maintain a safe distance from the other vehicles around them.

This will eventually lead to the totally driverless vehicle. The passenger will give voice instructions and the vehicle will simply drive to the destination. By eliminating the possibility of driver error, road travel will become faster, safer and more comfortable.

to design	*konstruieren*	n	design
car travel	*Autofahren*	vi	to travel (by car, etc.)
hazardous	*gefährlich*	≈	risky, dangerous
environmentally damaging	*umweltschädlich*	<>	environmentally friendly
smart	*intelligent*	≈	intelligent
artificial intelligence	*künstliche Intelligenz*	abbr	AI
on-board computer	*Bordcomputer*		
to improve	*verbessern*	n	improvement
engine performance	*Motorleistung*	vi	to perform
fuel economy	*Benzinverbrauch*	adj	economical
anti-lock braking system	*Antiblockiersystem*	abbr	ABS
to shorten	*verkürzen*	<>	to increase, to lengthen
braking distance	*Bremsweg*	vi	to brake
cruise control	*Temporegler, Tempomat*	vt	to control
to maintain	*aufrechterhalten*	≈	to keep
speed	*Geschwindigkeit*	phr	high ~, low ~
motorway (BE)	*Autobahn*	AE	freeway, highway, Interstate
satellite navigation	*Satellitennavigation*	abbr	sat nav
to monitor	*überwachen*	≈	to check
vehicle ['viːəkl]	*Fahrzeug*	adj	vehicular (formal) [və'hɪkjələ]
traffic	*Verkehr*	phr	heavy ~, light ~
safety feature	*Sicherheitsvorkehrung*	≈	safety device
hazard avoidance	*Gefahrenvermeidung*	vt	to avoid
to prevent	*verhindern*	n	prevention
collision	*Zusammenstoß*	v prep	to collide with
pedestrian	*Fußgänger/in*		
to change lanes	*die Spur wechseln*		
to exceed the speed limit	*das Tempolimit überschreiten*	≈	to speed
at the wheel	*am Steuer*	≈	behind the wheel
to ease	*erleichtern*	<>	to exacerbate
traffic congestion	*Verkehrsstau*	cf	traffic jam – *Stau*
satellite-based	*Satelliten*		
congested	*verstopft*	vt	to congest
destination	*Fahrt-, Reiseziel*		
car theft	*Autodiebstahl*	cf	car thief – *Autodieb/in*
to link to	*verbinden mit*	n	link
network	*Netz*	adj	networked
source	*Quelle*		
wireless connection	*Funkverbindung*	vt	to connect wirelessly
to exchange	*austauschen*	n	exchange
automated	*automatisiert*	n	automation
to steer	*lenken, steuern*	n	steering
driverless	*fahrerlos*		
to eliminate	*ausschalten*	n	elimination
driver error	*Fahrerfehler*	phr	to make an error

http://en.wikipedia.org/wiki/Alternative_fuel_car

Some alternatives to the petrol engine

For the last 100 years the petrol engine has dominated the automotive industry, but now the rising cost of petrol has encouraged car companies to develop alternatives.

Air car

The air engine is an emission-free piston engine that uses compressed air as a source of energy. The expansion of compressed air may be used to drive the pistons in a modified petrol engine. The only exhaust is cold air (15 °C). The source for air is a carbon-fibre tank holding air at high pressure.
Air cars have a lot of potential advantages. There are no emissions, the technology costs relatively little, the engine uses vegetable oil for lubrication and the cold exhaust air can provide air conditioning.

Battery electric car

Battery electric cars use the energy stored in a battery to run an electric motor. Up until now the high weight and low storage capacity of lead-acid batteries has meant that hybrid electric-petrol vehicles were the best way of using this technology. However newer battery technologies such as lithium-ion batteries are improving the performance and range of battery electric cars.

Biodiesel

Diesel engines have a 40% fuel burn efficiency compared with just 25–30% in petrol engines. This makes them capable of much better fuel economy. With modification, conventional diesel engines can run on biodiesel, a fuel made from vegetable oils.

Hydrogen

A hydrogen car uses hydrogen in one of two methods: combustion or fuel cell conversion. In combustion, the hydrogen is burned in engines in the same way as petrol. In fuel cell conversion, the hydrogen is converted into electricity which then powers an electric motor. With either method, the only by-product is water. Improvements in hydrogen storage should increase the range of hydrogen vehicles while reducing the weight, energy consumption, and complexity of the storage systems.
High-speed cars, buses, motorcycles, bicycles, submarines and space rockets already run on hydrogen, in various forms. There is even a working toy model car that runs on solar power, using a reversible fuel cell to store energy in the form of hydrogen and oxygen gas. It can then convert the fuel back into water to release the solar energy.

[Adapted: http://en.wikipedia.org/wiki/Alternative_fuel_car]

▸ **petrol**	*Benzin*	AE	gas(oline)
▸ **engine**	*Motor*		
▸ **automotive industry**	*Automobilindustrie*	≈	car industry
▸ **to develop**	*entwickeln*	n	development
▸ **air**	*Luft*		
▸ **emission-free** [ɪ'mɪʃn fri:]	*abgasfrei*	vt	to emit
▸ **piston engine**	*Kolbenmotor*	cf	piston – *Kolben*
▸ **compressed air**	*Druckluft*	n	compression
▸ **source**	*Quelle*	vt	to source sth from somewhere
▸ **energy**	*Energie*	≈	power
▸ **expansion**	*Ausdehnung*	vti	to expand
▸ **to drive**	*antreiben*	≈	to provide power to
▸ **to modify**	*modifizieren*	adj	modified
▸ **exhaust** [ɪg'zɔ:st]	*Abgas*	≈	exhaust gas
▸ **carbon-fibre**	*Kohlenstoff-Faser-*	cf	carbon – *Kohlenstoff*
▸ **pressure**	*Druck*	vt, v prep	to press (on)
▸ **vegetable oil**	*Pflanzenöl*	cf	mineral oil
▸ **lubrication**	*Schmierung*	vt	to lubricate
▸ **air conditioning**	*Klimatisierung*	adj	air-conditioned
▸ **to store**	*speichern*		
▸ **weight**	*Gewicht*	vti	to weigh
▸ **storage**	*Speicher*		
▸ **capacity**	*Kapazität*	≈	volume
▸ **lead-acid battery**	*Bleibatterie*	cf	acid – *Säure*
▸ **vehicle**	*Fahrzeug*		
▸ **performance**	*Leistung*	vti	to perform
▸ **range**	*Reichweite*	cf	mileage – *Reichweite (pro Liter Benzin usw.)*
▸ **fuel burn efficiency**	*Treibstoffverbrennungs-effizienz*	adj	efficient
▸ **economy**	*Wirtschaftlichkeit*	adj	economical
▸ **modification**	*Änderung*	≈	alteration
▸ **hydrogen**	*Wasserstoff*		
▸ **combustion**	*Verbrennung*	≈	burning
▸ **fuel cell**	*Treibstoffzelle*	phr	hydrogen ~, ~ car
▸ **to burn**	*verbrennen*	adj	burnt
▸ **to convert into**	*umwandeln in*	n	conversion into
▸ **by-product**	*Nebenprodukt*	≈	waste product
▸ **consumption**	*Verbrauch*	vt	to consume
▸ **complexity**	*Komplexität*	adj	complex
▸ **high-speed**	*Hochgeschwindigkeits-*	<>	low-speed
▸ **submarine**	*U-Boot*		
▸ **space rocket**	*Weltraumrakete*		
▸ **reversible**	*umkehrbar*	vt	to reverse
▸ **oxygen**	*Sauerstoff*		

www.spacefuture.com/tourism/gettingthere.shtml

Space tourism

The main problem about space is how much it costs to get there: it's too expensive! And that's mainly because launch vehicles are expendable – either entirely, like satellite launchers, or partly, like the space shuttle.

So we need reusable launch vehicles. The trouble is that these will not only reduce the cost of a launch – they'll also put the manufacturers out of business, unless there's more to launch than just a few satellites a year, as there are today.

Fortunately there's a market that will generate far more launch business than satellites ever will – passenger travel. Market research has shown that the idea of space tourism is very popular. And so, just like aviation, the launch industry is going to find that most of its business will be carrying passengers rather than payloads.

But space tourism isn't at all familiar to most people, including the space industry, who are used to the idea that space is for research or military activities. Few people are aware of how much work has been done to show that space tourism is a realistic goal, and how rapidly this work is now progressing.

Once travel to orbit becomes a commercial service, the question of how to get to space will be mainly one of saving up for a ticket – or looking for work in one of the many space hotels that will be built. Space offers unique pleasures, including the view, and zero gravity activities that provide a whole range of things to do on an orbital holiday – including space sports that take advantage of weightlessness.

Importantly, and contrary to what many people assume, the space agencies are not at all interested in space tourism, and are not trying to bring it about. This is a pity because space activities will never be profitable until tourism services begin.

Fortunately there is an increasing number of enterprises starting up in this area and we have already seen a number of private space flights. At the same time, many projects are under way to produce commercially viable reusable spacecraft. The solutions proposed range from conventional rockets with parachutes and jet-rocket hybrid spaceplanes to space elevators using carbon nanotube technology.

[http://www.spacefuture.com/tourism/gettingthere.shtml]

▸ **space**	*Weltraum*	phr	outer ~, interstellar ~
▸ **launch vehicle** [lɔːntʃ 'viːəkl]	*Startfahrzeug*	cf	vehicle – *Fahrzeug*
▸ **expendable**	*Einmal-, verbrauchbar*	≈	disposable
▸ **launcher**	*Trägerrakete*	vt	to launch
▸ **space shuttle**	*Raumfähre*	vti	to shuttle – *hin- und herfahren*
▸ **reusable**	*wiederverwendbar*	vt	to reuse
▸ **to put out of business**	*arbeitslos machen*	≈	to bankrupt, to ruin
▸ **manufacturer**	*Hersteller/in*	vt	to manufacture
▸ **to generate**	*erzeugen*	≈	to create
▸ **passenger**	*Passagier/in*	cf	freight – *Fracht*
▸ **travel**	*Reiseverkehr*	vi	to travel
▸ **market**	*Markt*	vt	to market
▸ **research** [rɪ'sɜːtʃ]	*Forschung*	vt	to research
▸ **aviation**	*Luftfahrt*	≈	aeronautics
▸ **payload**	*Nutzlast*	≈	cargo
▸ **military**	*militärisch*	<>	civilian
▸ **goal**	*Ziel*	≈	aim
▸ **to progress**	*fortschreiten*	n	progress
▸ **orbit**	*Umlaufbahn*	phr	to go into ~
▸ **commercial** [kə'mɜːʃl]	*kommerziell*	≈	profit-making
▸ **service**	*Dienstleistung*	vt	to serve
▸ **unique** [ju'niːk]	*einzigartig*	n	uniqueness
▸ **pleasure**	*Vergnügen*	adj	pleasurable
▸ **view**	*Aussicht*	cf	to have a ~ of
▸ **zero gravity**	*Schwerelosigkeit*	≈	weightlessness
▸ **orbital**	*in der Umlaufbahn*	≈	in orbit
▸ **to take advantage of**	*ausnutzen*	≈	to make use of
▸ **weightlessness**	*Schwerelosigkeit*	cf	weight – *Schwere*
▸ **contrary to**	*im Gegensatz zu*	≈	counter to
▸ **space agency**	*Weltraumagentur*	cf	European Space Agency (ESA)
▸ **to bring sth about**	*herbeiführen*	≈	to make sth happen
▸ **profitable**	*rentabel*	v prep	to profit from
▸ **enterprise**	*Unternehmen*	cf	entrepreneur – *Unternehmer/in*
▸ **space flight**	*Raumflug*	vti	to fly
▸ **viable** ['vaɪəbl]	*brauchbar*	n	viability
▸ **spacecraft**	*Raumfahrzeug(e)*	cf	aircraft
▸ **solution**	*Lösung*	vt	to solve
▸ **to propose**	*vorschlagen*	n	proposal
▸ **conventional**	*konventionell*	≈	traditional, standard
▸ **rocket**	*Rakete*	phr	~-powered
▸ **parachute**	*Fallschirm*	vti	to parachute
▸ **jet**	*Düse*	phr	~ engine, ~ aircraft
▸ **elevator**	*Fahrstuhl*	vt	to elevate – *heben*
▸ **carbon nanotube**	*Kohlenstoff-Nanoröhre*	cf	nanotechnology

Forum

Voxpop.com.au: GM agriculture – good or bad?

The ecological consequences of GM are unpredictable and could be devastating. For example, if crops are genetically modified to compete more successfully with weed species – to grow faster, stronger – they themselves could become 'superweeds' when they spread into the wild. Field trials of genetically modified plants are dangerous: how can you guarantee that their pollen or seeds won't spread over a wider area?

Brian D, Australia

Reply *Andrew Mossop, England*

Despite the hysteria created by the media and some pressure groups, I don't think GM is inherently good or bad, hazardous or beneficial. It depends on the uses to which it's put, and how thoroughly the potential dangers are researched. Genetics is a relatively new science, and we actually know very little about the functions of genes. It's foolish to rush into the widespread application of GM to food production. I think the public is right to be suspicious of GM – but not to reject it for emotional reasons.

Reply *Benjamin, Jersey*

Herbicide-resistant crops are being developed so that more and more toxic herbicides can be used to eradicate weeds on agricultural land. The results: barren agricultural 'deserts' and more toxins in the soil, the groundwater and the foodchain. Pest-resistant crops sound a better idea on the face of it, but they will remove important food sources for wildlife. Agricultural 'inefficiency' leads to greater biodiversity.

Reply *M. Blayney, Eire*

We are creating new forms of life which could never have existed naturally. How can we possibly foresee all the potential repercussions of interfering with nature in this way? I can accept the use of GM for medical reasons, but to tamper with our food and the balance of nature purely for the sake of profit is stupid.

Reply *Trudi Botha, South Africa*

Fact 1: the world's human population is growing rapidly and needs to be fed. Fact 2: over 900 million people are already chronically undernourished. Fact 3: intensive agriculture is not sustainable in the long term – it will exhaust and degrade the soil, as well as polluting the environment with chemicals. Put these facts together, and ask yourself: how can we afford NOT to research GM solutions?

▸ **consequence**	*Folge*	≈	result
▸ **GM**	*Genmanipulation*	=	genetic modification
▸ **unpredictable**	*unvorhersehbar*		
▸ **devastating** ['devəsteɪtɪŋ]	*verheerend*	n	devastation
▸ **to compete**	*konkurrieren*	n	competition
▸ **weed**	*Unkraut*		
▸ **to spread into the wild**	*sich in der freien Natur verbreiten*	n	spread
▸ **field trial**	*Feldversuch*	vt	to trial
▸ **to guarantee** [ˌgærən'tiː]	*gewährleisten*	n	guarantee
▸ **seed**	*Same*		
▸ **hysteria** [hɪ'stɪəriə]	*Hysterie*	adj	hysterical [hɪ'sterɪkl]
▸ **inherently** [ɪn'hɪərəntli]	*von Natur aus*	≈	intrinsically
▸ **hazardous** ['hæzədəs]	*gefährlich*	n	hazard
▸ **beneficial**	*nützlich*	<>	harmful
▸ **thoroughly** ['θʌrəli]	*sorgfältig*	n	thoroughness
▸ **to research**	*erforschen*	≈	to investigate
▸ **foolish**	*töricht*	<>	sensible – *vernünftig*
▸ **application**	*Anwendung*	vt	to apply
▸ **suspicious of** [sə'spɪʃəs]	*misstrauisch gegenüber*	n	suspicion
▸ **to reject**	*ablehnen*	<>	to accept
▸ **herbicide**	*Unkrautvernichtungsmittel*	≈	weedkiller
▸ **toxic**	*giftig*	≈	poisonous
▸ **to eradicate**	*ausrotten*	≈	to wipe out
▸ **barren**	*unfruchtbar, karg*	<>	fertile
▸ **toxin**	*Giftstoff*	≈	poison
▸ **groundwater**	*Grundwasser*		
▸ **foodchain**	*Nahrungskette*	≈	foodweb
▸ **on the face of it**	*auf den ersten Blick*	≈	ostensibly
▸ **wildlife**	*die Tierwelt*	≈	fauna
▸ **inefficiency**	*Unwirtschaftlichkeit*	adj	inefficient
▸ **biodiversity**	*Artenvielfalt*	cf	diverse – *vielfältig*
▸ **to foresee**	*vorhersehen*	adj	foreseeable
▸ **repercussion** [ˌriːpə'kʌʃn]	*Auswirkung*	phr	to have ~s
▸ **to interfere with**	*eingreifen in*	n	interference
▸ **to tamper with**	*herumdoktern an*	≈	to meddle with
▸ **balance of nature**	*Gleichgewicht der Natur*	adj	balanced
▸ **chronically**	*chronisch*	adj	chronic
▸ **undernourished**	*unterernährt*	≈	malnourished
▸ **sustainable**	*umweltgerecht*	n	sustainability
▸ **to degrade**	*abbauen*	n	degradation
▸ **to pollute**	*verschmutzen*	n	pollution
▸ **chemical**	*Chemikalie*	adj	chemical

Human cloning

Human cloning is the creation of a genetically identical copy of a human being, human cell, or human tissue. The term is used to refer to artificial human clones, although natural human clones – identical twins – are a common result of the natural process of reproduction.

The cloning procedure would involve taking an unfertilized egg from a female, removing the nucleus, which contains most of the genetic information, and replacing it with the nucleus of a cell from the person to be cloned.

If the technique is successful, the fertilized egg would grow to 50 to 100 cells and the embryo would then be transferred to a woman's womb. A baby clone would be born nine months later.

Human therapeutic cloning could provide genetically identical cells and organs for transplantation. This could improve treatment for serious diseases such as cancer, heart disease and diabetes, as well as reconstructive and cosmetic surgery.

Human reproductive cloning would produce benefits for couples who are infertile. Fertility treatment including cloning could allow them to have children who share some of their DNA.

Despite these potential benefits, there is strong political and public opposition to cloning. Some object that the danger of mutations remains too great. Others focus more on the unpredictable emotional and social effects of cloning humans. For example, how would you feel growing up knowing that your 'mother' is really your twin sister? Perhaps the strongest opposition comes from a belief that producing carbon copies of human beings is not acceptable.

To some extent the arguments against reproductive cloning are emotional rather than logical. Genes influence behaviour and personality, but 'genetically identical' does not mean completely identical; identical twins, despite having nearly identical DNA, are separate people, with separate experiences and personalities. People who wished to become 'immortal' through cloning themselves would be disappointed.

4 Biotechnology and medicine

▸ **human**	*menschlich*	<>	non-human
▸ **to clone**	*klonen*	n	cloning
▸ **genetically**	*genetisch*	cf	gene – *Gen*
▸ **identical**	*identisch*	≈	indistinguishable
▸ **human being**	*Mensch*	≈	person
▸ **cell**	*Zell*	adj	cellular
▸ **tissue**	*Gewebe*	cf	skin – *Haut*
▸ **artificial** [ˌɑːtɪˈfɪʃl]	*künstlich*	≈	man-made
▸ **clone**	*Klon*	adj	cloned
▸ **natural**	*natürlich*	n	nature
▸ **identical twin**	*eineiiger Zwilling*	<>	non-identical twin
▸ **reproduction**	*Fortpflanzung*	≈	giving birth
▸ **procedure**	*Verfahren*	≈	process
▸ **unfertilized**	*unbefruchtet*	n	fertilization
▸ **genetic**	*genetisch*	n	geneticist – *Genetiker/in*
▸ **to replace with**	*ersetzen durch*	n	replacement
▸ **to transfer**	*verpflanzen*	n	transfer
▸ **womb** [wuːm]	*Mutterleib*		
▸ **therapeutic** [ˌθerəˈpjuːtɪk]	*therapeutisch*	n	therapy
▸ **treatment**	*Behandlung*	vt	to treat
▸ **disease**	*Krankheit*	≈	illness
▸ **cancer**	*Krebs*	adj	cancerous
▸ **heart**	*Herz*	≈	cardiac (adj)
▸ **diabetes** [ˌdaɪəˈbiːtiːz]	*Zuckerkrankheit*		
▸ **reconstructive surgery**	*wiederherstellende Chirurgie*	vt	to reconstruct
▸ **cosmetic surgery**	*Schönheitschirurgie*	cf	surgeon – *Chirurg/in*
▸ **reproductive**	*Reproduktions-*	vti	to reproduce
▸ **benefit**	*Vorteil*	vt	to benefit
▸ **infertile**	*unfruchtbar*	<>	fertile
▸ **fertility**	*Fruchtbarkeit*	<>	infertility
▸ **political**	*politisch*	n	politics
▸ **public**	*öffentlich*	<>	private
▸ **opposition**	*Widerstand*	vt	to oppose
▸ **to object**	*einwenden*	n	objection
▸ **mutation**	*Mutation*	vti	to mutate
▸ **to focus on**	*sich konzentrieren auf*	≈	to concentrate on
▸ **unpredictable**	*unvorhersehbar*	vt	to predict
▸ **social**	*sozial*	n	society
▸ **belief**	*Glaube*	vt	to believe
▸ **carbon copy**	*(genaue) Kopie*	≈	identical copy
▸ **acceptable**	*akzeptabel*	vt	to accept
▸ **logical**	*logisch*	n	logic
▸ **to influence**	*beeinflussen*	adj	influential
▸ **behaviour**	*Verhalten*	vi	to behave
▸ **personality**	*Persönlichkeit*	≈	character
▸ **separate**	*getrennt*	≈	distinct
▸ **experience**	*Erfahrung*	vt	to experience
▸ **immortal**	*unsterblich*	<>	mortal

Describing charts and diagrams

World CO_2 emissions from fossil fuels (in million tonnes)

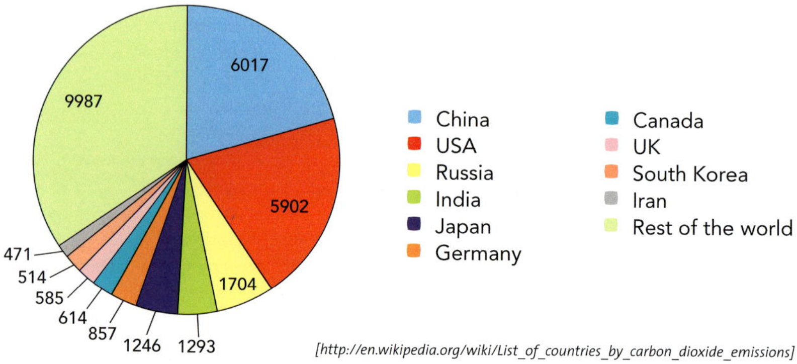

[http://en.wikipedia.org/wiki/List_of_countries_by_carbon_dioxide_emissions]

We can see from the pie chart that the biggest emitters of CO_2 were China and the USA, whose emissions were approximately equal. Four countries – China, the USA, Russia and India – together accounted for over half of the world's emissions. Japan came in fifth place, with only slightly lower emissions than India. Only two European countries were represented amongst the world's top ten emitters: namely Germany and the United Kingdom. Germany's emissions were significantly greater than those of the UK. The top ten countries were responsible for the vast majority of the world's CO_2 emissions, with a mere third of emissions coming from the rest of the world. However, it is important to realize that the chart only shows emissions of one greenhouse gas: carbon dioxide. Furthermore, it only takes into account emissions from fossil fuels and does not include other factors such as deforestation and agriculture.

Crime rate in England and Wales

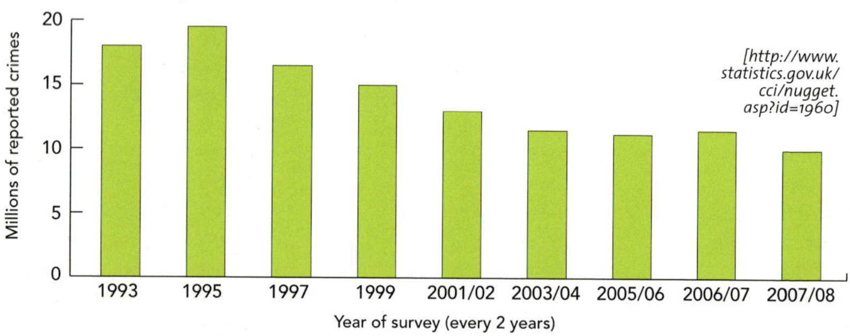

The histogram shows us that there was a drastic decrease in the crime rate in England and Wales over a period of 15 years from 1993 to 2008, by a total of nearly 50 per cent. From 1993 to 1995 the crime rate climbed slightly, hitting a maximum in 1995, but in subsequent years it fell steadily, levelling off in 2005–6 and then showing a slight rise in 2006–7, before resuming its fall in 2007-8.

Describing charts and diagrams

▸ **pie chart**	*Torten-, Kreisdiagramm*		
▸ **approximately**	*ungefähr*	<>	exactly, precisely
▸ **equal**	*gleich*	≈	the same
▸ **to account for**	*verantwortlich sein für*		
▸ **over**	*über*	<>	under, less than
▸ **half**	*(die) Hälfte*	cf	a third, a quarter, a fifth, a sixth, etc
▸ **to come in ... place**	*an ... Stelle kommen*	≈	to rank first, etc
▸ **slightly**	*etwas*	≈	a little
▸ **lower than**	*weniger als*	<>	higher than
▸ **to be represented**	*vertreten sein*	≈	to be, to figure, to feature
▸ **top ten**	*(die) obersten zehn*	<>	bottom ten
▸ **significantly**	*erheblich*	≈	noticeably
▸ **greater than**	*größer als*	<>	less than
▸ **to be responsible for**	*verantwortlich sein für*		
▸ **the vast majority of**	*die große Mehrheit (von)*	<>	minority
▸ **a mere third of**	*ein bloßes Drittel (von)*		
▸ **the rest of**	*der Rest (von)*	≈	the remainder of
▸ **to realize**	*sich bewusst werden/sein*	≈	to note
▸ **to show**	*(an)zeigen*	≈	to exhibit
▸ **to take into account**	*berücksichtigen*	≈	to bear in mind
▸ **to include**	*einbeziehen*	<>	to exclude
▸ **factor**	*Faktor*	≈	aspect
▸ **such as**	*wie (zum Beispiel)*	≈	like, e.g, for example
▸ **histogram**	*Balkendiagramm*	cf	bar chart – *Balkendiagramm*
▸ **drastic**	*drastisch*	adv	drastically
▸ **decrease**	*Rückgang*	vti	to decrease
▸ **rate**	*Rate*		
▸ **over a period of**	*über einen Zeitraum von*		
▸ **a total of**	*insgesamt*	vi	to total
▸ **nearly**	*nahezu, beinahe*		
▸ **per cent**	*Prozent*	n	percentage
▸ **to climb**	*klettern, steigen*	≈	to rise
▸ **to hit a maximum**	*einen Höchststand erreichen*	<>	to sink to a minimum
▸ **subsequent**	*folgend*	<>	previous
▸ **to fall**	*fallen, sinken*	≈	to drop
▸ **steadily**	*stetig, ständig*	≈	gradually
		<>	sharply
▸ **to level off**	*sich einpendeln*	≈	to level out
▸ **rise**	*Anstieg*	vi	to rise
		vt	to raise
▸ **to resume**	*wieder aufnehmen*	cf	to continue – *fortsetzen*
▸ **fall**	*Rückgang, Fallen*	≈	drop

Useful expressions for essay writing

1 Introducing the topic

- **Stating the opening proposition:**
  It is often claimed/said/asserted/ stated that …
  Today we are often confronted with the problem of …
  We often read in the newspapers that …
  X made the assertion that …
- **Calling the proposition into question:**
  One must ask oneself whether/why/ how …
  This assertion raises a fundamental question/issue: …
  We must examine the truth of this assertion.

2 Developing the argument

- **Enumerating the elements:**
  Firstly … secondly … thirdly
  On the one hand … and on the other …
- **Adding another point:**
  Furthermore, …
  In addition to this, …
  It must also be said that …
  We must also consider …
- **Introducing an example:**
  For example, …
  Take for example …
  To illustrate this, …
  … illustrates this point perfectly.
- **Introducing a quotation:**
  As X said/wrote, …
  In the words of …
  To quote X, …
- **Introducing a hypothesis:**
  It is quite possible that …
  … leads one to believe that …
  … may well be/have …
- **Expressing certainty:**
  All the indications are that …
  It is certainly true that …
  It is clear/certain that …
  It is very clear that …
  The truth is that …
  … as everyone knows.
- **Expressing uncertainty:**
  It is difficult to believe that …
  It is uncertain whether …
  This may be true, but …
  … seems likely/unlikely/probable/ possible.
- **Emphasizing a point:**
  It is important/vital/essential to realize that …
  We must remember that …
  … is an important/vital/essential point.

3 Considering counter-arguments

- **Signalling a change of viewpoint:**
  However, there are other issues to consider.
  However, this is just one side of the matter.
  However, we must not forget that …
  In X's view, however, …
  Let us now consider …
  Let us now turn to …
  On the other hand, …
  Turning to …

- **Conceding a point:**
  It must be admitted/conceded that …
  There is no denying that …

- **Denying a point:**
  It would be ridiculous to maintain that …
  On the contrary, …
  One cannot accept that …
  This completely contradicts/disproves …

4 Ending the essay

- **Summarizing the arguments:**
  Let us remind ourselves of the main arguments: …
  To summarize: …
  We have seen/established that …

- **Drawing conclusions:**
  All in all …
  All of these facts lead me to the conclusion that …
  From this I must conclude that …
  Having considered all these issues …
  Having outlined the main arguments …
  Having taken all these factors into account …
  What conclusions can be drawn from this analysis?

- **Stating one's own point of view:**
  I am convinced that …
  I personally believe that …
  In my opinion …
  It seems to me that …
  My own point of view is that …

A

D

E

F

G

H

I

J

K

L

M

N

O

P

Q

R

S

T

U

V

W

Y

Z

Bildquellen

RF photos:
Shutterstock: S.20, S.62, S.164

Wir bedanken uns für die freundliche Unterstützung: S.76/Fairtrade Foundation

Textquellen

S.14 www.netdoctor.co.uk/health_advice/facts/smokehealth.htm; S. 16 Slightly adapted: news.bbc.co.uk; S. 22 Slightly adapted: www.bullying.co.uk; S. 24 http://www.apprenticeships.org.uk/wanttobecomeanapprentice/faqs/; S. 26 Slightly adapted: www.vistawide.com; S. 28 http://www.helpguide.org/mental/blended_families_stepfamilies.htm; S. 34 Paragraph 1: http://www.racismnoway.com.au/library/understanding/index-What.html, http://www.abc.net.au/rn/counterpoint/stories/2006/1607107.htm; S. 36 Slightly adapted: www.independent.co.uk; S. 40 Adapted extracts: www.abc.net.au; S. 48 Adapted: www.eco-online.qld.edu.au; S. 50 Adapted and shortened: www.eco-online.qld.edu.au; S. 58 Adapted extracts: http://www.worldwaterwars.com; S. 60 Slightly adapted: http://www.sustainable-development.gov.uk/what/index.htm; S. 64 Slightly adapted: news.bbc.co.uk; S. 66 Shortened: www.greenpeace.org; S. 76 Adapted extracts: http://www.fairtrade.org.uk; S. 82 Shortened: http://www.direct.gov.uk/en/Employment/DiscriminationAtWork/DG_10026670; S. 86 http://www.bbc.co.uk/blast/art/articles/what_is_ethical_fashion.shtml; S. 124 Shortened: www.symantec.com/content/en/au/clubsymantec/socialnetsites/article.html; S. 130 Shortened and slightly adapted: http://www.abc.net.au; S. 132 Shortened and adapted: http://technology.timesonline.co.uk; S. 142 Shortened and slightly adapted: http://www.foet.org; S. 144 Adapted extracts: http://un.by/en/about/; http://www.unac.org; S. 160 http://news.bbc.co.uk/go/pr/fr/-/2/hi/technology/7549059.stm; S. 166 Adapted extracts: www.lifeaftertheoilcrash.net; S. 180 Adapted: http://en.wikipedia.org/wiki/Alternative_fuel_car; S. 182 http://www.spacefuture.com/tourism/gettingthere.shtml